RENAMO

TERRORISM IN MOZAMBIQUE

RENAMO

TERRORISM IN MOZAMBIQUE

ALEX VINES

Centre for Southern African Studies
University of York
IN ASSOCIATION WITH
James Currey
LONDON
Indiana University Press
BLOOMINGTON AND INDIANAPOLIS

Centre for Southern African Studies
University of York, York Y01 5DD

James Currey Ltd
54b Thornhill Square, Islington, London N1 1BE

Indiana University Press
Tenth and Morton Streets, Bloomington, Indiana 47405

British Library Cataloguing in Publication Data

Vines, Alex
  Renamo: terrorism in Mozambique.
  1. Mozambique. Resistance movements
  I. Title
  967.905
  ISBN 0-85255-354-4

Library of Congress Cataloging-in-Publication Data

Vines, Alex
  Renamo: terrorism in Mozambique / Alex Vines
          p.   cm.
  Includes bibliographical references and index
  ISBN 0-253-36253-9—ISBN 0-253-28880-0 (pbk.)
  1. RENAMO (Organization). 2. Terrorism—Mozambique.
  3. Guerrillas—Mozambique. 4. Mozambique—Politics and
  government —1975- I. Title
  DT3394.V56   1991
  967.905—dc20

                                                    91-13285
                                                    CIP

Typeset by Robert Vicat Ltd, London
Printed and bound in Great Britain
by Villiers Publications, London, N6

CONTENTS

MAPS, FIGURES AND TABLES

Maps

Figures

Tables

ACKNOWLEDGMENTS

Research for this book has continued on and off over five years. Fieldwork has been carried out in Mozambique, in its southern African neighbours and in Kenya. Further research has been carried out in the United States and Great Britain. The libraries consulted for published material on Renamo are at the School of Oriental and African Studies, London, the University of York, the Luso-Hispanic Council at Canning House, London, and the Library of Congress in Washington, D.C.

Many of the individuals that have given information, especially in southern Africa, did so on the condition that they remained anonymous. What I have done is to cite alternative sources such as press reports which reflect these private conversations. Where this has not been possible I have stated the source as anonymous or given a general indication of the category of the individual (ie. diplomat).

Of those whose comments and assistance I can acknowledge, I thank Landeg White. He has made the major contribution in supporting this project. He has thrown open his files and allowed me to use material from his own fieldwork in Lisbon carried out every summer since 1987, in addition to sharing his depth of knowledge and experience of Mozambique and giving generous advice. Jeanne Penvenne, Rob Turrell, Colin Stoneman and Herb Howe have also provided assistance. My parents, who have supported me while writing and have proof-read countless drafts, should be thanked too. My father, in particular, whose sojourn in Mozambique stimulated my interest in this subject, has provided insights into the country from his experiences of the Mozambican government. Finally, Karen Smith. She provided me with the opportunity to research in the USA: without her this book would have been much the poorer.

ABBREVIATIONS

AACC	Anglican African Council of Churches.
AEMO	Association of Native and Former Residents of Mozambique
AERM	Association of Mozambican Business and Property Holders.
AJEP	Association of Young Portuguese Businessmen.
AIM	Mozambique State News Agency.
ANC	African National Congress.
BND	West German Intelligence.
BOSS	Bureau of State Security.
BP	British Petroleum.
CAF	Conservative Action Foundation.
CANM	Associate Centre of Black Mozambicans.
CCM	Mozambique Council of Churches.
CDM	Democratic Convergence Movement.
CIA	Central Intelligence Agency.
CIO	Central Intelligence Organisation.
CNAM	African National Congress of Mozambique.
COMIMO	Commission of Mozambicans.
CONIMO	Mozambique National Independent Committee.
COREMO	Mozambique Revolutionary Committee.
CUNIMO	Committee for Mozambican Union.
DGS	General Security Directorate.
DINFO	Portuguese Military Intelligence.
FAM	Mozambique Armed Forces.
FCD	Cabo Delgado Front.
FPLM	Mozambique Armed Forces.
FRAUL	National Movement of Overseas Fraternity.
FRECOMO	Mozambican Common Front.
FRELIMO	Front for the Liberation of Mozambique.
FRESAMO	Salvation Front of Mozambique.
FUMO	Mozambique United Front.

FUNIPOMO	Popular United Anti-Imperialist Front for Mozambique.
GUMO	Mozambican United Group.
ICRC	International Committee of the Red Cross.
IFF	International Freedom Foundation.
IST	Institute for the Study of Terrorism.
MANU	Mozambique African National Union.
MANC	Mozambique African National Congress.
MFA	Armed Forces Movement.
MID	Military Intelligence Directorate.
MNR	Mozambique National Resistance.
MNRA	Mozambique National Resistance Army.
MOLIMO	Mozambique Liberation Front.
MONA	Mozambique National Association.
MONAMO	Independent Movement for National Reconstruction.
MRC	Mozambique Research Centre.
NRA	National Resistance Army.
PAC	Pan African Congress.
PADELIMO	Democratic Party for the Liberation of Mozambique.
PALMO	Mozambique Liberal and Democratic Party
PAPOMO	Monomotapa Popular Party.
PCN	National Coalition Party.
PRE	Economic Rehabilitation Programme.
RENAMO	Mozambique National Resistance.
RNM	Mozambique National Resistance.
SADF	South African Defence Forces.
SADCC	Southern African Development Coordination Conference.
SIM	Portuguese Military Intelligence, (ex DINFO).
SIS	Portuguese Civil Intelligence.
SNASP	Mozambique State Security.
SONAREP	Maputo oil refinery.
SSC	State Security Council.
STD	Special Task Directorate.
UDI	Unilateral Declaration of Independence.
UDENAMO	Mozambique National Democratic Union.
UDEMO	Mozambique Democratic Union.

UNAMI	Mozambique National Independence Union.
UNAMO	Mozambique National Union.
UNAR	African National Union of Rombezia.
UNITA	National Union for the Total Independence of Angola.
UK	United Kingdom.
US/USA	United States of America.
USSR	Soviet Union.
ZANU	Zimbabwe African National Union.
ZANLA	Zimbabwean National Liberation Army.
ZNA	Zimbabwean Army.

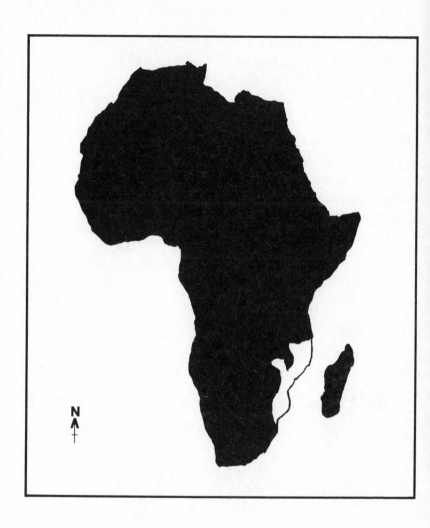

Map 1 Mozambique: location

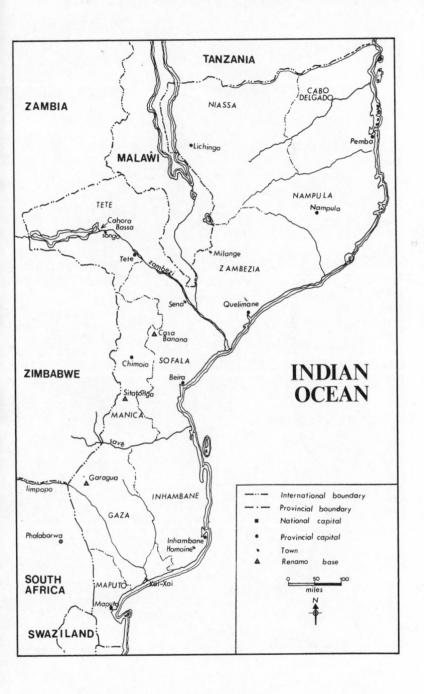

Map 2 Mozambique: topography and settlements

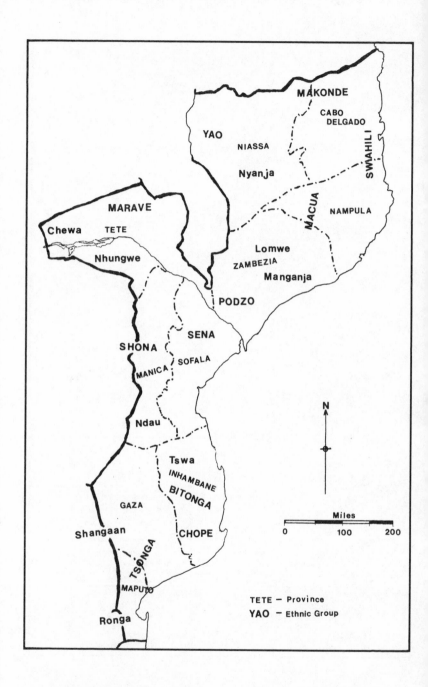

Map 3 Mozambique: ethnic composition and provinces

Source: adapted from Hall, 1990

INTRODUCTION

Mozambique is no longer portrayed as the new and revolutionary country that so much dominated the literature about it until the mid-1980s. Post-independence euphoria and optimism have given way to new interpretations. Titles, such as *The Revolution under Fire*, *Caught in the Trap*, *And Still they Dance* and *A Dream Undone*, illustrate the popular thesis that Mozambique's problems derive from external destabilisation, and in particular, the work of the rebel group, Renamo, which the South Africans have supported to keep Mozambique in turmoil so as to make it a "client" state subservient to apartheid power in southern Africa.[1]

Such perceptions are beginning to change, partly reflecting the fact that the old accusations of South African destabilisation do not hold credibility in the face of the reforms in South Africa under President de Klerk, such as the release of Nelson Mandela and the unbanning of the ANC, PAC and Communist Party.

The cruel conflict between government and Renamo, which began in a significant form in 1977, is likely to continue for the near future. It is obviously a war that Mozambique, already one of the most backward countries in the world at independence, can ill afford. The rebels have destroyed communications, commerce and health facilities. They have brought about a starving and increasingly fragmented and traumatised society.

Mozambique enters the 1990s with an estimated 4.3 million of its 14 million people displaced, and 100,000 deaths which may have been caused directly by the war. It has become increasingly necessary to go beyond previous studies and look directly at what Renamo is. Renamo is the cause of most of the conflict in Mozambique. Although its supporters depict it as a pro-western group of freedom fighters, struggling to impose democracy and individual freedom in place of a totalitarian communist dictatorship, such claims have very little realistic basis.

Renamo, nevertheless, is, by all accounts, a successful rebel movement. It has limited the secure government presence to the towns. It now operates in all ten provinces of Mozambique. Renamo's President Afonso Dhlakama has claimed that this is because "We are like fish in the water — if one drains off the water, the fish die. The People are the water in which we swim and survive ..."[2] As this study will show, this is untrue. What makes Renamo so different from most successful rebel movements is that the equation between popular support and rebel strength does not generally apply. Although Renamo obtains some support from the Mozambican peasantry, most of this is obtained through terror and coercion. This is why politicians such as Mrs Thatcher have described Renamo as one of the "most brutal terrorist movements that there is".[3]

Renamo is, nevertheless, a Mozambican phenomenon. Its 20,000 combatants are Mozambican, and many of its tactics, including the manner in which it commits its atrocities and organises itself, have historical southern African parallels. Renamo is a military organisation and many of its actions are coherent, deriving from a centralised leadership. The reasons why Renamo continues to fight a war that it itself acknowledges can not be won in the field will be discussed.

A decade of intense conflict against Renamo, and the lessons learnt from policy mistakes in the heady days of the 1970s, have forced the Mozambique government to reassess its strategy. Many decisions based primarily on ideological commitment and romanticism have been rethought. The effects expected from new policies, such as the government's "Economic Rehabilitation programme" (PRE),[4] have yet to be felt within much of Mozambique, where the war against Renamo blocks their implementation. This is why the Mozambique government has, since 1984, pursued a dual strategy of military and diplomatic initiatives towards Renamo. Dialogue with Renamo is an important example of this, with direct talks between the rebels and the Mozambique government in 1990 marking a further serious attempt to end the war.

The war, and Renamo's persistence against all the efforts against it, have rudely awakened the government to the geopolitical realities of Mozambique. The increasing insecurity in the countryside has fragmented centralised government. Eduardo Mondlane, the first President of Frelimo, the anti-colonial Mozambique freedom movement, had argued that in Mozambique:

> It was colonial domination which produced the territorial community and created the basis for a psychological coherence, founded on the experience of discrimination, exploitation, forced labour, and other aspects of colonial rule.[5]

The current situation in Mozambique implies that such experiences were not felt deeply enough to survive after independence once Renamo started playing on far older, and equally strongly felt, regional and ethnic frames of reference in rural areas, in order to obtain support and even some sympathy.

The areas where the government and Renamo hold their respective strengths reflect these traditional divisions. The intermediate zones are dominated by whichever force is strongest in that particular area. The fact of indigenous support for the rebels has been acknowledged by both the late President Machel and his successor, President Chissano.

One of the main issues examined in this study is the depth of South African influence over Renamo's tactics and objectives. The history of South African support and the politics behind it are analysed. It is concluded that while Renamo was initially trained by Rhodesia, and later by South Africa, it evolved its own style once it operated in the Mozambican bush. Its adaptation has taken varied forms, according to political and geopolitical circumstances, especially after the signing by South Africa and Mozambique of the N'Komati Accord in 1984, which loosened the direct external influences on its development.

It would be a mistake to compare too closely the liberation struggle of Frelimo before independence with Renamo's activities today, a comparison Renamo is frequently at pains to make. Renamo's origins, tactics and ideology are different from Frelimo's. Renamo lacks a sophisticated and centralised ideological commitment comparable with that hammered out by Frelimo in its 1960s disputes. This lack of coherent and consistent ideology has contributed to Renamo's brutality in action. Renamo has also failed, in contrast to Frelimo in its time as a liberation movement, to produce a convincing propaganda campaign to justify itself to the outside world. Frelimo's reforms have overtaken whatever worthy issues it has focused on.

This study attempts to demonstrate that Renamo is a real military-based organisation, not an umbrella for numerous groups of uncoordinated "armed bandits", or loosely aligned war-lords, as is sometimes depicted. As the chapters below show, a wider analysis of Renamo is well overdue. The research for this book, however, only uncovered fragments of what Renamo actually represents. Given that it is a study of a contemporary war situation, reliable information is frequently obscured by censorship and propaganda. In this respect what is recorded here remains very preliminary to what future research will reveal, once badly needed peace is allowed to return to a devastated and long-suffering Mozambique.

1 A BACKCLOTH TO DISORDER

"Independencia ou Morte! A Luta Continua! Venceremos!" This was the commonest of the call to arms issued by Frelimo during the thirteen years of its struggle to liberate Mozambique from Portuguese colonial rule. It appeared in all propaganda materials and beneath the signatures of all official correspondence. When independence was achieved in June 1975, the slogan was shortened to *"A Luta Continua!"* (the struggle continues). With an armed invasion expected daily from Southern Rhodesia and with South Africa a supremely dangerous neighbour, it seemed a cry of defiance directed against the remaining bastions of white rule in southern Africa. It was taken up by the schoolchildren of Soweto in 1976 and it has since been proclaimed at times of public protest by demonstrators throughout the region — in South Africa, in Namibia, in Zimbabwe and Zambia, even in Malawi. Within Mozambique, however, it was a double-edged slogan. During the nineteen months between independence in June 1975 and the Third Party Congress in February 1977, the continuing struggle was principally directed not against neighbouring white-ruled states but against what the party termed *"O Inimigo Interno"* (the internal enemy). This enemy was defined as those class enemies of Frelimo's revolution who were working through rumour, conspiracy and economic sabotage to undermine it. In sharp contrast to the appeals for national unity and reconciliation which had characterised Zambia's independence in 1964 and which (partly at Mozambique's urging) were to become so prominent a feature of victory celebrations in Zimbabwe in 1980, Frelimo came to power convinced of the need to continue its struggle within its national borders.

Frelimo had been preoccupied with *"O Inimigo Interno"* since the late 1960s when the movement had been torn apart by internal disputes. These disputes had erupted in the wake of Frelimo's successes, in its initial attacks launched across the Tanzanian border in September 1964, in driving Portuguese officials, traders and small farmers away from rural areas of the districts of Cabo Delgado and Niassa. The result was areas which could be described as having been "liberated". Questions of administration arose leading in turn to arguments about policy which soon turned to arguments about ideology.

There were three main areas of dispute. The first concerned power in the liberated areas, centring on Frelimo's relations with Makonde chiefs and elders who expected to dictate policy in neo-traditional terms. This question overlapped with disputes about the role of women, overlapping in turn with questions about access to land and land use. Northern Mozambique, like the rest of the country, had then, and still has, a great variety of customary systems. The second area of dispute concerned production policies, focusing in particular on the control of production and marketing and the profits derived from peasant cash-cropping within the marketing cooperatives which had flourished earlier in the 1960s. The third area of dispute

5

involved allegations of "tribalism" with the Makonde elders happy to proclaim a limited "independence" for their home area, neglecting the need to prosecute a national struggle in central and southern Mozambique and demanding of Frelimo only that the movement should proceed to liberate the northern towns of Mueda and Porto Amelia. Involved in all three areas of dispute was a generational struggle between young Frelimo activists, many of them trained in Algeria between 1962 and 1964, and an older generation which had left Mozambique only as labour migrants.

By 1970, following Eduardo Mondlane's assassination and the destruction of most of Frelimo's advance bases in the major Portuguese army offensive, *Gordian Knot*, these internal disputes were shelved rather than settled by Samora Machel's accession to power and his overriding emphasis on the successful prosecution of the military struggle. Propaganda about the economic, social and political achievements of the liberated areas played an important part in winning for Frelimo in its international relations the moral high ground of the war. In practice, the literacy classes and vaccination clinics, together with the communal production units where the "new men" already flourished, existed for the most part on paper. Absolute priority after 1970 was given to the war effort, particularly in Tete District where, for the first time after 1970, Frelimo had real targets for attack in the Trans-Zambesi and Beira railways and in the schemes associated with Cahora Bassa dam.

The disputes of the 1960s and their tragic consequences in the deaths of Mondlane and other party members haunted the government which came to power in 1975. By then, from Frelimo's perspective, Mozambique was no longer a war zone with scattered "liberated" villages for which policies existed on paper. It was a nation of towns and cities, plantations and industries, production systems and ethnic affiliations ranging from white Portuguese settler associations to the smallest village community. At every level of society, from the handful of white millionaires to the multitudes of impoverished labour migrants, strong links existed with Southern Rhodesia and South Africa. Potentially, *O Inimigo Interno* seemed everywhere, not least among the new recruits to the party as Frelimo assumed power.

The declaration of war against the internal enemy was, however, an extraordinarily dangerous strategy. Mondlane's speeches of the early 1960s, as he attempted to mobilise a constituency for Frelimo, had defined Mozambicans as a nation of "workers", of people who were united in the experience of seeing their labour exploited by colonial capitalism. This was a necessary tactic given that he was the leader of a movement based on a coalition of migrant workers' organisations, and it laid the essential groundwork of Frelimo's eventual adoption of a Marxist-Leninist programme. In retrospect, however, Mondlane would have been equally wise to have stressed Mozambique's extreme fragility as a potential nation.

Most African countries are defined by borders laid down in the European partition of Africa in 1890, borders which, as Nyerere once commented, have to be held sacrosanct because they are so absurd. Mozambique's present borders derive from Portuguese conflicts with Britain in Southern Rhodesia and Nyasaland, culminating in the humiliating ultimatum of January 1890. Despite its claim to have been the occupying colonial power since 1498, Portugal was allowed to retain only those regions for which Britain then had little use, and even this arrangement did not insure against frequent conspiracies by rival colonial powers over the next fifty years to redraw the map of Mozambique in British, French, South African, Southern Rhodesian or even German interests. In a country 1,800 km long and on average 500 km wide, the transport routes that developed flowed east to west rather than north to south, serving the stronger economies of the colonies of the interior rather than Mozambique itself. By 1909, it was already accepted that Mozambique's chief assets were its people and its coastline and that the bulk of its revenue would be derived from labour migration and from servicing imports and exports.

Even this economy depended on agreements with chartered companies and other foreign concessionaries to exploit Mozambique on Portugal's behalf. From 1890 until 1941, Mozambique was a patchwork of colonial districts and company concessions, administered from head offices in Lisbon, London, Paris, Monaco, Brussels and Durban. Travellers from Lourenço Marques to Quelimane, for example, in the 1920s, would drive the dirt road through state-administered territory as far as the Sabi River. At Mambone, they passed through a custom's post, paying duty on goods they were importing and changing their escudos for Mozambique Company pounds. At Beira, they faced two alternatives. One route took them on the dirt road to Vila Pery, Changara and Tete, changing their currency and paying duty once more as they crossed the Zambezi to Moatize as they entered Nyasaland and again at Mulanje as they left Nyasaland for the final drive to Quelimane. The second, shorter but slower route open only in the dry season, took them through Inhaminga to Lacerdonia on the Zambezi River, attending to customs formalities before crossing the river by pontoon into territory administered by the British company Sena Sugar Estates and continuing along another sand track to their destination. Those venturing north of Quelimane encountered similar difficulties — unsurfaced roads and more customs formalities until they reached Niassa Company territory in the north and the Tanganyikan border.

Only between 1941, when the last of the company charters lapsed, and 1974, when the Portuguese army rebelled in Lisbon, was Mozambique governed as a single administrative unit with a national economy. Only in 1955 when Portugal produced the first development plan for Mozambique was money derived from enterprise in Mozambique re-invested in the colony. Most of the very limited superstructure inherited by Frelimo at independence was created in the early 1970s to facilitate Portugal's war effort, Frelimo's greatest economic achievements arguably preceding the party's actual assumption of power.

Thus, even by the standards of colonial rule in Africa, Mozambique was a uniquely fragile creation. It had been hammered into shape by Portuguese-officered armies in expeditions against the chiefs and rival war lords of the late nineteenth century. But it was administered, for well over half the colonial period, by a variety of different agencies and the economic divisions inherited from that period remained until the 1970s stronger than any centrifugal pressures. The very strategies of resistance to colonial society, above all by the peasant majority, had necessarily been local and hence potentially divisive. The rushed economic development of the period 1961 to 1974, particularly in road-building and industrial development, had created for many Mozambicans, in colonialism's dying years, the flawed vision of alternative destinies for the country. Finally, the working class on which an incoming Marxist-Leninist government would depend for support (mainly the dock workers and railway workers of Lourenço Marques and Beira) was overwhelmingly white and Portuguese.

In the weeks and months following independence, the internal enemy was never defined except in the broadest of "class" terms as being those with "bourgeois" or "petit-bourgeois" or "capitalist" tendencies. There were frequent attacks on "saboteurs", and "collaborators", and sometimes more precisely on "alcoholics", "polygamists" and "Joes" (meaning American-style hippies). In practice, Frelimo's suspicions were directed at four loosely-defined groups.

The first target of suspicion was the white settlers, mainly Portuguese. They owned, or were the "comprador" face of foreign interests in Mozambique's farms and plantation companies. They owned or represented the import-export agencies and the new industries which had sprung up in the wake of the economic investments of the late 1960s and early 1970s. They included a small number of millionaires who had invested heavily in the dying years of Portuguese rule as foreign capital withdrew and looked to insure their wealth. But they also included a mass of much poorer whites manning the railway systems and the rural trade networks and keeping the ports of Lourenço Marques, Beira and Nacala operating. In 1975, this white working class came out on the streets, demonstrating with spanners and sledge-hammers their support for the new communist government — in sharp contrast to those other counter-revolutionary whites who seized the Radio Club in response to the Lusaka Accord which ceded Mozambique to Frelimo. By mid-1976, most whites of both groups had left for Lisbon, fleeing Frelimo's laws on the nationalisation of property and the socialisation of medicine and unwilling to sacrifice their Portuguese nationality for the uncertainties of a Mozambican future. As they departed, many of them sabotaged the possessions they were abandoning. A significant proportion of them, perhaps as many as 30%, were Mozambican-born blacks and mestizos, literate in Portuguese and experienced in urban wage employment.

The second target of suspicion was the handful of Mozambicans who, prior to 1974, had managed to acquire a higher education but who had not committed themselves directly to the armed struggle. Educational opportunities in colonial Mozambique were pitifully meagre, even by the standards of neighbouring colonies. At independence, 95% of a population of 12 million was pre-literate, the 5% who were literate including the white Portuguese. The new nation had one black doctor and one qualified black agronomist. Despite four generations of labouring in the gold mines of South Africa, there was not a single Mozambican mining engineer. A university had been founded in Lourenço Marques in 1961 as part of a reform package following the beginning of the war in Angola. It admitted a few black students, some of whom later found their way to Portugal for further studies. In Dar es Salaam, the Mozambique Institute opened under Frelimo's auspices, but it became the centre of bitter disputes when some students insisted on continuing their studies in the United States rather than join Frelimo's guerrilla army. There were also a small number of black Roman Catholic catechists training in the United States. In 1975, Machel denounced them as "the janitors that work in the toilets of white Americans".[1] Fifteen years on, many of these students have remained in exile, nursing their resentments. In contrast with Zimbabwe after 1980, the path to advancement under Frelimo has been through participation in the armed struggle.

Criticism of the catechists was but an aspect of Frelimo's suspicions of the third group of potential internal enemies, namely, Roman Catholics and Jehovah's Witnesses. The role of Christianity and Islam in independent Mozambique will be commented upon later in this study but one aspect is important here. It is that the churches (and mosques) provided the nearest equivalents to non-ethnic or supra-ethnic civil associations independent of party control. The Catholic Church, in particular, represented considerable networks of patronage. Catholic families, like most Mozambican families, tended to be large. But the range of mutual help and support within the family was enormously multiplied by networks of godparents and their own families, enlarging the scale of patronage across the divisions of race and class and the rural-urban divide. In its early hostility to the Catholic Church, Frelimo was in conflict with a social force stronger than anything the party had to offer.

Most serious of all, however, in its consequences for all involved, was Frelimo's ambiguous relationship with Mozambique's peasant majority. Throughout the colonial period it was the peasantry which bore the brunt of colonial oppression in the form of forced labour for men in the region's plantations and mines and for women in the compulsory cotton and rice schemes. The strategies of their resistance varied from place to place depending on their pre-colonial histories, the circumstances of their incorporation into the colonial economy and the nature of capitalism's demands. There were some groups who played the card of ethnic nationalism, negotiating space for themselves through tactics of limited collaboration. There were others who sought the patronage of individual employers, correctly identifying conflicts of interest between capital, particularly foreign capital, and the state. Others still took refuge in passive resistance, absenteeism, minor acts of sabotage or flight. All three of these strategies became unacceptable after 1975. What all three had in common was a fierce loyalty to their own lands and a hatred of governmental intervention.

The liberation struggle had been fought mainly in the rural areas of northern Mozambique and the experience led Frelimo to lay claim to a special, revolutionary engagement with the peasantry. When troubles arose, in the disputes of the 1960s, over authority, production and ethnic allegiances, Frelimo responded by talking of a combined process of self-education, the leaders listening to peasant grievances, and "conscientisation", the leaders giving the peasantry a political education. When this failed to resolve the tensions, Frelimo responded by complaining of "feudalism", "landlordism" and "capitalist tendencies" among people who had no shoes. In practice, Frelimo learned little from the the war about peasant societies, little at least that was carried over into policy making. At independence, when the party moved to take control of all local trading, arresting women head-loading baskets of rice to village markets, and when the policies of villagisation and collective production began to be imposed uniformly on Mozambique's great variety of soils, climates and production systems, peasant support for Frelimo was further eroded.

In attacking all four groups as potential or actual internal enemies, Frelimo was attempting to stand Mozambique's history on its head. Acutely aware of the fragility of the country it had liberated, the party was also acutely aware of the failures of neighbouring Tanzania and Zambia, their principal supporters during the struggle, to break their own economic bonds of neo-colonialism. The revolutionary project was both true to

Frelimo's origins and experience and had intellectual credibility in the southern Africa of 1975.

None of this explains directly the rise of Renamo and its success in despoiling Mozambique. As the following pages make clear, Renamo has its origins in counter-insurgency movements created by Southern Rhodesia and fostered by South Africa. Most of the young men fighting with Renamo were infants when Mozambique became independent and have no memory of these issues. However, this chapter does explain why, when the forces of white reaction launched their onslaught on Mozambique's revolution, they were able to recruit collaborators from all sections of Mozambican society, at home and abroad. Fifteen years on, Mozambican is fighting Mozambican in a situation which only casuistry refuses to call a civil war.

2 CREATED INSURGENCY

THE FIRST REBELS

Renamo, as we have seen above, was by no means the first opposition group to have arisen against Frelimo. A series of small movements, opposing Frelimo, on the grounds of elitism, ideology and the ethnic composition of its leadership arose following splits on these issues within Frelimo in the 1960s.

Frelimo was born of a coalition of three exile groups, MANU, UDENAMO and UNAMI. They coalesced together in June 1962 through the encouragement of Eduardo Mondlane, who had the advantage of not belonging to any of them. This union was fragile. Already by August 1962, Frelimo experienced its first schism with the expulsion of Matthew Mmole and Laurence Millinga (both former MANU officials) which arose from their disquiet over not being elected to Frelimo's Central Committee. They alleged that Frelimo's leadership was dominated by southerners who used the Makonde as ordinary rank-and-file troops without proportional representation in the upper levels of the party. Such allegations by disgruntled aspirants to the leadership were to resurface many times in the 1960s.[1]

Frelimo soon experienced another internal dispute. In December 1962, Frelimo's first publicity secretary, Leo Milas, was beaten up by about twenty Frelimo members in Dar es Salaam. A month later, in January 1963, Frelimo's Secretary-General, David Mungwambe, his deputy Paulo Gumane, the organising secretary, João Mungwambe, and Fanuel Mahluza were expelled from the Central Committee because of their alleged involvement in the beating. Milas had been sent to Dar by Mondlane to calm resentment over the election of Marcelino dos Santos as Secretary of External Affairs. Dos Santos was a mestizo, which embittered some black Mozambicans, who claimed he was actually Cape Verdian and should, therefore, be expelled from the party.

The sending of Milas could not have been a worse decision, as there was much uncertainty over his own claims to being Mozambican. Milas continued to be a cause of discontent within Frelimo even after the expulsions, and although warned to mend his ways and then reshuffled to a foreign posting, he refused to leave Dar es Salaam. Eventually Mondlane, with the aid of a private detective agency, investigated Milas' background which revealed that he was actually a black American, Leo Clinton Aldridge. Milas was expelled in August 1964 from Frelimo, from where he went to Khartoum, added Seifak-Aziz to his name, and began issuing pro-Chinese anti-Frelimo propaganda in the name of the defunct MANU.

Subsequent revelations may also explain why Milas was so difficult. It appears that Orlando Cristina, then an undercover Portuguese intelligence agent, based in Nampula, visited Milas in 1963 in Dar es Salaam, and arranged through Milas to be sent to Algeria for training as a Frelimo combatant. This early link probably explains how Cristina recruited Milas in 1977 into the newly launched Renamo.[2]

By late 1967 and early 1968, the further tensions generated by the unexplained death of Frelimo's Secretary of Defence, Filipe Magaia, in October 1966 and the encouragement of unrest by Fr. Mateus Gwenjere, exploded into violence. The disturbances took place at the secondary school operated by the Mozambique Institute in Dar es Salaam. Before 1967, much of the training there was the preparing of administrative cadres for an independent Mozambique. But with the death of Magaia, and Machel's rise in prominence, the military strategy dominated, being seen as the only way to obtain independence. As part of this process it was decided to de-emphasise academic preparation and stress military training. Many students, frightened by the prospects of fighting and having been led to believe they had been recruited solely for study, rioted. Students studying abroad refused to return to Mozambique to fight. This dispute culminated with the closure of the school and the sending of what remained of the student body to Rutambe settlement. Many of these students eventually fled to Kenya from where some reached the United States.[3]

Investigations into the unrest by the Tanzanian government and the OAU concluded that the revolt was the direct consequence of the presence of Fr. Mateus Gwenjere. Gwenjere, a Roman Catholic priest, had joined Frelimo at the end of 1967 with some twenty of his seminary students from Beira, and immediately supported the discontent amongst the existing students. The motives behind this probably included ambition. A late-comer to Frelimo, Gwenjere would undoubtedly have liked to have taken over the directorate of the Mozambique Institute.

In July 1968 Frelimo held its Second Congress. This time it was held within Mozambique, in Niassa province. Although the Congress outwardly depicted a unified and united organisation, there still remained discontent within the leadership. This included a dispute between Lazero Nkavandame (Frelimo's Cabo Delgado provincial secretary) and Mondlane on where the location of the Congress should be. Nkavandame wanted it held in Tanzania where he felt he had the strongest support for his bid for the presidentship. He and a small group of followers believed that Mondlane wanted the Congress to be held within Mozambique to counter this challenge by gaining maximum advantage in the competition for the leadership. When the Congress went ahead and was held in Mozambique, Nkvandame refused to attend.

These events contributed to Nkavandame's decision to defect to the Portuguese in April 1969. He accused the Frelimo leadership of being southern dominated and, as a result, of exploiting the Makonde people. As with the events in 1962-3 and the student revolts, these allegations did not obtain much support within Frelimo, even amongst the Makonde who the dissidents claimed to represent.

One other event was to cause Frelimo special difficulties in this period: the death of Mondlane by parcel bomb in February 1969. Mondlane's death generated a whole series of charges and countercharges between the leadership factions over responsibility. Although publicly Frelimo at the time blamed Portuguese agents, it is now admitted that Mondlane was also a victim of the leadership dispute, Nkavandame and Simango being blamed for assisting the assassination.

Following Mondlane's death, a triumvirate to be known as the Presidential Council was formed. Consisting of Simango, dos Santos and Machel, its sittings were not a success, with a continuing row over who was behind Mondlane's murder. One suspect, Silvero Nungu, Frelimo's Administrative Secretary, further fuelled the crisis by dying from hunger strike within Mozambique.

Simango responded to these events by publishing a statement in the press, protesting at the way Frelimo was run and blaming dos Santos, Machel and Janet Mondlane for Nungu's death. Although both the OAU and President Nyerere tried to reconcile the parties, Simango was purged from the Presidential Council. In February 1970 he was expelled from Frelimo for having attempted to launch a rival nationalist group. A reshuffling of the Central Committee resulted in Machel becoming President and dos Santos Vice-President.

These disputes, with their expulsions and resignations, produced a number of rival nationalist parties. Most of these were, however, little more than paper organisations and had no significant following or support. In 1962, Gwambe was expelled and organised UDENAMO in Kampala. This soon became reformed under the name UNDENAMO-Monomotapa. The expulsion of Mmole, Millinga and others in 1962 led to the formation of UDENAMO-Mozambique. In Kampala in 1963 UNDENAMO-Monomotapa, MANU and MANC came together to form FUNIPOMO. By June 1964, a further splinter group MORECO, UDENAMO-Mozambique, MANU and UNDENAMO-Monomatapa joined to form COREMO which was based in Lusaka and had a representative in Cairo.

COREMO was the only splinter group to have any support within Mozambique or indeed to be active inside the country against the Portuguese. COREMO cultivated an ultra-revolutionary image and links with the PAC of South Africa, attracting Simango to its leadership in 1971, after his expulsion from Frelimo. It was however never a serious threat to either Frelimo or the Portuguese. By 1966 it faced its own splits with a break-away group called PAPOMO being launched. A more serious splinter group emerged in 1968 from COREMO. Called the UNAR, it was based in Blantyre and stood for the unification of Rombezia, the area between the Rovuma and Zambezi rivers. Two other splinter groups emerged in Nairobi out of the student riots at the Mozambique Institute in 1968. These were MOLIMO and FUMO.

These splinter groups (which became known as phantom parties) provided a basis for black and multi-racial political opposition to Frelimo during the Caetano government in Portugal, when restrictions on political parties became more relaxed. Prominent amongst these small groups was GUMO, formed in 1973, and led by Maximo Dias and Joana Simião. It did not attack Frelimo but presented itself instead as a less bellicose party, calling for peaceful campaigns against the Portuguese. GUMO itself experienced a serious split in June 1974, over Joana Simião's links with Portuguese intelligence. Simião was suspended from GUMO's executive. She retaliated by expelling Maximo Dias from the executive. This complete disarray led to Dias winding up GUMO in July. Simião and her faction merged in June 1974 with another splinter group, the CNAM, to form FRECOMO. FRECOMO sought an end to the war. Its two main objectives were the holding of a referendum to decide Mozambique's future, and a meeting of a "Congress of the Mozambique People" to map out the result.[4] FRECOMO only lasted a couple of months, because, on 24 August, it fused with Lazero Nkavandame's UNIPOMO, Fr. Mateus Gwenjere's FREINA (sponsored by the Companhia Industrial de Monapo), Jorge Jardim's CDM, Amos Sumane's COREMO, and MONA to form the Partido de Coligacao Nacional (PCN). It was hoped that this coalition would obtain independence, by calling for a referendum on the country's future.

Another significant group in this interim period was FICO (meaning "I Stay"). FICO was an amalgam of white settlers, worried by what a future Frelimo government would bring. It campaigned for a federal union with Portugal and the right to have arms issued to whites to defend themselves against Frelimo. By September 1974 it was backing the PCN out of desperation. With the signing of the Lusaka Agreement on 7 September 1974, angry, bewildered and frightened groups of whites besieged and occupied the Radio Club of Mozambique for three days in a declared "revolt". They were led by a group called "Mozambique Livre", which was the successor to FICO. This revolt was echoed in the provincial capitals of Beira, Tete, Quelimane and Nampula. "Mozambique Livre" appealed to the Portuguese army to join in rejecting the Lusaka Accord and declaring UDI in Mozambique.[5] Gwenjere and Simango also broadcast on behalf of the PCN calling for black support. Appeals were also made for customs officials to open the borders, in the hope that South African troops would come in and support them. Reports at the time speak of P.W. Botha, then Defence Minister, sending a South African military task force to Komatipoort to wait for permission from Prime Minister Vorster to go into Mozambique to assist the revolt but, in line with South Africa's then policy of detente, this was never received.[6] Road blocks along the Beira corridor were also set up by Portuguese settlers in anticipation of support from a military force from Rhodesia led by Jorge Jardim (a wealthy Portuguese industrialist). This too never materialised.[7] The revolt eventually collapsed when it became evident that no external support was forthcoming and that the majority of Portuguese settlers were more inclined to leave Mozambique than follow the Rhodesian path of an UDI. A further revolt by a much smaller number of settlers and Portuguese commandos happened in October. This saw more violence, especially in the black suburbs of the capital where groups of armed white youth had been attacking blacks. This second upsurge of unrest forced the army to intervene both to crush the riots and to force the total capitulation of "Mozambique Livre". This marked the effective end of organised opposition to Frelimo rule before independence by both blacks and whites. It also marked a major increase in the flow of whites leaving the country.

With the swearing-in of the transitional government on 20 September 1974, all political activity other than that by Frelimo was suppressed. Several hundred supporters of the PCN were imprisoned. These included Paulo Gumane, Joana Simião, Uria Simango and Lazero Nkavandame. The PCN, being an urban phenomenon and lacking support outside the towns, was vulnerable to the pressure against it which Frelimo could mount. Even in the urban areas whatever appeal it had initially attracted amongst black Mozambicans was seriously compromised by its elitist approach and its desperate alliance with "Mozambique Livre" in the three day revolt.[8]

The first violent disturbances against the new government after independence occurred in late 1975 with a flare-up of unrest in the north of Mozambique among the Macua and Makonde ethnic groups. Frelimo alleged that this had been stimulated by the Frente de Cabo Delgado (FCD), partly out of discontent over the continued imprisonment of the former Frelimo Vice-President, Lazero Nkavandame, who originated from Cabo Delgado. Not much is known about the FCD, but Frelimo reports at the time refer to thirty-five members being arrested by the authorities in February 1976 in Nangada, and, a few weeks later, to the detention of a Frelimo political commissar in Montepuez, for involvement with the group.[9]

A third opposition group in early post-independence Mozambique was the reappearing Frente de Democracia de Mozambique (FUMO). It was however, for the most part, based externally in Lisbon under the leadership of Domingos Arouça (see below). Another anti-Frelimo organisation, calling itself "Magaia" (after Frelimo's first military commander, who died in unexplained circumstances in 1966) was launched by Orlando Cristina. It produced a clandestine publication called "Magaia's Voice". Distributed in 1976 in the Mozambique capital, it played critically on the disputes within Frelimo in the 1960s and the alleged southern origins of Frelimo.[10] "Magaia" had some popularity and its sympathisers had to be purged from the Mozambican army in the six months following the mutiny of 400 Mozambican soldiers at the Machava barracks near the capital in December 1975.[11] It was believed by the authorities that "Magaia" had encouraged the rebellion. The last recorded activity of "Magaia" was in December 1976 when it had its objectives and grievances aired on an early broadcast of the rebel radio station, Voz da Africa Livre.[12]

Three opposition groups claimed, by 1977, to be active within Mozambique. These were FUMO, the PRM (later renamed Africa Livre), and the MNRA. The PRM (Partido Revolucionario de Mozambique) claimed to be active in Zambezia and Tete provinces. It was an entirely African movement, run by two former Frelimo guerrillas, Amos Sumane and Gimo M'Phiri, who killed government soldiers in order to capture arms for further missions.[13] Even less is known about the other group, the MNRA. It claimed to be active throughout Mozambique — under the leadership of six former Frelimo commanders.[14] It is probable that this was Renamo under an earlier label, which had begun getting press coverage as the MNRA in July 1977 in the South African press.[15]

These groups were all small. They did not represent a major threat to Frelimo. In order to understand the levels of insurgency in Mozambique today, and the population's ambivalence to both forces — government and dissident — one has to turn to the roots of the problem.

RHODESIAN CREATORS

The origins of Renamo have been well documented.[16] It is widely accepted that it was established by the Rhodesian security forces. Rhodesian interest in sponsoring a rebel force within Mozambique has its roots in Frelimo's offensive against the Portuguese in Tete Province in 1973. Frelimo's successes led the head of the Rhodesian security forces (CIO), Ken Flower, to attempt to form, with Portuguese intelligence (DGS), an alternative rebel group to Frelimo that could gather information on Zanla and Frelimo operations. The efforts to form such a group were, however, frustrated by the political coup in Lisbon which led to the signing of the Lusaka Accord guaranteeing the transition of power in Mozambique at independence in 1975.[17]

These plans were revived in 1975, because of the now independent

Mozambique Frelimo government's hostility towards Rhodesian UDI, its support of Zanla and its closing of Mozambique's borders with Rhodesia. The Rhodesia CIO's initial plans took the form of sponsoring a small group of rebels, dominated by disgruntled Portuguese, who had either been associated with the DGS or had their property and economic assets abandoned to the new Mozambican government. This group was soon found to be cumbersome and ineffectual. It was, however encouraged to run the rebel radio station, Voz da Africa Livre, in an attempt to recruit more native Mozambicans. The broadcasts of Voz da Africa Livre coupled with recruitment drives amongst the large black Mozambican diaspora in Lisbon and Johannesburg had by 1977 already produced a steady trickle of recruits for the CIO to train.

Amongst the early recruits was a former Frelimo commander, Andre Matsangaissa. Matsangaissa had been sent to a Frelimo re-education camp for theft, from which he escaped to join the rebels. Matsangaissa was given the leadership of the group. By mid-1977 it had been named the MNR or MNRA, more commonly known by its Portuguese acronym, RNM or RENAMO (Resistencia Nacional Moçambicana).[18]

Renamo was still, to all intents and purposes, only a Rhodesian, anti-Frelimo fifth column operating in Mozambique. It relied entirely on Rhodesian aid for survival. It frequently operated as part of the operations of the Selous Scouts or other branches of the Rhodesian security forces. But, by late 1977, its role had become more clearcut: it was to "sabotage, to disrupt the population and to disrupt the economy" of Mozambique. It was, in addition, to obtain recruits, attack Frelimo and Zanla bases and gather intelligence on them. In concrete terms this represented the burning of villages, the plundering of agricultural co-operatives, shops and clinics, attacks on railroad lines and road traffic, the raiding of re-education camps and the disruption of commerce generally.[19]

With growing Zanla activity along the Rhodesian border in 1978, Renamo's operations were expanded by the CIO. Its tactics were slightly altered. More permanent bases were set up inside Mozambique as launch pads for counter-offensives against Zanla bases and infiltration routes. As an extension to this policy of reducing Zanla pressure, a plan was devised to cut Mozambique into three by severing land communications between the two main urban centres of Mozambique, Maputo and Beira, and the strategically important town of Tete. These plans were only in their first phase of implementation when Gorongosa mountain bases were attacked by the Mozambican Army (FAM) and Andre Matsangaissa was killed.[20]

Matsangaissa's death signalled the beginning of a major power struggle whose legacy is still evident within Renamo. Afonso Dhlakama (Matsangaissa's deputy) was his natural successor. But Dhlakama was unpopular, both with the Rhodesians and also with many of the black Mozambican dissidents. Dhlakama's support derived almost entirely from the N'dau speakers of central Mozambique and from Orlando Cristina, a white Portuguese, who had become a main link with the growing South African interest in Renamo and in destabilising "Marxist" Mozambique. The struggle resolved itself with the mysterious disappearance of the main challengers to Dhlakama's leadership bid, including Renamo's first deputy Commander, Orlando Macomo.

The most serious challenger to Dhlakama was Lucas M'langa, who was Rhodesian-backed. The Rhodesians attempted to resolve the conflict by dividing Renamo into two commands. This failed with the dispute being resolved by a gun fight between Dhlakama and M'langa's factions at Renamo's Chisumbanje base in then Zimbabwe-Rhodesia. M'langa was killed in this struggle. His surviving supporters fled back into Mozambique and handed themselves over to the FAM. At the same time Renamo's Political Commissar, Henrique Sitoe, and a radio operator surrendered to the Mozambican authorities.[21] This in turn caused further tensions and splits within Renamo's ranks, with supporters of other challengers defecting to Frelimo or going into self-imposed exile. The splinter group from Renamo known as MONAMO, which operated in Lisbon from late 1979, had its roots in this split. Even Dhlakama admitted in a report captured by Frelimo in 1981 from the re-established Garagua base that "many fighters died this year, including commanders and other heads and others were maimed and crippled — all because of a power struggle".[22]

Renamo was thrust into further disorder by the Lancaster House agreement on a timetable for ending UDI. By 1980 it found itself increasingly starved of logistical support from the Rhodesian CIO and more reliant on whatever it could get from the South African security forces (MID). As Dhlakama wrote in mid-1980 following Zimbabwean independence: "When Andre died the MNR was on the road to total destruction".[23] Renamo was only saved from being a sporadic irritant of armed banditry within Mozambique by the increased interest of the South African armed forces in maintaining it as a viable force.

Until 1980 the level of violence and the range of Renamo activity was fairly limited compared with the current levels. Production figures for 1980-81, following the lull in rebel activity after Zimbabwean independence, indicate that agricultural production reached the levels of 1974-75, the year of transition to full independence, an indication of Mozambique's economic potential, given peace. This improvement was sadly short lived. By 1982, Renamo had infiltrated 9 out of the 10 provinces of Mozambique. The level of violence and destruction steadily increased.

Between 1980 and February 1988 Renamo's activities rendered inoperable approximately 1,800 schools, 720 health units, 900 shops and 1,300 trucks and buses.[24] It is estimated that tens of thousands of people have died due to direct violence in the conflict. If the effects of conflict-related famine are taken into account this figure cannot be far from the 100,000 estimated for the State Department in the Gersony report. Human displacement has been just as dramatic. The number of refugees both internally and externally reached over 4.3 million in 1989, an indication of how devastating this conflict has become for Mozambique.[25]

To understand this dramatic revival of Renamo, it is necessary to look at South African policy towards Mozambique.

SOUTH AFRICAN RELAUNCHING

South African support for Mozambican rebels against Frelimo was not immediately forthcoming at Mozambique's independence in 1975. An informal understanding between the South African authorities and the new Mozambique government tacitly accepted that neither party should aid the others' opposition.[26] This changed by 1978 as a result of the increasing use by the ANC of the infiltration routes into South Africa through southern Mozambique.

Both the Rhodesian CIO and Orlando Cristina had already approached the South Africans for concrete support for Renamo, but they had been turned down on the grounds that this would contravene the policy of "detente" that South Africa's then Prime Minister, John Vorster, advocated that Pretoria should maintain towards the independent southern African states. This policy radically changed late in 1978 in the wake of the "Muldergate" information scandal. The scandal caused the fall of both Vorster and General Heneriek van de Bergh, head of BOSS, the South African civil intelligence organisation. Both Vorster and van de Bergh had been the main architects and protagonists of a policy of detente towards "front line states". As Prime Minister, Vorster was replaced by P.W. Botha, the Defence Minister. General Magnus Malan (a known hawk) became Minister of Defence. The result was to put South African military men in key positions of power. For the security forces this meant that BOSS (already undermined by scandal) would lose its power to the military intelligence organisation, MID. Following this reorientation a military perspective to the southern African region predominated.[27] The "Total Onslaught" theory, as part of the military "Total National Strategy" overall, became the dominant approach within the South African military establishment. Its major objective was to cut off outside support to the various domestic anti-apartheid opposition groups, creating a South African dominated security membrane around South Africa against incursion by armed and other reinforcements, such as leaders returning clandestinely from exile. In tactical terms this represented the neutralising of the Front Line States by a synthesis of diplomatic, economic and military policies. Against Mozambique this took the form of economic sabotage, direct attacks on the ANC there, and destabilisation through proxy warfare.[28]

By mid-1979 the MID were already supplying weapons to Renamo. They had already for some years organised supportive press coverage of the group. Colonel van Niekerk became the main liaison officer for this operation, the start of a long association with Renamo. It is estimated that by 1980 the Rhodesians had received over US$ 1 million from South Africa in support of Renamo operations. In this period of growing South African involvement plans were formulated, and an agreement was made between Magnus Malan and his Rhodesian counterpart, General Walls, that, in the event of the collapse of "white" Rhodesia, the groups that would be "compromised" by Zimbabwean independence would be integrated into the South African Defence Forces (SADF) and the MID.[29]

This is what happened in the period between the Lancaster House Agreement and the announcement of the independence election results. British pressure forced the CIO to close down its Renamo operations. The rebels were offered the choice of either continuing to operate as Renamo under South African management or reintegration into civilian life. To the surprise of several CIO officials the majority of the rebels opted to transfer to South Africa.[30]

The transfer to South Africa from Rhodesia was done mostly by air, using a shuttle of South African C 130s. These carried the equipment and staff of Voz da Africa Livre, Renamo personnel, their armaments and several instructors. The remaining rebels were ordered to regroup at a base already set up on Sitatonga mountain, opposite the Chimanimani mountains in Zimbabwe.[31]

The transfer of operations to South Africa meant a restructuring of

Renamo. This was effected by incorporating the rebels and their Rhodesian instructors into the South African Special Forces, the Special Forces being the operational arm of South African military intelligence. Although Renamo continued to be trained by former Selous Scouts and Rhodesian Special Force personnel, they acted on South African command — a situation which led several former commanders to resign over the conflict of interests about Renamo's future role.[32] Renamo's training and intelligence gathering were (until 1989) mainly at Phalaborwa in the north Transvaal. They were placed under the direction of Five Reconnaissance Regiment (5 Recce) which has Mozambique designated as an area of specialisation.[33]

The reduction of Rhodesian influence on Renamo resulted in the rise in importance of Orlando Cristina, who was made Renamo's first Secretary-General in 1980. The CIO had always kept Cristina at a distance from any direct involvement in Renamo's tactical decision making. Cristina, however, obtained greater influence in Renamo through his support of Afonso Dhlakama in the succession dispute following Matsangaissa's death.[34] It was through Cristina's publicity campaign that Dhlakama was able to consolidate his position and gain the Presidency of Renamo.

After the transfer to South Africa, Renamo's situation was, nevertheless, precarious initially. In June 1980, the FAM captured Sitatonga base and shattered the last concentration of rebels in Mozambique. With no base and no supplies, the remaining groups dispersed. They survived by pursuing a career of uncoordinated armed banditry.[35]

From Maputo's perspective, the threat was over. With the euphoria within the Mozambican leadership that the Rhodesian issue had been resolved and that the increased ANC presence in Mozambique was beginning to be felt within South Africa, Maputo appeared to be unable to strike a balance between its ideological commitment against apartheid and the necessity of a geopolitical pragmaticism in the face of the superior strength of South Africa. The SADF obtained without difficulty government backing for Renamo by arguing that the Mozambican government was committed to ending white minority rule in South Africa. A "political camp" was set up at Walmerstad, a former farm estate, some 50 km from Pretoria. Walmerstad was used (until N'Komati) to provide accommodation and facilities for Renamo's leadership and the rebel radio station staff. In addition to Walmerstad, Cristina was provided with an office and secretary at Zanza House, Pretoria, the SADF HQ. Renamo was also provided with military training facilities at Zoabastad and Phalaborwa bases in north Transvaal. By the end of 1980 the first of these newly trained units were ready for operation. Airlifted into Mozambique, with supplies, their initial base inside Mozambique was located at Garagua, well-placed in central Mozambique as a launch pad for wider infiltration. It has been estimated that, by 1981, between 6,000 and 7,000 rebels were active in Mozambique, a much higher number than under Rhodesian management.[36]

This infiltration marked the start of South Africa's new strategy for Renamo. Keeping a firm grip over Renamo, the South Africans tried to concentrate its operations on economic targets and communications. Its aims were to sabotage the newly formed SADCC (Southern African Development Co-ordination Conference) by reducing the independent states in the region to economic dependence on South Africa and to weaken Mozambique to a level of compliance with South African security considerations. A specific objective was the removal of the ANC from

Mozambique soil. Unlike the Rhodesian strategy, there was no consideration of a "hearts and minds" campaign to win over the local population.

A different approach was, however, launched for the benefit of international opinion. For external consumption a publicity campaign was mounted to establish the image of Renamo as a bona fide opposition movement
to Frelimo, worthy of external recognition. As part of this publicity drive,
Dhlakama and Cristina were funded to tour Europe in an attempt to
obtain financial, material and political support for the rebel cause. They
went to Portugal, West Germany and France. In Portugal they met the
business community and the Roman Catholic Church. They were inter-
viewed by the press, and met members of the Social Democratic Party. In
France they met an adviser to President Valéry Giscard d'Estaing. In West
Germany they met representatives of the Christian Social Union of Franz-
Josef Strauss, and the Christian Democratic Party.[37]

On 5 December 1981, the FAM overran the large Renamo base at
Garagua in Manica Province.[38] The capture of Garagua is significant in that
documents found stuffed down a latrine confirmed that the South African
objectives were to turn Mozambique into a destabilised buffer zone and to
curb ANC infiltration into South Africa. Renamo's operations were to be
concentrated on southern Mozambique as this was cheaper to supply.
However the infiltration by Renamo had already spread beyond these specific targets. By December 1981 only the province of Cabo Delgado in the
far north remained unaffected by insurgency.

Renamo insurgency was not, however, the only South African-spon-
sored violence in Mozambique at this time. South African special forces
attacked specified economic and ANC targets. Although some of these
incidents were admitted as having been direct South African action, the
majority were covert operations by special forces units.[39]

By 1983 a series of events in the political arena had brought pressure on
South Africa to reassess its strategy towards Mozambique. The growing
warmth in relations between Mozambique and the USA brought US pressure upon South Africa to reduce its destabilisation of Mozambique. The
rationale was that this created excess instability in the region and might
force Mozambique to call for direct Soviet or Cuban military intervention
to counter the South African threat. This was also the period of the finalis-
ing by the State Department of a more coherent policy towards southern
Africa, most widely known as "constructive engagement", developed by
the then Assistant Secretary of State for African Affairs, Dr Chester
Crocker. In the terms of this policy South Africa began to be seen as the
central contributor to unrest and tension in the region, which was increasingly becoming prejudicial to western interests. The USA therefore encouraged South Africa and Mozambique to negotiate over their differences.[40]

That South Africa agreed to enter into negotiations with Frelimo rather
than pursue its "Total National Strategy" of complete destabilisation of
Mozambique reveals a reassessment of its backing of Renamo. After six
years of destabilisation, Renamo appeared no closer to overthrowing
Frelimo or producing a coherent leadership. With this consideration in
mind, and with the diplomatic and propaganda advantage of being seen to
co-exist with Mozambique, South Africa decided to talk to Mozambique
(the "Mbabane" talks in late 1983). The culmination of these contacts was
the signing of the N'Komati Accord on Non-Aggression and Good
Neighbourliness on 16 March 1984.[41]

The N'Komati Accord took place just when Renamo found itself recovering yet again from a bitter internal dispute following the murder at Walmerstad of Renamo's Secretary-General, Orlando Cristina. This is believed by some commentators, including Renamo spokespeople, to have been orchestrated by MID, who were concerned that Cristina was becoming too independent-minded over the running and objectives of Renamo.[42] Given Cristina's history and subsequent events, this seems less likely than it being a consequence of a resurgence of the succession dispute of 1979-80 following Matsangaissa's death.[43] A faction of black Mozambicans led by Bonaventura Bomba and his brother, Adriano, had joined Renamo as defectors from Frelimo due to disenchantment with their lack of upward mobility and the diminishing success of the Government's domestic policies. This faction resented South African and Portuguese control of Renamo and N'dau dominance within Renamo's leadership. Although Cristina tried to calm this resentment it appears that he was murdered by Bonaventura Bomba. The murder threw Renamo into complete confusion. It brought, in particular, another dispute over who should take over the now vacant position of Secretary-General. Voz da Africa Livre went off the air for a few weeks.[44] Adriano Bomba obtained some publicity as the new Secretary-General.[45] However, in the now familiar manner, both Bonaventura and his brother had disappeared by late 1983. It is probable that they were eliminated by the faction led by Evo Fernandes (then European Representative of Renamo) who had South African backing.[46] By December, 1983 it was announced that Evo Fernandes (a Goanese) was to be the new Secretary-General as a measure to avoid tribalism.[47] Fernandes' rise to power was not only a response to the ethnic issue. It was also a reaffirmation of the old order. As such, it led to a series of resignations and expulsions from Renamo amongst the pro-Bomba faction. This group was to resurface in 1985-86 in the form of anti-Fernandes Renamo splinter groups.

The dispute probably served to encourage the South African government to pursue negotiations with Mozambique. It confirmed that Renamo remained deeply divided and relied visibly on South African support for its coherence.

Despite the N'Komati Accord, promising an end to South African support for Renamo, Renamo's activities within Mozambique intensified, forcing the South African to search for a solution to the conflict. By May 1984 the lack of tangible results from N'Komati led the Mozambicans to request a top-level meeting in Cape Town at which minister Jacinto Veloso presented a dossier documenting cases of Renamo allegedly being supploed by South Africa following the Accord. The South Africans responded by denying any government involvement, offering instead their good offices to bring about a negotiated settlement. Machel agreed to this, annoucing that a Permanent Commission of the Peoples' Assembly would introduce a law providing for an amnesty and the "reintegration" into Mozambican society of rebels who surrendered voluntarily. Following this announcement the South Africans arranged a meeting for a Mozambican envoy with Evo Fernandes in Frankfurt in May 1984 to present the Mozambican offer formally. Fernandes rejected this offer, reiterating Renamo's demands for a government of national reconciliation, a multi-party system and cabinet posts in return for peace.[48]

"Pik" Botha and General van der Westhuizen continued the attempt to bring the two sides to negotiation, visiting Maputo in June and July 1984. During van der Westhuizen's visit in July, Machel agreed to further talks with Renamo. With Mozambican blessing a Renamo delegation, led by Evo Fernandes, was invited to Pretoria in mid-August to discuss terms for laying down arms. Two senior Mozambican ministers, Jacinto Veloso and Sergio Vieira, were on hand in Pretoria, with South African officials acting as "interlocutors" between both sides. Renamo re-issued its terms, demanding the Mozambique government's resignation, the Peoples' Assembly's dissolution and the formation of "a democratic government based on free enterprise". Once the Mozambique government had resigned a coalition between Frelimo and Renamo could be worked out. In return for "accepting" Samora Machel as President, Renamo demanded for itself the portfolios of Prime Minister, Minister of Defence, Finance and Transport, changes in the constitution to "eliminate Marxism" and the abolition of the one-party state. If these demands were not met by September, Renamo threatened to "storm Maputo".[49]

A second round of talks commenced in late September, with two "unofficial" proximity meetings in Pretoria between Renamo and the Mozambique delegation, the South Africans acting as brokers and messengers between the two sides. By 2 October, the discussions had reached the point of collapse. The Mozambicans announced that they would return to Maputo, unless Renamo immediately stopped its attacks. Dhlakama compromised and agreed to the South African proposals.

The next day "Pik" Botha announced that Renamo had accepted a "joint declaration on a cessation of armed activity and conflict", "as a basis for peace in Mozambique". The declaration, unveiled at a press conference, stated:[50]

1. Samora Moises Machel is acknowledged as the President of the People's Republic of Mozambique;
2. Armed activity and conflict within Mozambique, from whatever quarter or source, must stop;
3. The South African government is requested to consider playing a role in the implementation of the declaration;
4. A commission will be established immediately to work towards an early implementation of this declaration.

For the first and only time the Mozambique government delegation appeared in public with Renamo. South Africa offered to send troops to Mozambique to help implement the terms of the declaration. It was also announced that the South African Deputy Foreign Minister, Louis Nel, would chair a commission on which both the Mozambican government and Renamo would be represented. The South Africans also approached Western diplomatic missions in Pretoria to solicit their countries' assistance in setting up an international fund to create employment for 8,000 reintegrated former Renamo combatants within Mozambique. South Africa also offered employment for a further 8,000 in South African mines.[51]

The following day it became clear that Renamo and the Mozambique government interpreted both the meaning of the declaration and the function of the commission very differently. The Mozambicans argued that by recognizing Machel as President, Renamo had recognized the "legitimate authority of our state and government" and that the commission was only empowered to discuss technical questions relating to the mechanics of a cease-fire. Renamo for their part argued that this merely recognized a "current fact" and that they had "not surrendered (their) political demands". Evo Fernandes announced "the war continues and we may have to escalate our actions. There is only speculation about peace or a ceasefire, but there is still no reality to it".[52] Renamo had, therefore, returned to its baseline demands — agreement on a "government of reconciliation", a change in the political system and the total withdrawal of foreign troops from Mozambique. Renamo continued to insist on cabinet posts in the Mozambique government, such as the Minister of Defence. "Honorary" posts, such as Ambassadorships, offered as part of the deal were not enough.[53]

Despite Renamo's return to its original demands, South Africa pursued the idea of the tripartite commission envisaged under Point Four of the Pretoria declaration. On 8 October Jacinto Veloso returned to Pretoria to discuss the proposed commission. He reaffirmed that further negotiation with Renamo could not take place before violence in Mozambique totally ended. Despite sticking to its own demands, Renamo continued to participate in the implementation talks. By the night of 11 October, an agreement with Renamo seemed imminent. All violence was to stop in 45 days. An extendable three-month ceasefire agreement, with a promise of continued negotiations through the Joint Security Commission, was under discussion. The agenda also included the reintegration of Renamo members into Mozambican society, with an understanding that certain political questions aimed at achieving "mutual political, social, economic and military accommodation" would be dealt with later. Renamo members as individuals would be allowed to stand for election to the Peoples' Assemblies in 1985. At this point, and after receiving a phone call which Fernandes said came from Portugal, from the then Deputy Prime Minister, Carlos Mota Pinto, Fernandes sought a one-week suspension of the meeting. It is said that Fernandes claimed that he had been told to return to Lisbon with Veloso for discussions before reaching any agreement. Fernandes then left the talks.

A second round of discussions took place 14–18 October, when Renamo finally withdrew. Jorge Correia (Renamo's European delegate) accusing "Pik" Botha of bias in favour of Mozambique's "communist regime". Correia claimed that Renamo was formally withdrawing from the peace talks because of this. It seems that, following Fernandes' rushed departure the talks declined to virtual hostility, reflected by Machel's return to a public hardline against Renamo, saying that "Mozambique will not negotiate with kidnappers, bandits and criminals. Instead, Mozambique will wipe them out, and that day is not far off".[54]

Although it was now evident that this peace initiative had collapsed, Pretoria still insisted that "peace efforts between the Mozambican government and Renamo are continuing". Only at the end of the month did the Mozambican themselves declare that the talks had failed. "Pik" Botha, nevertheless, tried to breath life into them by demanding Evo Fernandes' return to Pretoria to resume negotiations in January 1985. But this further attempt had to be quickly abandoned, once Fernandes demanded even more extreme concessions, such as the Presidentship of Mozambique for Renamo. As "Pik" Botha admitted in a press briefing: "I know in advance he (Machel) would not even read (it) halfway before he threw it away"; he would "think I was crazy even to imagine that they would be acceptable".[55]

Renamo's lack of negotiating consistency further reflects the divisions within its leadership, which had not recovered from the internal strife it had suffered following Cristina's murder and the diminishing extent to which, after N'Komati, Renamo was subject to South African government control. The Pretoria Declaration talks marked the peak of the influence of Portuguese nationals within Renamo, with Evo Fernandes and Jorge Correia appearing to hold much of the day-to-day decision power in Renamo. The conciliatory moves of Dhlakama and the black members of the Renamo delegation at the talks were overruled by Fernandes, as the principal negotiator. Fernandes' position was probably further encouraged by harder-line parties within South Africa who were not keen to see a settlement. It is generally understood that the South African military, like the Rhodesians before them, did not hold much respect for Dhlakama.

The events surrounding the Pretoria declaration can be seen to have a further explanation. In September 1985, Renamo's headquarters, Casa Banana, was captured in a joint Zimbabwean-Mozambican military offensive. The diaries of a Renamo National Council member and adjunct to Dhlakama, Fransico Vaz, were found there and subsequently given wide publicity by the Mozambicans. They reveal the intricacies and technicalities of the post-N'Komati relationship between Renamo and Pretoria, reflecting the continued contradictions which had developed within the South African political establishment as the military influence over Government thinking had increased.[56]

The Vaz diaries underline the continued SADF support for Renamo after the Mbabane talks and N'Komati when, technically, all support for the rebels from South Africa should have been terminated. The diaries record, for example, a meeting between Dhlakama and van der Westhuizen of MID in Pretoria, where Dhlakama was told that "We, the military, will continue to give them [Renamo] support without the consent of our politicians in a massive way so they can win the war".

The Vaz diaries revealed that General Constand Viljoen, Chief of the SADF; Lieutenant-General Andre Liebenberg, head of the SADF "Special Forces"; van der Westhuizen; van Niekerk; and Brigadier van Tonder of MID had all had direct dealings with Renamo. Furthermore the diaries showed that the then Deputy Foreign Minister, Louis Nel, had flown to Gorongosa on 8 June to meet Dhlakama for discussions on Renamo's future. The diaries also revealed that the separate negotiations at the build-up to the Pretoria declaration had been bugged by the military and that information on the Mozambican Government's secret discussions had been passed to the Renamo delegation.

The diaries quite clearly illustrate violations of the N'Komati Accord. They also indicate South African ill-faith, technically, in that they also record several contacts between Renamo and South African personalities in the period of negotiation of the Accord shortly before it was signed. It appears from the diaries and the circumstantial evidence of increased Renamo activity after N'Komati, that an enormous stockpiling of supplies by the SADF for Renamo took place within Mozambique. The objective appears to have been to equip Renamo with operational autonomy for at least six months. The South African military emphasised to Renamo that they should concentrate their operations during this period on attacking defined "soft" targets relating to the Mozambican economy — such as aid workers and projects, powerlines, railways, roads, bridges, factories and shops. Renamo was also advised for the first time to control the populations in the areas in which it operated. The aim of this advice was to teach Renamo, with its now reduced sources of supply, how to continue to operate and to cause the maximum impact for the minimum expense.

This advice appears to have been adopted by Renamo groups in that military targets were less frequently attacked from then on. For MID and its "Special Forces" this was an ideal solution to the N'Komati dilemma. Renamo operated more economically and autonomously, while the MID ensured that tabs were kept on Renamo's activities so as to ensure its survival, as well as maintaining continuing MID leverage on Renamo's actions.

In preparation for the N'Komati Accord the SADF arranged for the transfer of Renamo's headquarters from Phalaborwa to Gorongosa in December 1983. Renamo's communications and administration were then also decentralised into three (north, centre and south) zones, with Gorongosa as the central core for the system.[57] Phalaborwa remained an exchange for the Gorongosa command to communicate with its external representation, enabling South Africa thereby to continue to monitor Renamo's activities. To make this set-up work, a more efficient radio communication network between Renamo's main bases and its different fronts was established in early 1985. This continued to be co-ordinated at Phalaborwa as the communication exchange. The system operated on the transmission of messages in code on frequency-hopping radios, as was noted in August 1985 by two captured European engineers who saw such equipment.[58] They were told by the two proud radio operators that they had only just been trained on how to use the equipment on a course near Pretoria. This system was further improved in 1987 when the now "Special Task" directorate liaison officer, Brigadier van Niekerk, established a direct communication link with Renamo's offices in Lisbon and Heidelberg by installing fax and coding/decoding equipment in them. His intervention was in part also a reaffirmation of South African links with Renamo's external operations in the face of growing opposition in Renamo to external interference.[59] It seems that this equipment was withdrawn from Renamo offices by South African military officials in late 1989, an indication of the further decline in SADF support for Renamo.[60]

At the time of the N'Komati Accord itself the South African authorities had meanwhile acted in a way which can be interpreted as an intention to demonstrate some reduction of their direct support for Renamo. A witness who was at Phalaborwa at this time confirms that military personnel previously involved with Mozambique were transferred to Namibia in the months after the Accord.[61] Earlier, over 800 rebels had been sent across the South African border into Mozambique in the first few days of the Accord. [62] Being well supplied, they immediately became operational in southern Mozambique. The acquiescence of the army to this distancing of the South African Government from its more overt support for Renamo was, it seems, achieved only on condition that Renamo was given the material it needed to launch out on its own from then on. The result was, inevitably, an upsurge of violence inside Mozambique which prejudiced the goodwill generated by the Accord and cast doubt in Maputo on the value of the South African assurances that they intended to disengage from Renamo. South Africa had gained from the Accord the expulsion from Mozambique of all but a handful of the ANC resident there. What, it was asked, in the light of Renamo's fierce campaign in the south of Mozambique, had South Africa given the Maputo government in return?

Even before the Vaz diaries were captured, there had been numerous allegations of South African duplicity. The South African authorities themselves had revealed in early 1985 the discovery of a mafia-like criminal and political syndicate operating in South Africa, which provided funds for Renamo through sympathisers in the SADF. Five soldiers were dismissed over this.[63] Around the same time, and in the face of further reports from the Mozambicans of violations of the Accord, South Africa agreed to a number of measures proposed by the Mozambican government to further curtail any remaining support for Renamo in South Africa.[64]

Following the publication of the Vaz diaries, the South African government attempted to limit the damage from their revelations. At a press conference "Pik" Botha admitted that there had been continued contacts between South Africa and Renamo. He described these as being mostly of "humanitarian aid" and "technical breaches".[65]

The Vaz diaries focus also on the dilemma of the South African military. To drop Renamo totally would set an important and unwelcome precedent. It would send unwelcome signals to other groups dependent on South Africa such as UNITA in Angola. It would spawn a lack of confidence in MID. It potentially undermined South Africa's "credibility" amongst these groups. An added disadvantage was that it compromised intelligence sources and reduced leverage in front line states.

To drop Renamo also conflicted with the dominant military philosophy at the time. South Africa saw itself in a position similar to that of Israel. It believed that its future and stability were built up on its military might, and that to compromise this would undermine its position as a dominant regional superpower. If its Total National Strategy was to accommodate the dropping of Renamo, this would leave Mozambique open to reinfiltration by the ANC. In the eyes of the MID dropping Renamo would be to "compromise the sacred and vital security of our country".[66] The Vaz diaries are finally significant as confirming that there was a continuing division of interests within the South African government. It is evident that although "Pik" Botha, and, possibly, the then Prime Minister, P.W. Botha, supported N'Komati and the cessation of assistance to Renamo, the SADF was unhappy from the start. It is also significant that there were no serious repercussions within the leadership following the Gorongosa revelations. Those named in the diaries retired on schedule (Viljoen), or gained promotion or other important posts. Van der Westhuizen was moved from MID to the post of Foreign Affairs deputy to the State Security Council (SSC). Louis Nel was made Deputy Minister in charge of the State President's Information Bureau. Liebenberg was promoted to be an army commander, van Tonder to Major-General[67] in charge of MID and van Niekerk to Brigadier.[68] Only less important SADF members were dismissed for being Renamo sympathisers.[69]

The conflict of interests between the South African political and business community and the military remains the major factor in the South African approach to Renamo. In 1987 and again in 1988, there has been convincing evidence of MID sponsored supplies to Renamo in the form of parachute drops.[70] MID has also been involved in aiding Renamo to counter the damaging image of the Gersony Report, which had been commissioned by the US State Department. Two flights in 1988 from South Africa, taking journalists into Mozambique to interview Dhlakama, could not have been made without MID's knowledge.

Although Phalaborwa probably still monitors Renamo and remains a communication link, it is unlikely that it continues to provide services for the rebels. Continued changes within the Mozambican Government, with the reshuffling from key positions of anybody particularly unacceptable to South Africa, appear to be beginning to be appreciated at certain levels within the suspicious South African military establishment. In particular, the decisions of Frelimo's Fifth Party Congress in 1989 to abandon Marxism-Leninism as the dominant ideology strengthen this reappraisal. This is encouraged by pressure from the US, Great Britain and Portugal, all of whom have an increasing interest in the cessation of destabilisation in Mozambique and in a peaceful settlement of the rebel problem.

Renamo reflects this growing isolation in its recent performance. To maintain its presence it has had to rely more widely on captured armaments, and its own production. This has led to an increase in the level of violence and harsh treatment of the population in its areas, practices that grew in 1986 with the Malawian moves against the organisation's presence there.

Renamo has used attacks on the Cahora Bassa Dam's powerlines as a way to obtain publicity through little effort. As early as 1981, Cristina organised attacks on the pylons, in an attempt to strengthen Renamo's propaganda campaign depicting itself as a rebel force independent of South Africa, and in the belief that, as the powerlines only supplied 8% of South Africa's energy, no serious inconvenience would be caused. This publicity stunt backfired because South Africa experienced a particularly harsh winter that year, with a shortfall of electricity caused by increased consumption. The closeness of Renamo to South Africa at this time is illustrated by Renamo's announcement on Voz da Africa Livre the following year, that Renamo would not attack the power lines again and that it wished South Africans a "warm winter".

A further complication for Renamo has been Maputo's attempts to commit South Africa to the Cahora Bassa project through which it would be physically committed to act against Renamo. This is no new idea; it was suggested in 1981 that the late President Samora Machel hoped that ANC attacks on South African power stations might encourage South Africa to use Cahora Bassa, and thereby be committed against supporting Renamo.[71]

The South African Government itself used the power lines in its domestic defence of the N'Komati Accord. "Pik" Botha, in what was the first official South African public admission of previous support of Renamo, responded to an attack by the Verkrampte Conservative Party in the South African Parliament over government "betrayal" of Renamo by saying:[72]

> We have nothing to hide. Naturally there was a time when we helped train and support Renamo. There was such a time. Why? The honourable members are not so ignorant. South Africa's aid to Renamo had achieved its aim, as the Maputo Government realised what the result could be and had signed the Accord. We did not found Renamo; it was there. When South Africa's aim in helping Renamo had been achieved, help for the movement ceased. It's as simple as that. Some members would say it was wrong and reprehensible: but I had never considered it reprehensible to place my country's interests first. At present it does not serve my purpose for Renamo to blow up a powerline in which I have direct interest, nor

does it serve my purpose that it should blow up railway lines in which I have direct interests, nor does it serve my purpose that it should threaten the harbour in Maputo which is our exporters' cheapest channel of exports. Renamo must stop its violence. In any event, it can not achieve a decisive military victory.

The worst that will happen if things go on as they are is that President Machel will either be forced out or compelled to Moscow to request large-scale military aid, and what would happen then? Russia would comply with his request. Cubans would enter Mozambique and a disturbing and tense situation would develop between ourselves and Mozambique.

Interest in Cahora Bassa was revived in November 1987 when the Joint Security Commission, a consultative body that had collapsed over the revelations of the Vaz diaries, was resurrected. This commission had been originally set up after N'Komati in 1984. The 1984 Cahora Bassa agreement was one outcome of this body's work. The agreement was only to come into effect once there was one hour of uninterrupted supply on both power lines. South African investment in renovation and the possibility of some deployment of troops in defence of the lines was promised. This never happened. Renamo heavily attacked the powerlines to make implementation of the agreement impossible so that, in 1985, there was only a total of 15 days supply on one line. Before the first Cahora Bassa agreement only 11 pylons had been sabotaged. By the end of 1985 a further 513 had been destroyed, making repair of the lines impossible without heavy investment and military protection.[73]

The improvement of relations between South Africa and Mozambique, as well as Portuguese pressure (the dam is 82% Portuguese owned) and Cahora Bassa's capacity to supply South Africa with cheap energy (potentially sufficient to satisfy 8% of its energy requirements), encouraged the search for a solution. This took the form of a tripartite Portuguese-South African-Mozambican agreement on restoring the supply of electricity to South Africa.[74]

These developments culminated in September 1988 with the meeting of former President Botha and President Chissano at Songo in Mozambique.[75] Publicly, the meeting appeared as a firm official South African commitment to the project. Over 500 pylons would be replaced, the majority located north of the Sabi river in areas dominated by Renamo.

At the Songo meeting President Botha addressed this problem by issuing a clear warning to Renamo. He said that "these power lines which link us represent the future and let no one who has the interests of southern Africa disrupt them".[76] This was not the first such threat from South Africa. Renamo responded, as it had previously, by stating that it was by no means a South African surrogate and that it would continue to attack the power lines.[77] The power lines have always been an inviting target to attack for a Renamo which is increasingly anxious to prove its independence from South Africa. Sabotage of the power lines is an easy way to gain maximum publicity with a minimum of effort.

This appears to be what happened in the two months that followed the presidential summit. A second wave of sabotage by Renamo destroyed an additional 891 pylons, the majority in the northern sector between Cahora Bassa and Changara (Tete Province), doubling the estimated costs of rehabilitation from US$30 million to US$76 million.[78] It demonstrates Renamo's determination to be accommodated in any agreement on the dam's future by frustrating any initiative without its blessing. It is interesting to note that no pylons are reported to have been attacked by Renamo between 1985 and the end of 1987 until attempts to restore the power lines began again after the Songo Summit. Cahora Bassa therefore represents a challenge for South Africa. Although it really does not need the electricity at this stage, Cahora Bassa's potential of supplying a new power station able to cater for the predicted South African growth of energy consumption in the 1990's would be retained. Like the projects financed with South African capital to rehabilitate Maputo port, and the proposed improvement of the Ressano Garcia-Maputo rail link, it makes good economic sense for South Africa. On the other hand, the SADF has in the past shown little interest in such projects succeeding. Many of the pylons damaged in 1988 were buckled by highly corrosive acid, a technique not used by Renamo before. This suggests that some factions from the South African military were still training Renamo with later techniques, providing the rebel command with the right resources to bring into play when it wished to disrupt any imminent agreement of restoring production from the dam.

In spite of the set-backs in using Cahora Bassa as a locomotive to bring peace to Mozambique, South Africa called for formal peace talks involving South Africa, Mozambique, the United States and the Soviet Union in February 1989.[79] "Pik" Botha's proposal was probably inspired by the success of US mediated talks that led Angola, South Africa and Cuba to sign the New York Peace Accord in December 1988 on Namibian independence and direct talks between UNITA and the MPLA on ending the war in Angola. It is also likely that this was a South African attempt to muscle in on the process that led to the Nairobi talks on reconciliation in Mozambique in which South Africa had only played a marginal role.[79]

With the transition of the South African Presidency from P.W. Botha to F.W. de Klerk in 1989 a further thawing of relations between Mozambique and South Africa occurred. De Klerk twice visited Maputo on day visits in 1989, first in July, as head of the National Party, and then, in December, as President. Under De Klerk's policies South Africa has itself become a country in transition. The military now faces cuts in expenditure as the old relationship between government and military is redrawn by a less hawkish and less military-originated leadership. In his December visit to Maputo De Klerk reiterated South African claims that it does not aid the rebels by saying: "I can categorically say that the Government of South Africa does not aid Renamo in any way whatsoever", adding that it is not impossible that private individuals continue to do so, that his government is opposed to such aid, and that "we will take whatever reasonable steps we can to prevent that".[80]

The question of continuing South African support of Renamo has been the central polemic in Mozambican-South African relations. As illustrated above, South Africa now openly admits that it supported the rebels before N'Komati. But it has consistently denied giving them any subsequent official backing. Much of the post-N'komati period has nevertheless been dominated by Mozambican officials' accusations that the SADF has continued to be involved in recruiting and supplying Renamo. As early as 1985, an investigation was held by Major Craig Williamson on behalf of the Joint Security Commission, of Mozambican accusations that the South African police were officially recruiting for Renamo among Mozambican illegal immigrants in the Nelspruit area of the Transvaal. Speculation arose as to whether or not the South African government could control right-wing sympathisers amongst its security forces.[81] Such allegations from Mozambique have continued to this day. A further example occurred in January 1989 with reports of recruitment of Mozambican refugees for Renamo at Skukuza SADF base. These charges were raised at the Joint Security Commission meeting held at the Pequenos Limbombos dam site in January 1989 when Lt. Gen. Liebenberg confirmed that the reports of such violations were being investigated. He also said that the investigations promised after the Songo presidential summit into the nature of the forces in South Africa said to be supporting Renamo were proceeding and that the Mozambican authorities had been asked to assist.[82]

Some commentators continue to believe that South Africa is still the major source of support for Renamo. One report in particular, known as the Minter Report, is an assessment of Renamo compiled from interviews with thirty-two ex-participants who were active in Renamo up to November 1988. Minter concludes that Renamo is sustained by regular supplies of DC-3 parachute drops and sea landings and that it is organised through a highly centralised system of communications linked to the South African Special Forces. Although past history has shown Minter's results to be roughly correct, the conclusions appear exaggerated, as this study shows.[83] The exaggeration is probably due to the very small and selected sample of interviewees used to draw these conclusions. Additionally, the interest in government circles and media in depicting South African centrality in Renamo's successes must add to the temptations for interviewees to exaggerate.

Although assisting Renamo is not an official policy of the South African government, convenient loopholes of support for Renamo within South Africa undoubtedly remain. The SADF are unlikely to wish to give up completely the leverage and influence it offers upon the Mozambican Government's behaviour. This would be guaranteed by the strong supporters which Renamo can draw upon within the military establishment. The military intelligence Chief of Staff, Major-General C.J. van Tonder, and the Director of the Special Task Directorate (STD), Brigadier van Niekerk, have a long history of connections with Renamo. It is significant that the Mozambican authorities have asked both the United States and the United Kingdom to use their influence within South Africa to encourage such figures to drop Renamo. US officials have talked to van Tonder but an attempt by the former US Deputy Assistant Secretary of State for African Affairs, Charles Freeman, in March 1989 to meet van Niekerk was refused by the South African military.[84]

It seems likely that the South African military will do what they can to ensure that Renamo survives. The military logic is obvious: Renamo is a positive asset for MID. One approach might be to encourage Renamo to concentrate on central Mozambique, ensuring that the Beira corridor continues to be attacked, keeping Zimbabwe on the defensive and having its main trade route to the sea disrupted, while the south of Mozambique, with its economic value for South Africa, would be allowed to prosper. Such a plan was tabled in 1984, after N'Komati, but did not succeed. Renamo had become too uncontrollable and autonomous in its actions, following its restructuring. Its leadership would not respond subserviently to external orders. Its lack of authority over its many semi-autonomous branches, more concerned with rural politics and loyalties than operating under a distant central command, also created problems for its South African sponsors.[85] Renamo now appears nevertheless to be in a much less secure position than immediately after N'Komati. It has lost its rear bases in Malawi. Reports of the lack of new weapons currently used by Renamo suggest that it has also used up the large stockpiles of arms it once had. Renamo officials also freely admit that its sympathisers within the SADF are finding it increasingly difficult to assist them, for fear of losing their jobs. On the other hand it is theoretically more centralised and better co-ordinated through its sophisticated radio equipment, which might, having gained experience of operating it, even result in a lessening dependence on South African help.

Speculation continues to flourish over continued South African support for Renamo. In the wake of the revelations over the Civil Co-operation Bureau, a clandestine military unit within the SADF operating from secret funds and unknown to the South African authorities, there have been suggestions in the *Weekly Mail* that a similar unit may exist with the mandate to destabilise Mozambique.[86] Evidence supporting the existence of such a unit remains thin on the ground, most of it being several years old, and dating from the period before President de Klerk's election. What the *Weekly Mail* report does however confirm is that individuals, such as private businessmen, farmers and soldiers, continue to support Renamo within South Africa through funds and supplies. In this latter regard, it is also relevant that Renamo combatants (as they do in Malawi) cross the South African border to use the well stocked shops and markets of the Republic; and that it is probable that some South African sympathisers for their cause among police, immigration and other border authorities turn a blind eye to such comings and goings. Renamo's attacks on returning migrant labourers to Mozambique have also meant that Renamo continues to obtain amongst its booty a steady flow of Rand to use freely on visits to South Africa.

In contrast to Angola, Mozambique is the Front Line of South Africa. Its turmoil has given South Africa heavy leverage over her neighbouring independent black countries, through, in particular, the disruption of those of their trade routes which do not have to pass through South Africa, in turn forcing on poor black countries military commitments to defend them, at the expense of economic development. Expenditure on the enormous refugee influx is also a drain on their limited resources. Mozambique is of far more strategic importance regionally for South African security than Angola. A Mozambique in turmoil may be seen by individuals within the military and the die-hards among the Afrikaner establishment to serve South Africa's objectives far more than a peaceful country. It remains to be seen if the politico-economic argument against this will convince the SADF to agree to block any further support for Renamo, either from within or outside its own ranks.

3 THE INTERNATIONAL DIMENSION

Renamo's external wing has had the unenviable responsibility of explaining and justifying itself to a critical outside world. It also has the difficult task of trying to raise funds and obtain supplies and intelligence for Renamo. Until 1989 the wing was comprised of a group of semi-autonomous individuals usually holding their posts more from their status as persons with residence permission in a particular country than from a career structure determined by Renamo's central leadership. They are generally isolated and poorly informed on the situation within Mozambique. For this reason (and out of propaganda necessity), they issue communiques and statements which are frequently divorced from what is actually happening in Mozambique and which often contradict the line taken by Renamo's internal leadership.

The external wing should nevertheless not be discounted. Its members have a public profile. Several of them have in the past been important figures inside Renamo, deciding policy and formulating Renamo's public statements. It is also becoming increasingly evident that, in the wake of the Heidelberg meeting in late 1988, Renamo's congress in mid-1989 and the Nairobi meeting in December 1989, the external wing has been restructured to bring it more into line with Renamo's leadership within Mozambique.

PORTUGAL

Because of its close links with Mozambique from its colonial legacy, Portugal has been a natural destination for individuals, groups and factions that have found themselves in opposition to the Mozambique Government. These basically fall into two groups. The first comprises clubs and institutions such as ANERM,[1] AEMO,[2] FRAUL,[3] and the MIRN,[4] dominated by white and asian Portuguese who fled Mozambique at independence. This grouping is completely independent of Renamo, its main connection being as a source of occasional financial support and publicity for Renamo in Lisbon out of a general sympathy for anyone opposed to the Mozambique government. They also act as mutual support agencies, their reunions dominated by nostalgia for past glories and, especially in election years, as political pressure groups campaigning for "compensation" for lost possessions. Following the Nairobi talks and the moves towards direct dialogue between the Mozambique government and Renamo, members from these pressure groups have additionally coalesced to form the "Movement for Peace and Democracy in Mozambique". This group is led by Antonio Rebelo de Souza, an Assembly member and son of the last Minister for Overseas Provinces in the Caetano government. It has attracted members of the retornado community, such as Dr. Suleiman Valey Mamede, the Director of the Islamic Studies Centre in Lisbon. The main objective of the "Movement for Peace and Democracy in Mozambique" is to have the interests of the "retornados" recognised in any negotiations, especially that of compensation. For this reason de Souza visited Dhlakama inside Mozambique in March 1990 to discuss the peace process. It has been reported that Antonio de Souza has associations with Manuel Bulhosa (see below), but it remains to be seen what type of support Renamo can obtain from this group.[5]

The second group in Lisbon opposed to the Mozambique government, but independent of Renamo, is a mixture of black and mixed-race Mozambicans dedicated to political change in Mozambique. Their organisations, FUMO, MONAMO, MONALIMO and FRESAMO have their origins in disputes and splits within Frelimo and Renamo. They are notable only for their lack of success.[6]

The most important among these organisations was FUMO. Founded by a mestizo lawyer and plantation owner in Mozambique, Dr Domingos Arouça, its whole history is one of failed attempts to gain support. Arouça was a highly vocal opposition figure to the Portuguese in Mozambique. This led to his imprisonment between 1965 and 1973 for subversion because of speeches he gave as President of the black pressure group, the Centro Associativo dos Negros de Mozambique (CANM).[7] When freed in 1973, he campaigned for a pluralistic political system in a future Mozambique, again from the platform of the CANM. An already hostile Frelimo leadership ensured that Arouça remained distant from Frelimo. This became evident at independence when the new Mozambique Government did not offer Arouça a post. In reply, Arouça formed FUMO in July, 1976. FUMO was initially targetted at the sectors of Mozambique society which had become disgruntled with independence. In its manifesto it claimed that its policies would follow the "true" thought of Mondlane, creating a racially integrated state composed of ethnic divisions respecting the "ethnic and tribal realities" of Mozambique in a federal format, and that FUMO would integrate itself into a Lusitanian community. It would also maintain close ties with the West. By January 1977, FUMO claimed that it was in control of Cabo Delgado and spreading in the southern provinces, and that it had offices in France, Great Britain and West Germany. Both these claims were fantasy. FUMO had little support within Mozambique and its sole office was in Lisbon.

Although Arouça obtained access to the Voz da Africa Livre radio station in 1976 to broadcast his demands, he was unable to obtain support from either South Africa or Rhodesia.[8] Rhodesia was in particular concerned to encourage its own creation, Renamo, for which it recruited several FUMO members, including Evo Fernandes.[9] The South African refusal to get involved with FUMO reflected its policy at that time of detente and its unofficial understanding with the new Mozambique Government that neither party would support each other's opposition.

With the developing political settlement in Rhodesia, Arouça again attempted to obtain international support for FUMO. In 1977, and in 1979, he ran publicity campaigns in London.[10] But with the ZANU victory in Zimbabwe-Rhodesia in 1980, the sympathy he gained from Bishop Abel Muzorewa was worthless. Around this time Arouça also claimed the leadership of Renamo as part of the succession dispute after the death of

Matsangaissa.[11] This failed because Arouça, in Lisbon, was completely marginal to Renamo politics. In the face of these failures, Arouça retired as President of FUMO on the grounds of "ill health" and was replaced by João Khan.[12] Arouça remains in Lisbon as FUMO's "Honorary President". Although he has since been approached by both the Renamo splinter groups, CUNIMO and UNEMO, and also in 1987 offered an important Renamo position, he has preferred to remain in retirement.[13]

The official Renamo representation in Lisbon originates from its restructuring by Rhodesia in mid-1979. Lisbon has, since then, been Renamo's major location outside Mozambique and South Africa. Lisbon was for the Rhodesians a low-key operation, acting mainly as a post-box for Voz da Africa Livre from Evo Fernandes' flat in Cascais, and producing an occasional mimeographed Renamo newsletter called "A Luta Continua". From 1980, with South African encouragement and investment, Renamo's publicity and propaganda in Lisbon became much more sophisticated, with frequent glossy editions of "A Luta Continua" and the production of colour posters and Renamo programmes for distribution both internationally (these were printed in French, English and Portuguese) and within Mozambique.

Its activities in Lisbon between 1979-1988 were dominated by one man, Evo Fernandes. Fernandes, a Goanese lawyer, was a close friend of Orlando Cristina, who ensured that Fernandes obtained the Lisbon job. In 1983, following Cristina's murder, Fernandes, with South African backing, was able to take over Cristina's position as Secretary-General of Renamo. As such he became the major spokesperson and contact figure for Renamo internationally. His importance is illustrated by the fact that he led the Renamo delegation at the Pretoria Declaration talks.

Fernandes did not rely solely on South African support. He was closely connected to Manuel Bulhosa, a wealthy Portuguese businessman, who had been one-time boss to Jorge Jardim. Until the nationalisations of the Mozambique Government, Jardim had run the Maputo oil refinery, SONAREP for Bulhosa. Fernandes and Renamo's then European Representative, Jorge Correia, who had replaced Fernandes on Fernandes' promotion, were both employed by Bulhosa through his Lisbon publishing house, Livraria Bertrand.[14] Bulhosa has several times denied his connections with Renamo, a denial that has appeared even less valid with the revelations from the Vaz diaries in which Bulhosa was recorded as having sought a meeting with Dhlakama, through MID.[16]

A final possible link of Bulhosa with Renamo is reflected in the speculation on who was behind the urgent phone call received by Fernandes that stalled the Pretoria Declaration initiative on October 11 1984, towards a settlement in Mozambique. It has been suggested that it was Bulhosa in his capacity as Fernandes' patron who urged him not to accept the terms of the agreement. Fernandes suggested, however, that this call originated from Carlos Mota Pinto, of the Social Democratic Party (PSD), Deputy Prime Minister and Minister of Defence in the then Soares coalition government in Portugal. Fernandes claimed that he had been told not to reach any agreement in Pretoria before going to Lisbon for discussions.[17]

As already described above this action effectively torpedoed the initiative. What the circumstances surrounding this phone call suggest is that at this time Renamo had become very influenced by its Portuguese backers.

The historical ties between Mozambique and Portugal and Portugal's remaining economic interests there, such as Cahora Bassa, have contributed to the Portuguese government wishing to keep communication lines open to Renamo. A Portuguese officer, Lt. Col. Silva Ramos of Portuguese Military Intelligence, visited a Renamo base in 1983.[18] A further connection between SIM (formerly known as DINFO), the Portuguese Secret Service, and Renamo was revealed by Paulo Oliveira on his defection to Maputo in 1988. Oliveira claims that medicines and books were sent to a postbox number at Phalaborwa for Renamo. He also claimed that the Chief of the General Staff of the Portuguese Army, Lemos Ferreira, had helped arrange journalist trips to Renamo-held Mozambique. One of these visits was by a reporter from the Portuguese Army magazine, who visited the Gorongosa district in 1988 to interview Dhlakama. This was repeated in March 1990 when two SIM officers accompanied Antonio Rebelo de Souza and Jose Antas, a journalist, in visiting Dhlakama inside Mozambique.[19] Furthermore in late 1989, Renamo's Secretary for Foreign Relations, Raul Domingos, visited Lisbon, funded by SIM which had informed Maputo of the visit.[20] These examples illustrate the Portuguese government's desire to obtain independent intelligence on Renamo, which would be facilitated by showing sympathy for Renamo through unofficial channels such as SIM. The Nairobi talks in 1989 brought Portuguese officials (as it did those of other countries) for the first time in officially sanctioned fact-finding discussions with Dhlakama and his delegation.

The Mota Pinto connection is less easy to explain. Some commentators have argued that the phone call was a fraud organised by MID, given the subsequent revelations in the Vaz diaries. It is, however, strange that Mota Pinto never denied Fernandes' story. Another possibility, as suggested above, is that Mota Pinto acted on behalf of Portuguese political and business interests opposed to Frelimo who were unhappy with Renamo's initial recognition of Machel as President and with the principle of an unconditional cease-fire. In 1984 these influences had particular force in Portugal because of the balance of coalition politics in the government of Mario Soares.

The "retornado" vote was something that just could not be ignored because of its size and the funds that this constituency donated towards the costs of the PSD's campaigns. At this time the "retornado" community played a political role in Portugal far greater than its numbers deserved. Statements by "Pik" Botha further suggest that Portuguese politics contributed to the failure of the Pretoria Declaration. At the time of the phone call he declared that the talks were "being threatened by foreign interests" and he subsequently confirmed that a phone call from Portugal had taken place, which had in effect destroyed the talks.[21] A further indication of the level of Portuguese involvement in this affair was "Pik" Botha's attempt on October 12 1984 to travel to Lisbon to find out why there had been Portuguese interference, setting up a meeting with Prime Minister Soares. Just before he was due to depart Johannesburg he received a message from Lisbon saying that his visit would be "inopportune".[22]

Fernandes' close Portuguese and South African connections increasingly caused Renamo problems both with internal discontent and with its external image. It confirmed the image diffused by Maputo of Renamo being a movement comprised of disgruntled Portuguese settlers funded by South Africa.[23] This led to the USA from 1986 refusing Fernandes an entry visa. Fernandes dominated Renamo's operations to such a level in 1984-86 that communications and most policy decisions had to be channelled through him. This fuelled further discontent within Renamo following that which had already surfaced in 1979 and in 1983.

Opposing Fernandes, the US wing of Renamo demanded a greater black representation in Renamo and less external interference (this echoed feelings already present within internal Renamo). In August 1986, such pressures succeeded in bringing about the abolition of the post of Secretary-General. Fernandes was appointed Head of the Department of Studies, a ploy that removed him from his central position. In September 1986, Paulo Oliveira, the editor of Renamo's newsletter, "A Luta Continua", was promoted to become Renamo's European spokesperson. Jorge Correia was downgraded to Lisbon representative only.[24] The result was that all Renamo's communiques passed through Oliveira.

The dispute intensified in early February 1987, with the arrival in Lisbon of two Renamo figures claiming to be special envoys sent by Dhlakama to assess the situation of the Lisbon office and to make recommendations on this to Renamo's leader. One of them, Mateus Lopes, sided with Oliveira, while the other, Renamo's then Foreign Relations Secretary, Artur da Fonseca, appeared alongside Fernandes.[25] By February 27, 1987 the situation had become clearer, with Mateus Lopes reappearing with orders from Dhlakama to expel not only Jorge Correia (as a supporter of Fernandes), but also Evo Fernandes himself, from Renamo's National Council. One reason given was Correia's and Fernandes' initial claims that Renamo had been behind a bloody car bomb explosion in downtown Maputo, an incorrect claim according to Dhlakama. João Ataide (a former Mozambican Ambassador who had defected to Portugal in 1983) was recommended to take Correia's place. Ataide, who had joined Renamo in 1986, had been its European delegate for propaganda and information. His appointment to Lisbon appears to have been aimed at revitalising Renamo's Lisbon office after the years of its domination by Evo Fernandes.[26]

Ataide was however a vulnerable figure in Lisbon because he was not a Portuguese citizen, holding only refugee status. Portuguese law requires that refugees should refrain from conspicuous political activities. This meant that Ataide was the target of considerable pressure from the Mozambican Government for his residence permit to be annulled because of his "abuse" of this refugee status. This law has been one of the determining factors in Renamo's choice of representation in Lisbon. Fernandes, Correia, Oliveira and Manuel Frank all hold Portuguese passports and can therefore freely campaign in Portugal, subject only to the normal requirements of Portuguese law.

Unable to stay in Lisbon as an active Renamo figure, Ataide moved to Paris, as a first step in opening a Renamo office there. He is thought to have been carrying the papers from Dhlakama confirming his appointment to Paris, when he died in an unexplained car crash in Malawi in November 1987.[27]

With Ataide's removal from Lisbon, the focus returned on a new struggle by Evo Fernandes to regain influence. This appears to have been encouraged by the South African MID, who regarded him as their most dependable contact in Renamo's external wing. This struggle produced the sacking in August 1987 of Paulo Oliveira as Renamo spokesman, and to Oliveira's return to the editorship of the newsletter "A Luta Continua". Oliveira was replaced by Manuel Frank, a young student closely associated with Fernandes. In effect this was a re-affirmation of Fernandes' control over Lisbon operations. This fact was not lost on Oliveira, who was any-how more sympathetic to the Ataide, Lopes and US wing's vision of a Renamo more autonomous and independent of external influences. Fernandes' regaining of stature in Lisbon led to Oliveira and four other Renamo members in Lisbon resigning in October 1987.[28]

This swing was further consolidated on November 30, 1987, with the deaths of Ataide and Lopes in the unexplained car accident while transit-ing Malawi from Mozambique on their way from Blantyre to Lilongwe's Kamuzu International airport. Ataide and Lopes were returning from con-sultations with Dhlakama within Mozambique. It is believed that Mateus Lopes, acting at this time as a special envoy of Dhlakama, was returning to Lisbon to attempt again to reform the office there.[29] What both men actual-ly stood for was a continuation of the campaign against South African con-trol and Fernandes' dominance of Renamo's external operations.

The official explanation of their deaths is that they were speeding along the Lilongwe road and collided with an oil tanker on a section of road under repair. The car is said to have rolled over several times and burst into flames, burning the bodies beyond recognition. The incident has, not surprisingly, been the cause of several rumours alleging that they were "accidentalised" — the Malawian phrase for this type of murder. Given the context of the accident, it was highly convenient for the Fernandes wing and its backers. One theory is that the crash was arranged by Malawian security officers at the request of their South African counter-parts. The links between these two organisations are well known.[30]

Confirmation of the struggle within the Lisbon wing has come from the defections of Paulo Oliveira (March 1988)[31] and Chanjunja Chivaca João[32] (November 1988) of that wing to Maputo. In a press conference in Maputo Oliveira revealed how Renamo in Lisbon was connected to South African Military Intelligence at Phalaborwa through sophisticated communications equipment. He also confirmed that Fernandes remained the most trusted Renamo figure in the external wing for the South Africans. South African pressure removed Oliveira from his position, enabling Fernandes to regain his influence through Manuel Frank. This was strengthened when the South African Intelligence flew Fernandes into Mozambique to have talks with Dhlakama in January 1988.[33]

Fernandes' regaining of influence was, however, short lived. In April 1988 he was found murdered on the outskirts of Lisbon. This murder remains unsolved. The US wing of Renamo blamed the Mozambique Security Forces (SNASP).[34] The Lisbon wing blamed the Washington wing, with South African help.[35] The Mozambican authorities suggest that it was a revenge killing by the Washington wing for the deaths of Ataide and Lopes. They claim to have evidence of a Puerto Rican hitman being hired by Thomas Schaaf (an informal Renamo lobbyist) to do the killing.[36] These alle-gations are in themselves illuminating. They demonstrate the specific pre-occupations of the different groups at this time. (The bitterness of the strug-gle between the Lisbon and Washington wings of Renamo is, for example, revealed by Evo Fernandes' widow's allegations of the US wing's involve-ment. The Mozambican interpretation seemed to have been targetted at the least penetrable area of Renamo's external wing — the Washington office — so as to discredit it.)

Lisbon police investigations are probably the most reliable source of what actually happened. Their findings suggest that this was a SNASP operation that went badly wrong. It appears that SNASP was led to believe by one of its agents, Joaquim de Conceicão Messias, that Fernandes might, like Oliveira, be persuaded to defect to Maputo. In fact, when Fernandes was formally approached, driven by Messias and accompanied in the car by Alexandre Xavier Chagas (also found to have connections with Maputo) to a beach restaurant where the full details of the offer of defection were presented, Fernandes, contrary to what was expected, did not respond favourably. In the confused situation it was decided to save face by killing Fernandes rather than letting him go and risk a major scandal. Chagas then murdered Fernandes. The extent to which the Portuguese authorities believed that SNASP was involved in this murder is illustrated by the Portuguese Prime Minister, Anibal Cavaço Silva, postponing his visit to Mozambique until September 1989 as a sign of anger over the murder of a Portuguese citizen by suspected foreign agents. The expulsion of the Mozambican Third Secretary, Rafael Custodio Marques, from Portugal in March 1989 because of evidence showing that he acted as a paymaster for the operation confirms this belief.[37]

The outcome of the court hearing into the murder of Fernandes contained a further twist. Chagas told the judge he had admitted Mozambican involvement under police pressure, and that he actually worked for South Africa. The eventual court decision was to convict Chagas with imprisonment (18 years) and Messias (8.5 years). An accomplice, Pinto da Costa, was ordered to pay Ivete Fernandes (Evo Fernandes' widow) an indemnity of 165,000 Escudos. Allegations of third party involvement in the case were dropped because, in the words of the judge, "allegations can not be proved".[38] It appears that some sort of out-of-court agreement was struck whereby any damage to Portuguese-Mozambican relations was limited and the bereaved party compensated (Ivete Fernandes is known to have had several meetings with aides to the Portuguese Prime Minister in the run-up to the trial in Cascais in April 1989). The result of this deal is seen in the very successful official visit to Mozambique by Cavaço Silva in September 1989 and a return visit by President Chissano to Lisbon in April 1990. It is also shown by the down-playing of the incident by Mozambican officials, a major change of tune.

The death of Fernandes further disrupted the Lisbon wing. Maputo has continued to encourage Renamo's disgruntled Lisbon members and sympathisers to defect to Maputo and accept its amnesty. Jorge Correia has been approached by Maputo with offers to defect. Renamo in Lisbon meanwhile became increasingly out of tune with its internal leadership. In 1989, Manuel Frank several times contradicted statements made by Renamo's delegation at the Nairobi talks. It also lost its direct link to Gorongosa, with the SADF withdrawing its communication equipment in late 1989. The link with the SADF is now through Col. Rosa de Oliveira, a SADF officer of Portuguese origin, who is known to be close to Brigadier van Niekerk. His posting to Lisbon, as part of South Africa's defence delegation in Lisbon, reflects the increasingly loose relationship between the rebels and the SADF.[39]

The growing isolation of Manuel Frank, as a protégé of Evo Fernandes and his continued divergence from the Renamo line in public policy statements, contributed to Renamo's decision at its Nairobi meeting in December 1989 to eventually replace him. He was to be succeeded by João

Almirante, a figure from inside Mozambique. The visit by Raul Domingos to Lisbon in late 1989 without informing Manuel Frank was partly in preparation for this change, to obtain the necessary documentation for Almirante to reside in Portugal. This reshuffle, the rebels hoped, would bring the divided Lisbon office into line. This was not to be. Almirante found himself to be the victim of divided Portuguese policy on Mozambique. Although SIM (military intelligence) had supported his presence in Portugal as a more authoritative contact with Dhlakama, its rival SIS (civil intelligence) campaigned for his removal. Eventually, following a speaking tour to Madrid in April 1990, Almirante found he was denied a renewal of his visa when he tried to return to Portugal. He has since returned to Mozambique. Renamo responded to these events by sending Jose Augosto to Lisbon as European Representative. Nevertheless Renamo continues to find the Portuguese government divided on how to deal with them. A visit to Lisbon by Raul Domingos sponsored by SIM in September 1990 was cut short by Renamo over government hostility to the visit. SIM continues to be the acceptable link of communication with the rebels.

THE PORTUGUESE DIASPORA

Portuguese former residents of Mozambique living in other countries are also known to be sympathetic to Renamo. Such communities in West Germany, France, Malawi, Australia , and, more importantly, in Brazil and South Africa have in the past given Renamo assistance.

In Brazil, attention has been focused on the activities of Manuel Bulhosa, already described above. The seriousness with which the contribution of individuals in Brazil to Renamo is regarded is reflected by the statements made to the Brazilian press by the former US Deputy Assistant Secretary of State for African Affairs, Charles Freeman. Freeman, who stopped over in Brazil in March 1989 after an official visit to southern Africa, stated (with Brazil in mind) that countries in which financiers of Renamo lived had a moral obligation to use political or legal means to persuade these people to end this support.[40]

South Africa, with its 600,000 strong Portuguese community, is the other major expatriate source of support for Renamo. In 1989, this community has twice been lobbied to persuade it against supporting Renamo. The first mission was by the Portuguese Secretary of State for Co-operation, Jose Manuel Barroso, who visited South Africa in late May, to talk with the Portuguese community. This visit was followed in September by Mozambican Minister Jacinto Veloso who met the Portuguese community, and especially the AJEP, to encourage them to invest in Mozambique, instead of supporting the country's destruction. What many Portuguese continue to seek is compensation for property lost at Mozambique's independence.[41]

WEST GERMANY

The evolution of the Renamo Office in West Germany mirrors that of its representation in Portugal.[42] It began as a spin-off from Dhlakama's European tour in 1980. Based in Heidelberg for much of the time it was closely associated with Evo Fernandes, operating initially through sympathetic individuals, particularly Professor Werner Kaltefleiter and a former student, then colleague, Andre Thomashausen of the University of Kiel, providing venue space, academic respectability and introductions. Thomashausen was at this time the main link, having become a close friend of Fernades through his student days in Lisbon. This relationship continued when Thomashausen went to South Africa to become the Director of Foreign and Comparative Law at UNISA in Pretoria. Thomashausen has become close to Renamo's leadership, having provided it legal assistance. He has assisted in drafting policy documents and treaties and is acting as a consultant for the rebel's options during peace talks.

Formal Renamo representation in West Germany began in November 1983 with the appointment of João Rajabo da Costa as representative. The decision was made during Dhlakama's visit to West Germany that month. This decision to formalise Renamo's presence in West Germany brought into the open the divisions and tensions in the movement as a whole at that time. Mozambican exiles in West Germany complained of being treated along ethnic lines by da Costa. With Renamo also being thrust into general crisis following Cristina's murder and the subsequent expulsions of members wishing to break away from South African/Portuguese domination, a gathering of Renamo sympathisers was held in St Peter Julian Convent in Duren in February 1984. This was organised by João Rajabo da Costa as representative and Horacio Leven as his deputy with the objectives of trying to recruit new members, to raise funds and to iron out differences within the Mozambican exile community, especially over the allegations of da Costa's discriminatory approach.

These efforts were not successful. With Cristina being succeeded by the South African-backed Evo Fernandes, many exiles continued to see Renamo as fully compromised by non-Mozambican interests. The fact of Fernandes also being non-black aggravated the already tense situation, in effect maintaining the divisions among Renamo's supporters in West Germany. The forming of splinter groups resulted (which will be discussed below). The splits however led to the replacement in June 1987 of Rajabo da Costa, who was regarded as being too sympathetic towards the US wing of Renamo, by Horacio Leven, although the real power from 1985 within Renamo in West Germany was Renamo's then Foreign Relations Secretary, Dr Artur Janiero da Fonseca. Because of Fonseca's close ties with Fernandes (he was with him in Mozambique at the January 1988 meeting with Dhlakama), the West German office has been very closely linked to the Lisbon wing with its South African connections. Like Lisbon, Heidelberg was connected with Phalaborwa by communication equipment set up by South African military intelligence. This placed Heidelberg in direct conflict with the Washington wing, which was highly suspicious of Fonseca.[43] Fonseca's closeness to Fernandes was a cause of tension and unpopularity, leading to his dismissal at Renamo's Congress in June 1989 from his positions as a National Council member and as Foreign Relations Secretary of Renamo.

Fonseca also fostered connections with West German intelligence, BND. According to Oliveira on his defection to Maputo, Wolfgang Richter (connected to the BND) gave Evo Fernandes one million Marks to buy SAM-7 anti-aircraft missiles on the black market via Poland. These were not the first reports of West German intelligence interest in Renamo. In 1983 the West German government had been seriously embarrassed by allegations of contacts with the rebels. The seriousness with which these allegations were taken at the time is shown by the official protest which a US State Department official, Frank Wisner, made to the West Germans. He told West German officials that the US government was worried about the activities of the BND agent in South Africa. US intelligence indicated that this agent had been involved in supporting Renamo and that this endangered US foreign policy towards Mozambique. Renamo has also received some support from the Konrad Adenauer Foundation's Institute for International Solidarity which has organised several Renamo-related seminars, the Hans Seidel Foundation, and the International Gesellschaft fur Menschenrechte (IGFM).

There is, however, little direct evidence to link the West German government with Renamo. It would appear that as with the security agencies in the US (as we shall see below), the West German security forces were, from a mixture of right-wing political affiliations and a sympathy towards Renamo among some of their members, prepared to give limited support to Renamo, in spite of this being counter to federal government policy.

Domestic support for Renamo probably arises from Renamo's contacts with the Christian Social Union of the late Franz-Josef Strauss, the then Bavarian Prime Minister. There is evidence of several such contacts, especially in the period preceding Strauss' official visit to Maputo in January 1988. It has been suggested that Strauss had been encouraged by the West German government in 1987 to act as a go-between for Renamo with the Mozambique government in an attempt to find a basis for a solution of their differences.[44] The CSU had already been involved the year before in supporting the Renamo splinter group, CUNIMO, in the hope of reviving the peace dialogue between Renamo and the Mozambique government. The channel used was Dr Holger Ludwig Pfahls who had once been Head of Department for State, Society and Foreign Politics in the office of Franz Josef Strauss and who subsequently became Deputy President of Federal Defence of the Constitution (BVS). In this latter capacity he coordinated the activities of all three security services (BND, BVS and MAD). Pfahls appears to have arranged for funds to be given to CUNIMO by the security forces.

Renamo's Heidelberg office, however, obtained the major part of its support from West German right-wing sympathisers and the large community of Portuguese migrant labourers in West Germany. Many of these are originally from Mozambique. They remained bitter about Frelimo's policies at independence, which they saw as having been the cause of their decision to leave Mozambique and their relatively comfortable life there.

Dhlakama has visited West Germany three times. Firstly in 1980, when he met delegations from the opposition parties, the Christian Democratic Union and the Christian Social Union. This was followed up in November 1983 by a six week visit arranged by Professor Kaltefleiter, then a political adviser to Helmuth Kohl. The Renamo delegation visited the Konrad Adenauer Foundation (closely connected to the CDU) and the Hans Seidel Foundation (linked to the CSU). The visit's climax was a meeting with the late Franz Josef-Strauss.

Heidelberg was chosen by Afonso Dhlakama in September 1988 as the location for his meeting with the external representatives of Renamo at that time in Kenya (Manuel Lisboa, Jose Munhlanga & Jose Vaz), Portugal (Manuel Frank, Ascenscio Freitas & Sebastião Temporario), USA (Luis &

Simão Serapião) and West Germany (Artur de Fonseca).[45] The meeting was important as it marked Dhlakama's determination to bring the external wing into line and to diminish the Heidelberg/Lisbon versus US wing confrontation. The meeting was also used to brief the representatives on the developments towards talks with the Mozambican church. After the Heidelberg meeting, Dhlakama visited Belgium and Italy to lobby for additional support from sympathetic individuals and organisations and to brief them about Renamo.

THE UNITED STATES

In the first ten years of Mozambican independence (1975-1985), there was very little need for Renamo activity inside the United States. Frelimo's closeness to the Soviet Union and its hostile rhetoric against the West meant that little US aid was channelled to Mozambique. With a deteriorating economic performance, intensified Renamo activity and the rejection of Mozambique's application to join Comecon, the Mozambican leadership reassessed its policies and sought to reorient Mozambique by reducing dependence on the Soviet Union and becoming more genuinely non-aligned.

With this shift in Mozambique's international policy, the State Department's relations with the Mozambique government improved from 1983 onwards. The N'komati Non-Aggression Pact with South Africa in March 1984, was seen as a vindication of the US policy of "constructive engagement" in southern Africa. By October 1985, US-Mozambican relations had warmed sufficiently for President Reagan to receive the late President Machel at the White House, a gesture repeated in 1987 with Machel's successor, Joaquim Chissano. The relationship has continued to strengthen under Chissano as President, a fact reflected in the continuing increase of US aid to Mozambique to a peak in 1989 and 1990 of just over US$ 100 million, making Mozambique the largest recipient of US aid in southern Africa. But the increased aid has in turn given rise to US domestic opposition to the State Department's approach. US right-wing organisations claim that this is a flawed policy, supporting a regime that still remains Marxist at heart.[46]

The existence of anti-Frelimo elements in the United States is nothing new. During the 1960's the US had become a destination for Mozambican Catholic ex-seminarians who had split with Frelimo over student participation in Frelimo's military operations within Mozambique and over the issue of élitism within Frelimo's structure. Such tensions continued after independence. President Machel characterised this group in 1976 as "the janitors in the toilets of white Americans",[47] who were bourgeois deviationists of the Mozambique revolution and therefore collaborators or already integrated members of the rebels. Although Machel had, by 1983, become far more conciliatory towards the Mozambican diaspora in the US, for its part, it was sceptical of Frelimo and sympathetic to Renamo's cause. In 1982, Renamo formally approached this group in a recruitment drive by Orlando Cristina in the USA. The visit was not particularly successful, with the single exception of Artur Vilankulu, who joined Renamo with the enticement of a leadership position. In 1984 another visit took place, this time by Cristina's successor, Evo Fernandes. This visit was equally unsuccessful, but did achieve contact with the US right-wing and obtained some media coverage. These contacts were to become increasingly important in assisting Renamo's higher profile the following year. Two of Renamo's head US spokesmen — Artur Lemane (1984-1986) and Luis Serapião (1986-1989) — emerged from this "seminarian group".[48] From 1986, until he was replaced in December 1989, by Julius Seffu, Serapião was the leading Renamo figure in the US from his base as an associate Professor at Howard University, Washington, D.C.

The major catalyst for the emergence of an active Renamo presence in the US was, however, the visit of President Machel to Washington, D.C. in 1985. Machel's appearance in Washington as an official guest was distasteful to a right-wing used to seeing Machel portrayed as a ruthless pro-Soviet, anti-American, Marxist dictator.[49] This led to a campaign, mobilised and funded by an organisation called the "Conservative Caucus", to stop Machel's visit.[50] Unable to stop it, the Caucus organised a series of anti-Machel meetings during the visit. Renamo's Secretary for Foreign Affairs was funded to attend these and to speak on behalf of Renamo.[51] The spin-off was to put Renamo on the US political map for the first time, creating interest in Renamo from a greater variety of American right-wing organisations.[52]

All this helped to mobilise support for Renamo among Senators and Congressmen.[53] Renamo was depicted as the victim of a flawed, soft policy towards communism and as an example of State Department feebleness. Renamo was (it was argued) no different in its objectives from the Contras, UNITA or the Afghan Mujahedin, all of whom received aid from US official funds.[54] This has continued to be the thesis of the right ever since.

As a result of the growing conflict between State Department policy towards Mozambique and the US right-wing's interpretation Renamo obtained a greater profile in the US and continued to gain fresh support from right-wing bodies. As within the US government itself, there has been, and is, much competition within the different segments of the American right. This surfaced in 1986 in a bizarre dispute between Free the Eagle (an organisation heavily funded by the Heritage Foundation) and the Conservative Action Foundation (CAF). The protagonists were Free the Eagle's backed Renamo representative, Luis Serapião, and the CAF's supported Artur Vilankulu, both men claiming to be the legitimate Renamo representative in the US. The dispute was eventually resolved through the mediation of Renamo's then Secretary for Foreign Affairs, Artur da Fonseca, who visited Washington to throw his support behind Serapião. Further supporting credentials for Serapião were brought to Washington by the Executive-Director of the then newly opened Mozambique Information Office (MIO) in Washington, who had visited Dhlakama in Mozambique to obtain his blessing for the MIO and for its affiliation with the Free the Eagle organisation.[55]

From 1986 to 1988, Free the Eagle remained the major benefactor of office space, telephone access and expense funding for Renamo. It sponsored the Mozambique Research Centre (until mid-1987 it had been called the MIO). The MRC incorporated the Free Mozambique Business Council and the Mozambique Relief Fund. It continues to be run by Thomas Schaaf (he sometimes uses the pen name Tom Curran). Schaaf, a white American, had worked in Rhodesia for the Ministry of Agriculture from 1978. After Zimbabwean independence he continued in this job, but was later transferred to Agritex in Mutare in September 1982. His work for Agritex included visits to Manica province in Mozambique in connection with his agricultural project against blue mole disease.[56] In this capacity and through Mutare's One Way Christian Centre mission programme for Mozambique he became interested in Renamo and began to help it along the Zimbabwean border until, according to the Zimbabweans, he was asked to leave on account of these contacts. Schaaf however denies this, saying he left voluntarily. It seems that in early 1986 Schaaf got wind that the Zimbabwean authorities had become aware of his illegal activities and left the country hurriedly.

The Mozambique Research Centre (MRC) is primarily an informal lobbying office for the Renamo cause in Washington. It lobbies Capitol Hill and the International Agencies. It issues press statements and raises funds for Renamo. To obtain favourable press coverage, the MRC has sponsored visits by sympathetic academics and journalists to Renamo areas in Mozambique.[57]

The main objective of Renamo in Washington is lobbying against State Department policy towards Mozambique. To this end it tries to establish contact with US government officials to gain a constituency of support for Renamo in the US Administration. In this respect it has obtained some success. In August 1986, Patrick Buchanan, then White House Director of Communications, and John Philip, the Africa Advisor of the National Security Council, met Renamo's former Secretary for Foreign Affairs, Artur da Fonseca, its former European spokesman, Jorge Correia and its former US representative, Luis Serapião.[58] It is also believed that this Renamo delegation met the then head of the CIA, William Casey. In November 1987, Frank Carlucci, President Reagan's former National Security Advisor, and Herman Cohen, then National Security Africa Advisor, met a group of conservative lobbyists, including Thomas Schaaf. This latter meeting particularly embarrassed White House officials, who claimed that they had not been aware of Schaaf's presence.[59]

The honeymoon days for Renamo in Washington with the right-wing ended in late 1987 with the graphic reports of the Homoine massacre by Renamo in Mozambique. After this Renamo found that obtaining favourable coverage became difficult. Its task was further complicated by the publication of the Gersony Report in April 1988, a survey of refugees' accounts of their experiences of Renamo, commissioned by the State Department.[60] Schaaf admits that fund raising has been made considerably more difficult since then. The MRC's removal from Free the Eagle office space from September 1988 is a further indication of the growing difficulties Renamo is meeting with US right-wing organisations. The State Department has also ensured that Dhlakama does not visit the US, threatening to extradite him to Maputo if he is found in the States.[61]

Renamo's constituency of support in the US nevertheless remains strong amongst a small group of wealthy American businessmen, ideological conservatives and evangelical Christian missionaries. Among these is a Louisiana businessman, James V. Blanchard 3rd. Blanchard has contributed medical supplies and radios to the rebel cause. Since 1986 he admits to supporting the operational costs of the MRC, which has cost him between $50,000–75,000.[62] Blanchard has been particularly important in financially supporting Renamo during the Nairobi talks: he was even present in Nairobi for the first round of talks in August 1989.

Another key supporter of Renamo is Major Robert C. MacKenzie (aka Jordan, aka McKenna), until recently, Executive-Director of a conservative group called Freedom Inc. Mackenzie's interest in Renamo goes back to his service with the Rhodesian "Special Forces" in the late 1970s. Mackenzie has several times since been inside Mozambique with Renamo.[63] His visit to Mozambique in November 1987 was sponsored by the MRC, with the support of Senator Jesse Helms, when he successfully returned with an American missionary, Kindra Bryan, who was held by Renamo.[64] This visit was designed to counter a publicity campaign which had been embarrassing Renamo's supporters, including Senator Jesse Helms, for the fact that a so-called pro-Christian movement had kidnapped and kept captive an American missionary.

Mackenzie, and Freedom Inc's owners, Harry Schultz and Larry Abraham,[65] organised and financed in July 1988 the flying of a party of US journalists from the *New York Times*, *Washington Post* and *Newsweek* into Renamo-held areas to interview Dhlakama.[66] This was a desperately needed publicity stunt by Renamo's supporters to counter the damage from the Gersony report. They were also behind the mission to free a British journalist, Nicholas della Casa, in late 1988. Freedom Inc, which is now based in Seattle, owns the influential right-wing magazine *Conservative Digest* and continues to lobby and fund raise for Renamo. It has, for example, struck a Renamo silver proof "Freedom Fighter Commemorative" coin to raise funds for the rebels.

The flight which took the three US journalists into Renamo-held territory in 1988 also transported solar-energy battery chargers, laptop word processors and printers which could be linked to the TR-48 radios used by Renamo. This suggests that messages from sympathisers based in Malawi (see below) can be picked up by Renamo's radios in the bush, and can interface with printers used in the shifting Renamo headquarters. The donation of this equipment was intended to enable Renamo to receive the required flight schedules and destinations of ICRC relief flights. Planning this had been one of the main activities of the MRC, with Tom Schaaf and Antonio Rocha (Director of Research at the MRC) visiting the ICRC headquarters in Geneva in the summer of 1988, to finalise the details.[67]

Radio equipment continues to be an important priority in the aid Renamo is given by its US based sympathisers. Because of the internal politics of Renamo, the US wing has increasingly tried to strengthen Renamo's ability to operate without back-up from South Africa. The disputes within Renamo's Lisbon wing, with its deaths, defections, resignations, and sackings, also reflect this struggle for greater independence. The Lisbon and Heidelberg offices were seen by Renamo in Washington, and its US sympathisers, as being completely discredited by having been infiltrated by South Africa. This is the picture Paulo Oliveira confirmed on his defection to Maputo; according to his account only the Washington office was really independent of South African or Portuguese influence — a matter of pride for the US wing and its supporters.

To preserve this autonomy (and given its experience of South Africa blocking its communications), the US wing did not operate through the Lisbon, Heidelberg and Phalaborwa communication networks when contacting Renamo inside Mozambique. It relied on sympathisers in Malawi for relaying its messages to Renamo inside Mozambique. The main sources of sympathy and relay for the US orientated Renamo in Malawi are provided by the evangelical Christian missionaries operating in southern Malawi. The evangelical contacts of Thomas Schaaf (a committed evangelical) have enabled him to develop a network of missionaries operating from Malawi into Mozambique on evangelical campaigns. Schaaf admits that this is an important source of information for him, which is further confirmed by the amount of Malawian-derived missionary information available at the MRC.

The success of this network is best illustrated by the case of an Australian missionary, Ian Grey of Shekinah Ministries. Shekinah Ministries, a pentecostal organisation, has been active in areas of Mozambique dominated by Renamo. The Rev. Michael Howard, the organisation's director, has admitted that "tent meetings" have been held in such areas and that the rebels have been given clothing, bibles and other religious literature at them.[68] Ian Grey's case suggests that this aid went one step further. Grey was detained and imprisoned by Frelimo for being found to have carried messages from Renamo's US wing received in Malawi and for taking these to Renamo inside Mozambique when on missionary duty.[69] Grey's arrest, highlighting the need for a more consistent and reliable communication link, has been one reason why more sophisticated radio equipment has been donated by the US wing which needed to improve its contact with Renamo inside Mozambique.

Evangelical Christianity remains an area targetted by Renamo in the US for funding and aid. Schaaf is known to have solicited churches and evangelical Christians for financial support. One of those approached was Thomas Demery, the Reagan administration's Assistant Secretary for Housing from October 1986 until January 1988. It appears that Demery used his official status to solicit $290,000 for his own favourite charity, "FOOD for Africa". Developers who stood to gain from housing programmes became donors to this charity. Demery is also known to have joined a South African evangelical minister, Peter Pretorius, at a number of fund-raising dinners held in various cities in the US for FOOD for Africa as "honoree" or "guest speaker", some calling for donations of $1,000 a plate. At one particular dinner in Washington, D.C. organised by Demery in honour of Peter Pretorius, Maureen Reagan (daughter of the former President) who had shown interest in Mozambique by making a trip to Maputo, made a personal donation to FOOD for Africa. Demery and other Housing and Urban Development (HUD) officials are to be charged with insider dealing.[70]

Before joining HUD, Demery had in fact been the US funding director of FOOD for Africa, closely linked to the charity work of Peter Pretorius and his Jesus Alive Ministries which are allegedly financed by the Rhema Church of South Africa. Although Rhema denies any connections with Renamo, it is widely accepted that FOOD for Africa, otherwise little known, is active inside Renamo-held areas. Robert Mackenzie of Freedom Inc has admitted "I do know of Rhema and I know of their efforts inside Renamo areas". In the same interview he confirmed that a religious group closely associated with FOOD for Africa had donated medicines and run soup kitchens for Renamo rebels.

Demery is also said to have solicited $25,000 from Pat Robertson, tele-evangelist and a public advocate of providing food for distribution in Renamo camps. Pat Robertson has on several occasions in the past been known to encourage donations for humanitarian aid to Renamo. Another tele-evangelist, Jimmy Swaggart, is also thought to have funded mission work in Renamo areas.

Further evidence came to light in late 1989 of the continuing link between evangelical Christianity and Renamo with the capture by FAM troops of six American and two South African church workers illegally inside Mozambique. The Americans are members of a California-based mission group, the Christian Emergency Relief Team (CERT), which focuses on "war-torn areas" such as Afghanistan, Nicaragua and the Philippines, but which has not been known before to have any African experience.[71] The group were detained close to the Malawian border in the company of a Cape Town Baptist pastor, Peter Hammond, and his South African co-worker, George Bezuidenhout. Peter Hammond heads a pro-Renamo group of Christians, known as Frontline Fellowship, which has been very active within Renamo-held areas in the past.[72] As well as its reports on the state of Christianity in areas Renamo dominates, Frontline Fellowship's links to Renamo are highlighted by the testimony of Ian Grey. Grey reports having seen Hammond leading groups that visited Renamo in Mozambique in 1986.[73]

The capture of the missionary group suggests that CERT was thinking of expanding its operations into Mozambique and that the six Americans were on a fact-finding mission which went wrong, due to their inexperience. In spite of their relatively lenient treatment and short detention (six days) by the Mozambican authorities, Hammond continued to be completely hostile to the Mozambican authorities, an indication of how sections of the Christian community still see events in Mozambique.[74]

Another source of support for Renamo within the US comes from Jack Wheller and his Freedom Research Foundation in La Jolla, California, dedicated to the study of anti-Soviet insurgency around the world. Wheller went into Renamo areas in June 1985 to study the movement.[75] On return he tried to obtain aid for Renamo from his contacts in the US. Among those approached after his visit was the then member of the National Security Council, Lieutenant-Colonel Oliver North (of Iran-Contra scandal).[76] North turned down the request because he felt that all resources should be concentrated on Central America. General John Singulab and his US Council for World Freedom (the US branch of the World Anti-Communist League), based in Texas, have also shown interest in Renamo. It is known that large donations of thousands of dollars were made by them to Renamo between 1986 and 1988. Although these seem to have diminished, Singulab continues to favour Renamo. In 1989 he lectured in the US about his visit to Renamo areas in late 1988 with Freedom Inc.[77]

With direct talks taking place between the Mozambique government and Renamo in 1990 and the prospect of free elections in Mozambique in 1992, Mackenzie and other Renamo sympathisers met at the annual *Soldier of Fortune* magazine conference to plan a new strategy of support for Renamo. Their strategy is now to be based on a comparison with events in Nicaragua in 1990, in which the Sandanista government was defeated at the ballot box and the Contras reintegrated into mainstream Nicaraguan society. The conference agreed that the emphasis of their activity towards Mozambique should be shifted to fundraising, and to supporting any party in opposition to Frelimo as well as assisting Renamo to obtain political acceptance in Mozambique in the hope that free elections in Mozambique in 1992 will bring about a situation comparable to that of Nicaragua.

As already noted Renamo's lobbying of support against State Department policy, especially on Capitol Hill in Senate and Congress, is persistent. After the success of the anti-Frelimo demonstrations during President Machel's visit to the White House it obtained a small core of sympathetic right-wing Republican senators and congressmen. Seven senators and two congressmen invited Dhlakama in November 1985 to visit the US to testify for Renamo before Senate.[78] A similar invitation was made at the end of 1987 by Congressmen Jack Kemp and Dan Burton with 17 others.[79]

The most successful achievement of the pro-Renamo lobby on Capitol Hill so far is, however, the blocking of the nomination of Melissa Wells as American Ambassador to Mozambique by a group of Senators led by Helms, Kasten, Symms, Humphrey and Wallop. Wells was made to answer a record 146 questions before the Senate Foreign Relations Committee over her nomination. Although the committee approved her nomination on March 31 1987, this was challenged. With the decision in early May 1987 by the powerful Senator, Robert Dole, to join forces with Helms in opposing Wells' nomination and to press for a more positive stance towards Renamo, the blockage to Wells within the Senate was greatly enlarged. An unprecedented bi-partisan group of 28 senators urged that the nomination should not be brought to a vote. The blockage continued until a Senate procedural vote on the nomination on September 9 confirmed her nomination (64, with a record 24 votes against). By this time the nomination had been delayed on the issue of Renamo by eleven months and two days, another record.[80]

The decision of Senator Dole to embrace Renamo at this time should, however, be seen more in terms of American domestic politics than foreign policy. Dole was an undeclared GOP (Republican) presidential contender. He appears to have recognised Renamo as an issue from which he could secure the vote of the extreme right in his campaign against George Bush in the primaries in late 1987-88. Until the publication of the Gersony Report in April 1988, domestic politics made support for Renamo a litmus test of credibility in the early campaigns for the Republican nomination for the 1988 Presidential elections. The Gersony Report's conclusions, however, made any further support of Renamo by Dole impossible. Since then he has distanced himself from the issue.

There are other reasons beyond those already stated (adverse publicity following the Homoine massacre and the Gersony report), why the pro-Renamo lobby in Washington has become weaker since 1987. By the spring of that year the most powerful advocates of Renamo on the National Security Council, William Casey, Pat Buchanan, Phil Nicolaides and Phil Ringdahl, had left the administration. In combination with the growing tide of adverse publicity over Renamo this meant that mid-1987 was probably the watershed for Renamo's operations in Washington. Staunch supporters of Renamo, such as Jack Kemp and former UN Ambassador, Jeanne Kirkpatrick, have been less willing since to come out in its support. The same is true of the right-wing Institutes and Foundations which have at one time or another shown sympathy towards Renamo. Since 1988 they have distanced themselves from the MRC and Renamo, to such an extent that Renamo in Washington appears badly informed and isolated.

Senator Jesse Helms and Congressman Dan Burton remain the most consistent constituency of support for Renamo on Capitol Hill. Whenever possible both continue to challenge State Department policy on Mozambique. Helms attempted to obtain a guarantee from Herman Cohen, US Assistant Secretary of State for African Affairs, in the latter's confirmation hearings, that he would talk to Renamo. Between October 1989 and January 1990 there was lobbying against plans to remove Mozambique by presidential decree from the black list of non-qualifying communist countries for EX-IM Bank loans and guarantees.[81] This failed with President Bush decreeing that Mozambique was a "communist country" in transition, thereby meriting EX-IM services.

All this reflects the difficulties that Renamo's publicity campaign now finds itself in the US. With Frelimo's reforms and growing pragmatism, Renamo's previously successful rallying calls of religious persecution by the Mozambique government and its pro-Sovietism have lost their sharp edge. Nevertheless, US policy towards Mozambique has lacked coherence and consistency. Events such as the Iran-Contra scandal illustrate how US policy is fragmented between different interest groups within the administration as a whole. A lack of a consistent overlap between various departments and agencies concerned with their own empire building and specific interests continues to affect the Bush administration. But unless the Mozambique government makes a drastic return to its old policies, the more relaxed State Department policy towards Mozambique seems likely to remain the key-note of the US administration's approach.

Although Renamo is likely therefore to continue to be shunned in official US policy, it appears that some parts of US intelligence may continue to have an interest in it. This is suggested by the level of funds still reaching Renamo through the third parties above. It is not unusual for the CIA to sub-contract to private sector interests with good security connections, delicate, but not crucial, operations (a strategy that was masterminded by the late CIA director, William Casey).[82] The approach of US intelligence to Renamo probably derives from a mixture of anti-communism, a wish to receive independent information on Renamo, and a desire to weaken whatever South African influence there is over Renamo's affairs. Areas of government which have in the past shown, and appear to continue to show, sympathy towards Renamo are the Defence Department and the Defence Intelligence Agency (DIA). With the demise of Renamo's popularity, DIA officials have become reticent in their vocal support of Renamo. It is however rumoured that DIA analysis documents about Renamo continue to be favourable towards the rebels, a reflection that sympathy remains in the DIA towards Renamo.

The Nairobi talks in 1989 also brought Renamo its first official contact with the US State Department. Two rounds of talks were held there on August 12 and on December 7, between the US Chargé d'affaires in Harare, Ed Fugit, and Afonso Dhlakama. Both meetings were held to try and break deadlock in the dialogue over peace. These contacts were part of the current State Department policy of offering a facilitative role in the search for peace in Mozambique, by encouraging both sides to talk to each other.[83] The importance of the USA in the peace process is demonstrated by President Chissano's visit to Washington in March 1990. During this visit, after discussions with President Bush on the subject, Chissano announced that direct talks between the Mozambican government and Renamo would take place.

With Renamo in Washington increasingly isolated and uninformed about Renamo's activities inside Mozambique a further bitter dispute within its organs then took place. Great tension and jealousy between Luis Serapião and Tom Schaaf over Schaaf's high profile and success came to a head at the Heidelberg meeting where, in response to this tension, but also to the re-imaging process of Renamo, Serapião was advised to conduct Renamo operations independently from the MRC and not to deal with Schaaf. This caused a skirmish of typical exile bickering, with Francisco Nota Moises, the Renamo Information Secretary, backing Schaaf by writing an open letter to Dhlakama in November, 1988, criticising Serapião and Fonseca for laziness and incompetence. By producing a newsletter called "Mozambique Today", Serapião attempted to continue operating as Renamo spokesperson but, after two issues, the project collapsed. Without the technical back-up that Schaaf used to provide for Renamo's publicity, and without Schaaf's contacts, Serapião could not respond to the increasing demands for publicity with the build-up to the Nairobi talks. Schaaf continued to lobby for Renamo support for his operations by visiting Gorongosa in June 1989 as an observer at Renamo's Congress. He also attended the August round of the Nairobi talks. Schaaf appears, with Antonio Rocha, to have been able to force the removal of Serapião from his position, on the grounds of ineffectualness, getting him downgraded after the December 1989 Nairobi meeting to the minor position of Renamo's Director for Further Education. The appointment of Julius Seffu, a neutral figure in the Serapião-Schaaf dispute, as Serapião's successor as representative in Washington, is part of internal Renamo's attempt to bring the external wing into line. It seems that Tom Schaaf continues to be too important, both in efficiency and in his contacts, to be dropped by Renamo, even if his presence continues to be embarrassing to Dhlakama, in his attempt to project Renamo as a completely African movement. The compromise position is that Schaaf is to take a lower profile outside the US in favour of Antonio Rocha, and that the MRC will not publicly issue Renamo communiqués or statements, although it will act, as it has in the past, as a Renamo information office.

UNITED KINGDOM

Britain has become an increasingly important source of aid to Mozambique. The official visit of the late President Machel to London in 1983 marked the beginning of an improved and increasingly serious relationship between the Mozambican and British governments, drawing on the important Mozambican contribution to the success of the Lancaster House negotiations over Zimbabwean independence and the personal relationships between Mozambican ministers and officials and their British counterparts then established. The rapid increase of British aid to Mozambique between 1984 and 1987 was in part a repayment of that debt.

It was also a reflection of Britain's response against criticism by the pro-sanctions lobby that Britain was upholding apartheid. Britain argues that its aid to Mozambique, which is directed mainly at transport route improvement, is helping the land-locked Frontline States to reduce their dependence on South Africa. Aid to Mozambique, which peaked in 1987 at around $66 million was not by any means the largest contribution from the West.[84] What made it significant was the fact that Britain was the first to take Mozambique seriously amongst major western NATO donors, whose opinions might carry some weight, however slight, with South Africa and whose views would be noticed by the US Republican administration.

The good relationship first forged between the late President Machel and Mrs Thatcher following the Lancaster House Conference and during the transition to Zimbabwean independence also played its part. The fact of this relationship helped to persuade President Reagan to see Machel on his visit to Washington in 1985. Her support of Machel was also crucial when the US Congress voted in 1985 to provide covert support for the UNITA rebels in Angola. The right-wing lobby in Washington then saw Renamo as the Mozambican equivalent of UNITA. Mrs Thatcher's position that support for Machel would help bring Mozambique into a genuine non-alignment enabled the State Department to keep official US government policy behind the Frelimo government.

Under Mrs Thatcher, official British government policy has always been to refuse to acknowledge South African support for Renamo (unlike the US State Department), although, privately, British diplomatic officials increasingly acknowledge that South Africa has, in the past, supported the rebels. During her official visit to Zimbabwe in April 1989, when she accompanied President Mugabe and President Chissano to watch the British Military Advisory and Training Team (BMATT) at Nyanga training Mozambican troops, Mrs Thatcher denounced Renamo in public as "terrorism of a particularly brutal and cruel kind".[85]

In spite of this public statement, it is clear that the British government does not believe that Frelimo can defeat Renamo militarily. At her April 1989 meeting with President Chissano, it is suggested that Mrs Thatcher urged him to talk to the rebels and was reported to have been frustrated when he appeared to be uncompromising. Britain, like the US, has used the Nairobi talks to contact Renamo and obtain a clearer picture of what the rebels want. During Mrs Thatcher's official visit to Kenya in 1988 the agenda for the talks with President Moi included the issue of Renamo.[86] President Moi also briefed Mrs Thatcher on the progress of his mediation attempts during his visit to London in November 1989, while President Chissano, during his twelve hour stopover in London following his visit to Washington in March 1990 briefed Mrs Thatcher on the Mozambique government's moves towards direct talks with Renamo.

British government involvement in Mozambique is most visible in its training since 1986 of two battalions of Mozambican troops by BMATT at Nyanga in the Eastern Highlands of Zimbabwe. In addition, officer training for Mozambican officials at Sandhurst has been on offer since 1984. Overt British military assistance to Mozambique has been supplemented by the use of Hall and Watts, a private weapons and procurement company, and Defence Systems Ltd (DSL), a private security firm which has links with Lonhro.[87] DSL at present protects Lonhro's interests within Mozambique and has already trained an élite team to protect the power lines supplying Maputo with electricity from South Africa. These lines are frequently attacked by Renamo (six times between August and October 1989).

Lonhro has been particularly active within Mozambique since the early 1980s. Its ownership of the Beira oil pipeline has meant that it has a particular interest in curtailing Renamo's activities. Renamo, recognising Lonhro's importance in Mozambique, has tried to develop informal contacts with it, so as to gain further credibility and leverage over Frelimo. It has frequently been pointed out by the rebels that Lonhro has supported UNITA, while Renamo has been ignored.[88] Although this is the position publicly, it increasingly seems that Lonhro has talked to Renamo. Lonhro has been rumoured to be one of the major players behind Renamo's cessation of attacks on the Nacala line. Lonhro has always been secretive about such contacts but it appears to be increasingly active in looking for ways to end the war. Just as Lonhro's own company planes had earlier helped transport the Mozambique delegates to South Africa (1984) when special discretion was required, Lonhro's close continuing interest was shown in 1989 by the flying to Lisbon of Tiny Rowlands and his then Mozambique representative, Alves Gomes, to have talks with the Portuguese Prime Minister, Cavaço Silva, on the eve of his departure for an official visit to Maputo.[89]

Since it recognised that Britain played an important role in foiling its attempts to win US government recognition, Renamo's Washington office has been looking since 1985 for ways of running a pro-Renamo campaign in Britain to counter the adverse image it has with the British press and public opinion. Initially they established contacts with sympathetic journalists and with British right-wing figures, such as the Marquess of Salisbury, and his son, Lord Michael Cecil. Lord Michael Cecil twice visited Renamo areas, first in 1986, and more recently in 1987. His 1987 visit witnessed the brutal fighting for Caia, and its heavy casualties, which appears to have dampened his support for the rebels.[90] A more coherent source of support had however already materialised by 1987 when some small right-wing "Institutes" and "Foundations", staffed by young British right-wingers, showed interest in Renamo.[91] Hitherto little known organisations such as Western Goals (UK), Mozambique Solidarity Campaign, and the better known bodies such as the now defunct Institute for the Study of Terrorism, International Freedom Foundation and the International Society for Human Rights (ISHR) began to produce sporadic literature sympathetic towards Renamo. With the exception of the Institute for the Study of Terrorism (IST) and the ISHR, it appears that these groups were launched initially with US right-wing funds from similar organisations in the US, such as the Heritage Foundation, the Freedom League and the now defunct Western Goals Foundation.

Everything about these groups resembles the US models that sponsored them. After initial capital input from the States, it was expected that they would be self-financing through US style direct-mail techniques to solicit their running costs from British businessmen. Their objectives and political position are also a mirror image of the stance taken by their US counterparts. The Director of the International Freedom Foundation, Marc Gordon, spoke, for example, in the same rhetoric as the US right-wing, describing Renamo as "the best anti-Marxist campaign of the 1980s" and its aim as being "to replace a totalitarian state with a free democracy".[92]

Renamo's objective appears to have been to use these organisations as pro-Renamo pressure groups, with a long-term aim of establishing a Renamo representative in London. The Director of Western Goals (UK), Stuart Northolt, travelled to Mozambique in 1987 via Malawi to visit Renamo. His visit was organised by a South African businessman, Duncan Beckman, who was in contact with the MRC in Washington. In late 1988 Thomas Schaaf and Antonio Rocha (of the MRC) visited London to make such preparations. Rocha and Schaaf visited the media (BBC World Service, Times, Telegraph and Independent), Amnesty International, Marc Gordon (IFF) and Jillian Becker (IST).[93] This visit came to nothing due, in part, to decisions on administrative matters taken at Renamo's Heidelberg meeting being held at the same time. The growing coolness of former Renamo sympathisers in London, reflecting the fact that Renamo was no longer in fashion with the right internationally, also diminished the impact of their visit. The emphasis has therefore returned to cultivating sympathetic individuals. The journalist Nicholas della Casa is a recent example. He was invited by Dhlakama to return to Mozambique with Sybil Cline and Robert Mackenzie of Freedom Inc in May 1989, to interview Renamo officials and make a documentary on Renamo for British Independent Television as a public relations exercise (this was broadcast in autumn 1989).

Nevertheless Renamo continues to look at London as a priority location for rebel representation. Pro-Renamo campaigns in London have been particularly concerned with two issues, the policies of the British Foreign Office towards Mozambique, and those of Lonhro. Renamo's British sympathisers attack (in terms similar to their US counter-parts) the policy of the former British Foreign Secretary, Sir Geoffrey Howe, and his successors, John Major and Douglas Hurd, for "working to encourage the growth of democracy and liberalism in countries very different from ours (Britain) but not impervious to change".[94] They argued that the Mozambique government will, in fact, never introduce a multi-party state, nor break its close ties with the Soviet Union. This has now changed, as in the US, to comparing Mozambique with Nicaragua.[95]

None of those groups which publicly supported the rebels in 1987 does so now. This is also reflected in the lack of contact in Britain now with the MRC in Washington. The Mozambique Solidarity Campaign supported by the IFF has collapsed (it only ever distributed compilations of photocopied pro-Renamo newspaper cuttings with comment). David Hoile, who published a pro-Renamo book in 1989, remains the main UK contact with Renamo via its Lisbon office (in September 1990 they arranged for him to meet Afonso Dhlakama and Raul Domingos in Nairobi).[96]

One other source of support for Renamo in Britain is found amongst right-wing fundamental Christians. One group in particular, "The Good Hope Fellowship", is closely connected with Peter Hammond's Frontline Fellowship, which as stated above, has a very active programme of support for Renamo.

MALAWI

Relations between the Malawi of President Hastings Banda and Frelimo have traditionally been tense, both before and after Mozambique's independence. The roots of this lie in the fact that both parties were, until recently, at the opposite extremes of the ideological spectrum. Malawi was one of the most conservative pro-western countries in Africa. Frelimo was, on the other hand, ideologically committed to Marxism-Leninism. During the liberation struggle for Mozambican independence, Malawi came under great pressure from the Portuguese not to give large scale assistance to Frelimo. This led to President Banda giving limited assistance to both sides. It was only in 1973, with mounting Frelimo successes, that Malawi began to play any major role as a launch pad for Frelimo operations into Mozambique.[98]

Contributing to this policy of "non-alignment" and the underlying hostility to Frelimo was the presence on Malawian soil of splinter groups from disputes within Frelimo. Both FUNIPOMO and PAPOMO relied on Malawian hospitality. PAPOMO was eventually closed down by the

Malawian authorities for its sympathies towards communist China. Another group, the UNAR, was a little more successful, appearing to have obtained support from both Jorge Jardim and President Banda. The UNAR stood for an independent state in the northern half of Mozambique, to be called Rombezia, in the area between the Rovuma and the Zambezi Rivers.[99]

On the eve of Mozambican independence the tensions between Banda and Machel became more evident. Machel bitterly attacked Malawi for its friendship with Portugal and for supporting anti-Frelimo groups such as the UNAR. There was some truth in these allegations in that opponents of Frelimo like Jorge Jardim (who had been Malawian Honorary Consul in Beira) and Orlando Cristina (who had helped train President Banda's Young Pioneers in the early 1970s) had fled initially to Malawi in the weeks after the 1974 coup. By 1976, the tension between Banda and Machel had focused itself on a revival of support in Malawi for opposition groups to Frelimo.[100]

The continuing Malawian involvement with anti-Frelimo groups after Mozambican independence might seem at first sight inexplicable, given that Malawi is a land-locked country dependent upon Mozambique for its trade routes (prior to heavy Renamo disruption in 1983, 60% of Malawi's trade transitted Mozambique). In logical terms it would seem a self-defeating policy to pursue.[101]

President Banda's decision to support Africa Livre, and possibly Renamo, may have its roots in 1967 in his support of the UNAR. Behind this may lie territorial ambition. It has been reported that President Banda sought in the 1960s to convince then President Julius Nyerere that northern Mozambique was historically part of Tanzania and Malawi.[102] What Banda was suggesting appears to have been a revival of the disputed concept of the 17th century Maravi confederacy. If this were achieved, Malawi would obtain direct access to the Indian Ocean and secure its own trade route. Both Africa Livre and the UNAR were based on regional goals. One possible scenario is that Banda's ambitions led him to make an informal agreement with South Africa and Renamo groups for the partition of Mozambique in return for Malawian territory being used by Renamo for transit and services.

Until severely weakened by the Mozambique Army's counter-offensives in late 1980, Africa Livre was publicly described by the Mozambican authorities as an extension of Renamo. This has subsequently been denied by both former CIO officials and figures in Renamo who had earlier been associated with Africa Livre.[103] Little information has ever been forthcoming about Africa Livre other than that it operated from about 1976 to 1982 and was led by the former Vice President of the UNAR, Amos Sumane. It apparently gained some grass-root support by penetrating the local Frelimo political structure in the Milange district of Zambezia province. It is known also to have attacked Government administrative establishments and the increasingly unpopular state stores. One eye-witness speaks of it killing officials, raiding stores and setting up road blocks with impunity around the town of Milange in late 1977.[104]

The facts about its foundation remain enigmatic, however. It has been speculated that Jorge Jardim used his influence in Malawi to relaunch the UNAR, for two possible reasons. Firstly, Jardim is known to have held a similar dream to that of Banda over creating a "greater Malawi" incorporating parts of northern Mozambique.[105] Secondly, Jardim, was, it seems, refused access to the Rhodesian operations of Renamo, because of his falling out with the the Rhodesians over oil supplies from SONAREP, which he had managed, in early 1970s sanction busting. Although this was partly due to Rhodesian policy, it was also orchestrated by Cristina, whom Jardim had arranged to be expelled from Malawi. The choice of the group's title is tantalising. Commentators initially assumed that it was part of Renamo as it shared the name of the rebel radio station located in Rhodesia, Voz da Africa Livre, but the title was probably copied due to the popularity of the latter's broadcasts in Zambezia in the late 1970s.[106]

By 1981, Africa Livre had become sufficiently successful, in spite of its set-backs in 1980, to require a meeting between Machel and Banda. Reports of its outcome indicate that Banda promised to curtail Africa Livre's activity on Malawian territory.[107] It appears the promise held, for, in 1982, Sumane was reported to be in Frelimo's hands and the movement shattered. Two trials of Africa Livre combatants took place, firstly in February 1981, when four were sentenced to death and 27 given prison sentences. A second trial, in June 1982, sentenced two prominent Africa Livre members to death. These were Matias Tende, who had left Frelimo in 1967 to join Coremo, and became a founding member of Africa Livre, and Joaquim Veleia, Frelimo Commissar for Gurue in Zambezia, who had joined Africa Livre in 1979. Around the same time its major external supporter, Jorge Jardim, died.[108] With the death of Jardim, Renamo's Secretary-General, Orlando Cristina, with South African encouragement, began talks with Africa Livre about joining forces and opening up a joint northern front. These contacts were made through Gilberto Fernandes, an Indian trader from Tete and associate of Cristina and Africa Livre's military chief, Gimo M'Phiri. The union was agreed and came into effect in late 1982, when some 600 Renamo combatants crossed the Zambezi to join what remained of Africa Livre.[109] This union led to a second serious flare-up of insurgent activity in Zambezia at the end of 1982.

In response to this, another meeting was held, this time between the then Foreign Minister of Mozambique, Joaquim Chissano, and President Banda, on the continued harbouring of rebels in Malawi.[110] But this intensification of insurgency probably represented a fresh input of arms and personnel from the now South African supported rebels who, for the first time, attacked Malawian access routes to the coast, a point made forcibly by Chissano at the meeting. Given the then heavy South African involvement in Renamo the latter's objectives were probably as much targetted at disrupting Malawi's involvement in the SADCC initiative as at destabilising Mozambique. It remains unclear whether, after the 1981 meeting, the President himself was aware of Renamo's presence in the Malawian border areas, a fact that President Machel illustrated in his 1984 visit to Malawi by insisting on visiting the sites of former Frelimo safe houses and transit camps on Malawian soil that were used during Mozambique's liberation struggle. The point was clear: if Frelimo could have utilised Malawi as a spring-board for operations inside Mozambique, often without the Malawian authorities being informed, why not Renamo?[111]

From 1983, rebel activity in areas adjacent to Malawi became increasingly common. Malawian complicity with Renamo was alleged to be a factor in Renamo's growing success. This culminated in Samora Machel threatening to place missiles on the Malawian border if support for Renamo was not terminated. A summit of major Front Line States' leaders was held in Malawi on 11 September 1986, at which Machel, accompanied by Prime Minister Robert Mugabe and President Kenneth Kaunda (as Chairman), gave Banda a folder that "contained documentary support, evidence of the allegations" that Malawi was supporting, and abetting, the Mozambique rebels,[112] a fact that had been independently noted by a British journalist visiting Malawi. Machel was even more blunt at a press conference he held in Maputo after his return from Blantyre, alleging that "the Malawian police, security, and military are controlled by South Africa and are being used to destabilise Mozambique".[113]

Banda responded by sending a 16 member team to Maputo, led by John Tembo, to answer these charges.[114] In spite of this gesture, tensions continued. A flurry of diplomatic activity occurred. "Pik" Botha visited Banda in Blantyre on September 26 encouraging Banda to defuse the crisis. On September 29 Tembo led another delegation to Maputo, followed by visits to Harare and Lusaka on October 17 to try further to curtail the allegations of Malawian support for Renamo and to provide assurances that Malawi would not allow further Renamo violations of its soil. During this period an enormous flare-up of Renamo activity in areas bordering Malawi occurred, rapidly spreading throughout the whole Zambezi valley and beyond. This would seem to suggest that Malawi responded to the Front Line States' demands by pushing the Renamo groups resident in Malawi across the border. The results of this displacement were horrifying. As the newly arrived groups attempted to carve out territory for their operations in Mozambique, a new level of violence and intensity of fighting occurred. By 1987, the whole Zambezia basin was in anarchy, except for the few strongly defended towns. The situation only began to improve in 1988. Malawi was to suffer too, through an enormous influx of Mozambicans to add to the already serious refugee problem. The escalation of violence created by Renamo's need to be more self-sufficient led in turn to a greater disruption of civilian life, providing few alternatives other than fleeing to neutral territory or becoming embroiled in the conflict. With such limited options and the growing insecurity in both Renamo and Frelimo dominated areas, only Malawi and the more strongly Frelimo held towns offered the civilian any sense of relative security. Renamo publicly boasts how the international efforts to deprive it of rear bases have backfired on the government and played into the rebel's hands.[115]

The fact that John Tembo was chosen to head the team sent by President Banda to respond to the Front Line allegations of Malawian support for Renamo is seen by some commentators to be significant.[116] John Tembo has long been thought of as having fostered elements in Renamo as an extra support for his bid to obtain the Presidentship after Banda. Tembo has been very close to Banda, helped by his kinship tie (uncle) to "the official hostess" — Mama Cecilia Kadzamira, the person with most influence over the President. Tembo's attempts to consolidate his position began when he held the important position of Governor of the Malawian Reserve Bank between 1971 and 1984. He is also known to have fostered close connections with the security police, South Africa and, through the "Official Hostess", the CCAM — the women's movement, which has great influence in matrilineal Malawi. Tembo is also a member of the Central Executive Committee of the Malawi Central Party (MCP), holding the post of Treasurer-General. In spite of these credentials, his position is, however, still insecure as he failed to gain the important position of Secretary-General of the MCP which became vacant on the death of its former Secretary-General in an accident. Although this was officially described as an "automobile accident", some commentators claim that the car was found riddled with machine-gun bullets.[117] This has led to the widespread conviction that Tembo was behind the incident, the motive being that the Malawi constitution dictates that when a President dies, his successor is to be chosen by the Secretary-General of the ruling party and two Cabinet Ministers. If Tembo, who lacks support amongst the civil service and the Malawian army, had gained the Secretary-Generalship, his position would have been considerably strengthened.[118]

It has also been suggested that Tembo tried to strengthen his hand by wooing support from Renamo groups as a "third force" to improve his position in the event of some type of armed struggle over the Presidentship.[119] If this is the case, the Front Line States' confrontation with Malawi over its support for Renamo in late 1986, and the escalated cost to Malawi of having its trade routes through Mozambique closed by Renamo, would have persuaded President Banda to restrain such dealings with Renamo.

Political developments within Malawi since late 1986 confirm this interpretation. On 4 December 1986, as a direct result of Front Line pressure and the unleashed anarchy of Renamo groups pushed out of their rear bases in Malawi, the setting-up of a Mozambique-Malawi security commission was agreed. This was followed up on 18 December by the signing in Lilongwe of a security pact.[120] This is thought to have given the FAM permission to enter Malawian territory in transit or in hot pursuit during anti-Renamo operations. It also prepared the way for the deployment from April 1987 of the Malawian army in defence of the Nacala line.[121] The many Malawian casualties from Renamo attacks have hardened feelings against Renamo in the Malawian army. Both General Khanga and Major-General Yohane, although fiercely loyal to President Banda, are known, like much of the Malawian army, not to favour Tembo or Kadzamira. They may have used their growing access to the President's ear (because of the Armed Forces' operations against Renamo) to try and limit Tembo's influence.[122]

All these factors are additional obstacles to John Tembo succeeding President Banda. Although it was widely believed that Banda regarded Tembo as his heir-apparent, it now seems the situation is more ambiguous, especially as Tembo's unpopularity within Malawi continues to grow. One indication that President Banda may have distanced his backing of Tembo over the succession came at the annual convention of the MCP in Zomba in 1987. In his address Banda referred to "Mama" Kadzamira by name as not having any aspirations over the succession and suggested that in the future there should be five, not three, nominees who would choose any future president.[123]

Tembo is, nevertheless, still regarded as the most likely person to succeed President Banda. With Banda's ailing health and greater unpredictability (such as his actions in 1989 against northerners), Tembo is being increasingly courted by the international community, as heir-apparent. Lonhro has been particularly active in this manner, making Tembo responsible for its Malawian operations. It is also probable that the cessation of Renamo's attacks on the Nacala line, following Dhlakama's statement in Nairobi on August 20, 1989, that all attacks on the line would cease as one of "the first steps towards the peace process in Mozambique", involved more than goodwill. Lonhro has been active in secret contacts with Renamo, and it is probable that Tembo, with his influence and experience of Renamo, was part of this process. Some sort of deal has evidently been made over the Nacala line which must have had Malawi and Lonhro as central players to a background of known diplomatic activity by Kenya, France and Portugal.

Within some circles in Malawi there seems to remain a continued benevolence towards Renamo and its splinter group, UNAMO. UNAMO continues to operate and to hold meetings in Blantyre without interference from the authorities. The frequent crossings by Renamo into Malawi in the Mulanje area, such as those after the FAM's recapture of Milange in 1988, when the rebels fled into Malawi to escape capture, the attack on Milange town by Renamo in late 1989, and the hot pursuit of fleeing FAM troops across the Malawian border for up to two miles within Malawi without any Malawian counter-action, suggest that there are still some sympathies for Renamo amongst Malawians.[124]

Another indication of this is the blind eye turned by the Malawian authorities to the most obvious remaining constituency of support for Renamo on Malawian soil, the various missionary groups (such as the Blantyre Christian Centre of Rodney and Ellie Hein) operating along the border areas. Although Ian Grey revealed that, since 1987, the Malawian authorities have been much more hostile to pro-Renamo activities, giving as example the putting under house arrest and deportation from Blantyre of Holger Jensen, then a reporter for *The Washington Times*, and Jack Wheller, because of their Renamo activities, the link nevertheless still continues, the MRC continuing to receive missionary material from Malawi.[125] This remains an important bridge between Renamo and its right-wing Christian sympathisers in the USA, Europe and South Africa.

Renamo itself confirms that it is finding Malawi increasingly difficult to operate in. Its attempts to place a mobile pro-Renamo radio station on Malawi soil have been blocked by the Malawian authorities.[126] Although Renamo still uses Malawi for transit purposes and as a market for trade, there does not seem now to be any official support for Renamo. With around one million Mozambican refugees having had to flee to Malawi by late 1990 (one in every eight persons in Malawi is now a Mozambican refugee), Renamo has become increasingly unpopular there for having created this heavy burden on the community. Already suffering from natural disasters, the local population have experienced spiralling inflation and a shortage of commodities aggravated by the demands of this large refugee influx.

The Malawi government has in its turn become active in assisting the process of bringing Renamo and the Mozambique government into dialogue. After Dhlakama and his top-ranking officials were nearly captured or killed during a FAM offensive in 1989 as they waited for transport to Nairobi for the talks with church leaders, Malawi assisted Renamo with safe passage and accommodation in Blantyre. It would appear that a main consideration in Renamo's decision not to attack the Nacala line since August 1989 is a gesture of gratitude for Malawian assistance. Recent Malawian dealings with Renamo have been encouraged by the Mozambique government who are briefed and informed on the progress of such contacts, in contrast to the suspicions of Maputo about such Malawian involvement with Renamo pre-1987.

KENYA

Since the late 1960s Kenya has also been a refuge for persons opposed to Frelimo. The core of the Kenyan group are former Catholic seminarians who fled from Dar es Salaam after the dispute over Fr. Mateus Gwenjere in 1968 at the Mozambique Institute. Kenya has always been an important contact point for the Mozambique Government with the rebels. For this reason a Renamo office was opened in Nairobi in 1984. The original Renamo delegation was led by Vincente Ululu (who was in Nairobi studying for a Kenyan degree at the time) and Armando Khembo dos Santos. This line-up did not last long, with Ululu returning to Mozambique once he had finished his course, and Khembo Santos becoming disenchanted with Renamo because of Evo Fernandes' dominance. In late 1985, Khembo Santos resigned from Renamo and formed a splinter group in 1986 called PADELIMO. More recently, in August 1989, he relaunched MANU, with the help of three other former MANU leaders now residing in Kenya, Antonio Nguala, Rafael Namacokola and Agostinho Malepande, to try to obtain a Makonde voice in the discussions for peace in Nairobi. Khembo Santos hoped that MANU's historical ties with Kenya (it was originally founded in Kenya with Kenyan encouragement and modelled on the ruling party KANU) would give it access to any peace talks in Nairobi.[127]

Through Khembo Santos, Leo Milas (of the 1960s disputes in Frelimo and prominent in early Renamo) resurfaced as a Renamo spokesperson. Between 1985 and 1987 he was the main Renamo contact in Nairobi, although never an officially sanctioned representative from Gorongosa. Francisco Nota Moises, a National Council member and Information Secretary, replaced Khembo Santos in 1986. After his departure in 1987 to Canada, he, in turn, was replaced by Manuel Lisboa. Lisboa remained Renamo delegate to Kenya until December 1989, when it was decided to replace him with Faustino Mateus during the Nairobi meeting of Dhlakama with his external representatives. Renamo in Nairobi is linked to its internal leadership through a radio transmitter supplied by its US supporters.

Since 1984 Kenya has been a source of passports for internal Renamo officials who otherwise found it impossible to travel, not being recognised by the UN as political refugees. This arrangement has been more recently formalised with the Mozambican government agreeing to Renamo negotiating teams travelling to Rome in 1990 on Kenyan passports.

The Kenyan government has increasingly become involved with Renamo since mid-1988 when President Moi began to show interest in becoming involved in mediating over the conflict in Mozambique. One of his first actions was to jointly call with US Senator Jesse Helms for the release of a British journalist, Nicholas della Casa, from Renamo captivity. This call was timed to coincide with the successful intervention by Freedom Inc and the MRC for della Casa's release. President Moi has since played an important role as joint-mediator with President Mugabe (as we shall see below) in seeking to bring Renamo and the Mozambique government to the negotiating table. But he also seems to have played a double role, favouring the rebels. It has been reported that in early 1990, President Moi withheld from Presidents Chissano and Mugabe an important Renamo document relating to talks with Frelimo. His reason for doing this is not known. It is also reported that a Kenyan delegation, including a major and a captain of the Kenyan armed forces, crossed into Renamo-controlled Mozambique in April 1990.[128]

Reports of Kenyan involvement with Renamo continue to grow. It is now suggested that Kenya is replacing South Africa as the logistical rear base of support for the rebels. Diplomatic sources have been quoted as saying that at least one Renamo training camp is now on Kenyan soil, whose fighters, once trained then fly to Malawi, are assisted to transit the country by vehicles of Malawi's Young Pioneers and cross into Mozambique. The Mozambique government has reported that a rebel battalion trained in Kenya became active in Tete province in early August 1990. There is also speculation that Renamo arms purchases in Europe in 1990, principally from West Germany, have been shipped to Kenya before delivery to rebel controlled Mozambique.[129]

Kenya's motives for becoming so involved with Renamo are puzzling. President Moi's mediation attempts are depicted in Kenya as reflecting his statesmanship as father of the nation, welcome publicity in the face of domestic problems.[130] There are suggestions that the failure in June 1990 to hold direct Frelimo-Renamo talks in Malawi was due to Kenyan advice to Renamo to continue to try and force negotiations to take place in Nairobi. The closeness of Kenya's relationship with Renamo is illustrated by Dhlakama having travelled from Nairobi to Malawi with Kenya's foreign ministry Permanent Secretary Betwell Abdu Kiplagat, under direct orders from President Moi, on the eve of those failed talks.[131]

Dhlakama has become very reliant on Kiplagat as an adviser. Kiplagat is known to have travelled frequently with Dhlakama in 1990. They travelled together to Malawi in mid-March for briefings on the result of President Mugabe's meetings with President Banda. Kiplagat was also seen on 2 April in Malawi meeting Dhlakama and Ululu following a meeting with Banda, and also in late April associating with the Kenyan delegations, some of whom crossed into Renamo-controlled Mozambique. In fact, Renamo claims that Kiplagat accompanied this delegation to Gorongosa and was favourably impressed by what he saw. Dhlakama's reliance on Kenyan advice is no doubt partly a response to the fact that his other sources of outside support and advice have diminished notably since 1988. This reliance is further reflected in the second round of direct talks with Frelimo in Rome in August 1990 when Renamo requested that Kenya should mediate in any further talks. But this is only the visible side of the story and it may be some time before it becomes fully clear why Kenya has become so involved with Renamo.[132]

SWAZILAND

Swaziland was at first a destination for large numbers of Mozambicans who fled at independence. Many of these are Portuguese or mixed race "retornados", who feel deeply embittered by the losses they incurred at independence. A growing community of illegally resident Mozambicans, fleeing Mozambique for the relative safety of the kingdom, has established itself there since. Renamo has recruited out of both groups. Such activity has enjoyed varying levels of tolerance on the part of the Swazi government, depending on its relationship with Maputo at any given point of time. For example, in 1983, Renamo had an official delegate in Mbabane, Francisco Nota Moises.[133]

It appears that, for a short while after the N'komati Accord, Renamo bases were set up in the Swazi mountains near the Mozambique border. These were well placed to make raids into Mozambique, with the aim of cutting off Maputo from outside. In February 1985, Mozambique protested to Swaziland. It appears that such bases were then moved across the border into Mozambique due to Swazi government policing of such areas. Swaziland remains a transit area for Renamo rebels but is not now seen as being a location for Renamo bases, as has sometimes been alleged in Maputo.[134]

ZIMBABWE

Zimbabwe became increasingly involved with the conflict in Mozambique in order to guard its own economic life-line — the Beira corridor — and as repayment for Mozambican sacrifices in support of the Nationalist cause before independence. Mozambique's role in the successful Lancaster House Agreement in bringing independence to Zimbabwe has also been recognised in this way.

The war in Mozambique, and especially South Africa's take-over of Renamo in late 1979, was also interpreted as an attempt by Pretoria to weaken Zimbabwe through a stranglehold on the Beira corridor. Renamo was regarded as a South African surrogate group primarily targetted to disrupt Zimbabwe through its destabilisation activities in Mozambique. Zimbabwean support for the Mozambique government in combatting Renamo was therefore seen by some Zimbabweans as fulfilling Zimbabwean domestic needs rather than repaying Mozambique for supporting Zanla during the 1970s.

The legal basis for Zimbabwean military involvement in Mozambique is the 1981 Zimbabwe-Mozambique Defence Agreement. This led in 1982 to a special "task force" of 1,000 Zimbabwean troops (ZNA) being deployed along the Beira corridor to safeguard the economic life-line in response to increasing Renamo activity and the blowing-up of the country's petrol tanks in Beira that year. By 1984 with an increasing number of attacks along the Beira and Tete corridors this contingent was expanded to around 3,000 troops.[135]

In the aftermath of N'Komati and the failed Pretoria Declaration proximity talks, ZNA forces became more involved within Mozambique. The turning point marking this greater involvement came in 1985, when a former Rhodesian CIO official acquainted with Renamo led élite Zimbabwean paratroopers in an assault that captured Renamo's headquarters in Gorongosa, known as Casa Banana. This move, in response to a request from President Machel, marked a deeper involvement by Zimbabwe in Mozambique than mere defence of its own strategic interests. Zimbabwean troops also played a major role through air and ground support in 1987 and the first half of 1988 in the FAM's counter-offensive to return small towns in Mozambique's Zambezia province to government control. With this accomplished, Zimbabwean troops have again concentrated their efforts on protecting the Beira corridor, and preventing Renamo incursions into Zimbabwe. President Mugabe stated then that Zimbabwe would be prepared to commit up to 30,000 troops in Mozambique.[136] Although this level of military presence has never been reached, it is estimated that there are currently around 10,000 Zimbabwean troops on Mozambican soil.

The increase in Zimbabwean troops in Mozambique and their fighting directly against Renamo, has led the latter to threaten to disrupt Zimbabwe. These threats gained force on June 20, 1987 when Renamo declared war on Zimbabwe. Since then it has attacked tea estates, schools, health clinics, shops, farms and peasant communities, destroying and looting property and killing and abducting the local populations. Over 450 deaths on Zimbabwean soil have been reported following Renamo attacks.[137]

Renamo activity in Zimbabwe is a mirror image of its tactics within Mozambique. The maimings and brutal, very visual, murders have happened with an eye for media coverage. The levels of rumour and physical fear of such occurrences among the local communities indicate the success of Renamo's methods. The majority of Renamo incursions into Zimbabwe are, however, cross-border raids. Renamo has no permanent presence in Zimbabwe so far. Many of its incursions are by groups ranging in size from five to fifteen, transiting Zimbabwean territory to avoid detection within Mozambique. Other incursions involving looting are intended to obtain commodities needed by Renamo within Mozambique. Zimbabweans are also kidnapped on such incursions for forced labour. The Zimbabwean authorities estimate that some sort of Renamo incident occurs every second day.[138]

Renamo aims to increase domestic pressure within Zimbabwe for a disengagement from the war in Mozambique. After a long and draining liberation struggle many sections of Zimbabwean society feel unenthusiastic about being committed to a seemingly endless struggle in Mozambique. This sentiment has grown with knowledge of the rising costs. It is thought to cost Zimbabwe around Z$ 1,000,000 a day to sustain operations there. The increasing number of Zimbabwean casualties in action in Mozambique further feeds these sentiments. Zimbabwean soldiers with first hand experience of the war are particularly ambivalent about their deployment in a conflict they do not believe in.[139]

Known by many Zimbabweans as "our Vietnam", the military involvement has increasingly been utilized by the political opposition as a rallying issue. Beginning as a private reservation only, it has recently been voiced in public. Back-bench MPs in the Zimbabwe Assembly (especially Sidney Malunga and Alexio Mudzingwa) began in January 1989 to criticise the government over the Mozambique commitment, calling, in direct opposition to their party line, for the withdrawal of troops from Mozambique.[140]

Withdrawal of the "Task Force" has now become one of the prominent features of the programme of the opposition party of Edgar Tekere — the Zimbabwe Unity Movement (ZUM).[141] It has also increasingly been a campaign issue of the Rev. Ndabaningi Sithole's Zanu-Ndonga party. In May and November 1989 letters sent by Sithole to President Mugabe described the war in Mozambique as a conflict between Mozambicans, adding that Zimbabwe should pull out of the conflict so as to aid the peace process.[142] He has reiterated this line in interview. He has said:[143]

> I am utterly opposed to Zimbabwean forces in Mozambique. The conflict is one between Mozambicans, in other words, differences between Renamo and Frelimo. Zimbabweans are foreigners, unwanted foreigners in this conflict. They have a role to play — the one of mediator rather than combatant.

Such public calls for withdrawal and negotiation have been ridiculed by the Zimbabwean authorities who have tried to link them with the activities of Renamo and South African destabilisation. Soon after the launch of ZUM in May 1989, the Harare daily, *The Herald*, republished a story on a "friendship and co-operation agreement" between Zanu-Ndonga and Renamo of August 1986.[144] According to *The Herald*, this agreement was signed by three Renamo representatives in Washington, D.C. when they visited Patrick Buchanan at the White House. That such an agreement was ever signed has been utterly rejected by Sithole who claims that the story was published to denigrate Zanu-Ndonga and that it was aimed at under-mining Edgar Tekere's ZUM in response to its popular calls for an end to the Zimbabwean presence in Mozambique.

However, both Renamo and the MRC in Washington claim that such an agreement was signed and that Sithole has developed cold feet.[145] They say that the agreement was not recognised by Dhlakama, who was never consulted (it was Fonseca's, Fernandes' and Sithole's idea), or by Zanu-Ndonga in Zimbabwe, which has distanced itself from Sithole's exile politics. The Zimbabwean government continued to attempt to link Zanu-Ndonga and ZUM with Renamo during its election campaign in March 1990, allegations strongly denied by both groups.

Renamo has recognised that the war is unpopular, especially amongst the young Zimbabwean conscripts fighting in Mozambique. It has therefore produced literature in Shona and in English which it leaves in areas where the ZNA is active. It has smuggled such propaganda into army bases. In its more dramatic attacks within Zimbabwe, Renamo has left similar material, including hit lists with the names and addresses of prominent Zimbabweans, justifying its actions and threatening to increase its incursions in the future, unless Zimbabwe withdraws its troops from Mozambique.[146] Renamo has tried to link any peace process in Mozambique with a demand for Zimbabwean withdrawal, as point 11 of Renamo's 16 point declaration released at the end of the first round of talks in Nairobi in August 1989 (see Appendix 2) and as its arguments against talks in Malawi illustrate.

The Zimbabwean authorities' response to Renamo's incursions along the eastern border has been to herd people into what are described in the Zimbabwean press as "security planned village settlements" — protected villages, reminiscent of the Smith years. The talk in the press about these settlements being attractive for "development activities" refers in fact to security considerations, such as better roads which are difficult to mine. The return of protected villages has brought about the familiar popular complaints heard during UDI in Zimbabwe and over the aldeamentos of colonial Mozambique, such as the lack of fertile land, the distance from ancestral territory, inadequate essential services, abuses by the security forces. Along the south-east border complaints about the inadequate security given by the army are still commonly heard.[147] In an area already marked with severe and growing land pressure from thousands of landless peasants (denied access to land because of private, and mostly white-owned, commercial farming, or because of security restrictions, as well as a well-founded natural fear of cultivating land in areas frequently visited by Renamo), there is concern that Renamo will be able to recruit freely in this climate. What is especially worrying for Zimbabweans is that this particular area is where the N'dau, a Shona clan, reside, not least because the N'dau on the Mozambican side of the border are the nucleus, and continue to be the leadership core, of Renamo, providing the organisation's lingua franca. CIO officials begin to worry that, as with the Mozambican N'dau, there is very little to stop their Zimbabwean counterparts from becoming increasingly involved with Renamo.

It is not insignificant that both Zanu-Ndongo and ZUM have their stongest support in these areas. In the 1985 general election Chipinge was the only non-Ndebele constituency to return an anti-government representative, Goodson Sithole of Zanu-Ndongo.[148] Such feelings were reiterated in the voting during the 1990 elections. All three opposition seats (two ZUM, one Zanu-Ndonga) were won in the eastern highlands, a serious indication of the government's unpopularity in this region. Renamo's use of a mixture of violence, the skilful exploitation of local grievances (such as communalism) and the enlisting of religion, especially the *Svikiro* (Spirit mediums), to obtain support within Mozambique is a strategy that is not enormously different from that utilized by Zanla during the war for independence. Although Renamo's use of violence is clearly far greater than that of Zanla, the combination is not entirely dissimilar.

In public, the Zimbabwean authorities deny that there are any potential problems along the eastern border. Their actions suggest otherwise. The ZNA has attempted to create a 40 kilometre-wide *cordon sanitaire* on the Mozambique side of the border to prevent further Renamo incursions and has forcibly removed the local population. Various segments of the border area are then technically "frozen" to flush out and make "contact" with the rebels in order to destroy them before they reach Zimbabwean soil. This is made particularly difficult by the cultural, ethnic and kinship ties between the peoples on both sides which have created a traditional fluidity of movement across the border. Recognising Renamo's combatants in this situation is extremely difficult.

The successful targeting of Renamo's operations within Zimbabwe has suggested to the Zimbabwean authorities that a network of Renamo informers has been established amongst the Mozambican migrants working in the country as well as being placed in protected villages and the refugee camps. The estimated 100,000 Mozambican refugees remaining in Zimbabwe today have therefore been placed in camps at Tongogara, Mazowe River Bridge, Nyangombe and Nyamatiki, which are heavily policed by both the CIO and the regular police force. These camps have nevertheless increasingly become centres of discontent. Shortages of firewood and tensions over land among an already impoverished and land hungry local population have caused serious riots.[149] Although there have been some attempts to encourage education and training, to make the camps self-supporting and to isolate them from Renamo influence, these programmes continue to suffer from lack of funds and consistent government commitment. Zimbabwe has responded to these problems by summarily expelling many refugees to Mozambican government reception centres inside Mozambique (between 8-9,000 in 1988) with the result of increasing hostility and uncertainty in the camps.[150]

Refugee influx to Zimbabwe has slowed to a trickle. This is not a reflection of any improvement in the situation inside Mozambique but rather of the refugees' realisation that they will receive a warmer, and safer, welcome in Malawi, a fact supported by recent arrivals in southern Malawi who have fled from south of the Zambezi river.

All these factors add to the growing domestic desire within Zimbabwe to find a negotiated settlement within Mozambique which will include Zimbabwean withdrawal from Mozambique. Both Renamo and critics of the Zimbabwean government point out that part of the reason for Zimbabwean involvement inside Mozambique is chauvinism and arrogance. They point to talk of "Mozambabwe", a joint country whose President would be Mugabe and the Prime Minister, Chissano. This is crude propaganda, based on the views of a couple of extreme MPs in Zimbabwe. Although many Zimbabweans continue to stereotype Mozambicans as incompetent, the majority of Zimbabweans want Mozambique to be a peaceful neighbour where the more prosperous of them can invest and again have access to the coast. There is no general desire for any type of union or permanent presence in Mozambique.

The Zimbabwean authorities have privately become far more realistic about the situation inside Mozambique. They held several informal meetings with Renamo in early 1989 as part of the build-up to the Nairobi talks and the official role President Mugabe played as a joint mediator with President Moi of Kenya. Elleck Mashingaidze, a foreign affairs permanent secretary, directly participated in the September and October rounds of the Nairobi talks in an attempt to break the deadlock. As part of this process the CIO has also been increasingly involved in informal liaison with Renamo, both in Nairobi and inside Mozambique. They have also been closely monitoring the situation inside Mozambique, regarding Renamo as a successful rebel force, as leaked documents suggest.[151]

The growing domestic unrest in Zimbabwe about government dogmatism, incompetency and, in particular, corruption has left Mugabe vulnerable. The Willowgate scandals, the Sandura Commissions, and their aftermath of acquittals and cover-ups of all those close to the President, are regarded as a sham by most Zimbabweans and interpreted in ethnic terms. The detention of trade union leaders, the student riots at the University of Zimbabwe followed by its temporary closure, and the challenge to the judicial system by the party all represent a growing uncertainty within Zimbabwe about the plans of President Mugabe and his supporters to impose one party rule. This was all a build-up to the general elections in March 1990 and the tenth anniversary of independence, when legislation came into force allowing President Mugabe to amend the Bill of Rights by a two-thirds vote of Parliament, and to abolish freedom of political association. The 1990 election results, with 46% of the electorate staying away from the ballot boxes are a further indication of a growing ambivalence towards the government in Zimbabwe. The result may be to re-ignite the powder-keg of domestic grievance that became so explosive in Matebeleland with South African-backed intervention and political opposition.

One can only hope that, with the reduced role of the South African military and a greater pragmatism by President Mugabe over Mozambique, the additional potential powder-keg of discontent along Zimbabwe's 1,200 mile long border does not catch alight. The recipe for further disaster is in place. It is clear that many Zimbabweans hope that lessons were learnt by the government in Matebeleland, so that there is not a repeat of a dissident problem in Manicaland. As one peasant from Chiredzi said:[152]

> The chefs (leaders) do not understand. They are the ones who grow fat. We want schools and peace. Let the cock crow again (ZANU) to our song. The one of the povo (people).

TANZANIA

Tanzania has, like Zimbabwe, deployed troops within Mozambique in an attempt to bolster Frelimo and to curb the war for the government's benefit. Tanzanian support for Frelimo against its opposition was a continuation of its pre-independence role of providing Frelimo with rear bases. In the run-up to independence in 1975, Frelimo placed detained opposition figures, such as Lazero Nkavandame, in one of its southern Tanzanian bases. Nkavandame was moved after independence to Cabo Delgado, and continued to be guarded by Tanzanian troops.

The Tanzanian decision to commit troops within Mozambique was not made solely from solidarity with the Mozambique government. Troops were sent to Mozambique to ensure that rebel activity did not spread across into Tanzania. It was possibly also a way of employing restless troops from the Ugandan campaigns rather than having them stationed at home, with the potential problems that they could cause.

The size of this commitment has never been publicly declared. In June 1985 Tanzania publicly pledged training facilities for the FAM in southern Tanzania at Nachingwea. By 1989 this was estimated to have cost Tanzania $3.5 million. However, it seems that just over 1,000 Tanzanian troops had been stationed by 1983 in Cabo Delgado inside Mozambique. This commitment only became public in September 1986, following a Mozambican request, when Tanzania announced that it would send a brigade group of 4,000 soldiers to assist the Mozambique government to regain control of the countryside. Tanzania's contribution seems to have peaked in 1987, with between 5–7,000 personnel stationed by then in Zambezia province and in Quelimane town in support of the FAM offensive to recapture the small towns occupied by Renamo in late 1986 and early 1987 during its infiltration of Zambezia following its loss of Malawian support. In December 1988, Tanzania decided to pull out the majority of its troops from their bases in the north and north-east of Mozambique, due to the costs which they felt increasingly to have been ineffectual. Tanzanian officials talk of the intervention having cost 60 lives and over $120 million.

Renamo has only been active sporadically on Tanzanian soil. It is thought that there is some sympathy for it amongst muslims, especially on Zanzibar and along the coast, due to rumours of Islamic repression by Frelimo. In 1984 the Tanzanian authorities foiled an attempt by Portuguese sympathisers to construct an airstrip in southern Tanzania from where air-drop supplies to Renamo could be launched. Renamo has also made direct cross-border incursions. The Tanzanian authorities have officially recorded that five incursions have taken place between late 1987 and April 1989. One Tanzanian had been killed, many others abducted and large amounts of property, food and money stolen from villages. By late 1989 reports of incursions had become more frequent, a reflection of the growing presence of Renamo along this border region, which is confirmed by the growing number of refugees in Tanzanian camps (60,000 in 1990).

ZAMBIA

Although it does not have troops committed within Mozambique, Zambia has increasingly suffered from incursions by Renamo since 1987. Renamo's raids into Zambia's Eastern province were first recorded in March 1987. Throughout 1987 there were minor cross-border actions involving abduction, cattle rustling and other types of pillaging. However, it is difficult to distinguish in the reports of such activities between the freelance banditry and smuggling syndicates that operate in this border area and Renamo. The first definable Renamo action occurred in December 1987 when an immigration post and cooperative store in Chadiza district were attacked. The Renamo group, which was well armed, killed a Zambian national during this raid. A poster of Dhlakama was left near the body, together with copies of an open letter to the Zambian government warning that such attacks would continue until Lusaka stopped supporting the Mozambican government.

Since then attacks by Renamo have consistently intensified in typical Renamo frontier style — attacking and looting of clinics, shops, schools, farms and local villages, with the ubiquitous sequestration of civilians and brutal treatment of inhabitants. Between March 1987 and May 1989, Zambian officials speak of 75 dead, over 171 abductions, 152 huts burnt and 9 stores looted, with the greater number of incidents taking place in 1989, a further reflection of Renamo's growing need to plunder to survive as its external support dries up.[153]

In an attempt to discourage the rebels the Zambian army has mounted cross-border raids after such attacks. This has included offensive action. In May 1988, for example, the Zambian army pursued raiders 19 km into Mozambique's Tete province, killing 73 rebels and destroying 2 bases.[154] Because of the deteriorating security situation in Eastern province in 1989 a Zambian-Mozambican Security Commission was set up to look at ways of improving security. That one of its main proposals was that government-sponsored open fairs should be set up to try to obtain some benefit from the smuggling and booty trade with Renamo confirms that a major reason for Renamo's incursions is to obtain supplies. The Commission's hope is that the fairs will encourage peaceful barter rather than further bloodshed and destruction.

OTHER COUNTRIES

Other countries that have at one time or another been named as being sympathetic towards Renamo are the Comoros, Israel, Morocco, Oman, Saudi Arabia and Zaire. Comoros Islands' assistance to Renamo was first reported in 1984. A report appeared in the South African *Sunday Tribune* that Renamo was receiving arms from Oman and Saudi Arabia through Somalia and the Comoros. No further supporting evidence of Comoros involvement has materialised. Most commentators believe this story to be part of a South African disinformation campaign at the time designed to shift attention from continued South African violations of the N'Komati Accord.[155] Possible Comoros involvement in Renamo was, however, reported again in late 1987, when dhows were suspected of being loaded in the Comoros with supplies for Renamo donated by sympathetic individuals in South Africa, Oman and Saudi Arabia. These dhows then shipped the supplies to the Querimba islands, just off the Mozambique mainland (also strongly muslim), in preparation for Renamo's new offensive into Cabo Delgado. The Mozambique authorities took this seriously at the time as Mozambican archaeologists were forbidden to carry out field work on these islands during this period. It is also alleged that Saudi Arabia donated $500, 000 to the rebels in early 1990, an indication of continued support.

The common denominator between the Comoros link and continuing sympathy amongst some individuals in Oman and Saudi Arabia for Renamo is Islam. Renamo propaganda, especially that disseminated from Lisbon, has targetted Islamic countries with accounts of past Frelimo religious intolerance, trying with these to raise funds for its cause. For this reason, as well as the islands' known close links with South Africa, the Comoros have probably been used as an occasional transit point for supplies for Renamo. This may continue, even following the military coup in late 1989 and a new government in the country, as long as individuals within the international Islamic community perceive the Mozambique government as anti-muslim.

SPLINTER GROUPS

Splinter groups within Renamo emerged after the death of Andre Matsangaissa, which had resulted in a dispute over his succession. The first such groups, based in Lisbon, were Maximo Dias' MONAMO (1979) and Zeca Caliate's FRESAMO (1981). Both attacked Renamo for being South African-dominated and the Mozambican government for being multi-racial, although it is known that MONAMO signed an agreement in September 1979 with Renamo to supply material for Voz da Africa Livre. Yet another group emerged from a similar dispute over the succession following the death of Orlando Cristina, and the rise to power of Evo Fernandes. Further discontent, expulsions and defections from Renamo flowed from this struggle for power. These various factions eventually coalesced into the groupings known as PADELIMO[156] in Kenya (1986) and CONIMO (1985/6) in West Germany,[157] both, in their turn, amalgamated quickly into the "Cologne Group"[158] which, by June 1986, had decided to call itself CUNIMO.[159] As an umbrella organisation CUNIMO attempted to attract Mozambican dissidents who felt unable to support either Renamo or a reforming Mozambican government. Another splinter group calling itself "Veterans of Renamo", appeared in Lisbon in March 1988.[160] It too accused Dhlakama of being a "traitor and unfaithful henchman of Renamo", but has not been heard of since. A further attempt by the splinter groups to form an alternative to Renamo was made in August, 1989, when MONAMO, FRESAMO and a previously unknown group called COMIMO decided to form a single organisation. Called UDEMO, it only held together several months, collapsing into its founding groups and stimulating the formation of yet another splinter group, MONALIMO.[161] In August 1989, MANU, a party that was dissolved in the 1960s on forming part of the newly formed Frelimo under Mondlane, was relaunched in Kenya.

None of these splinter groups has any relevance inside Mozambique. Although FRESAMO claimed to have an internal organisation, this was never evident inside Mozambique.[162] CUNIMO, like its predecessors (CONIMO and PADELIMO), was more concerned with pushing for reforms within Renamo's structure. It particularly urged the removal of Evo Fernandes. Its platform was largely based on a black Mozambican backlash to Renamo's continued dominance by asians and whites, such as Fernandes, Correia, Schaaf and by South African military intelligence. The one uniting factor was the call for the end of Evo Fernandes' dominance.[163] With Fernandes' loss of authority in 1986, CUNIMO rapidly fragmented. By mid-1987 it was, in effect, a spent force. Many of its members had reintegrated into Renamo or returned to their original splinter groups.

The rapid appearance of CUNIMO and its related groups within only a year, and its equally rapid decline, need further explanation. CUNIMO held three meetings. The first in Nairobi served only to get it on its feet. The second was little more than an administrative follow-up to Nairobi. Its most important session was held in Cologne from which it sent two representatives to Malawi.[164] Its final meeting was held in late 1987 in Philadelphia, where the proceedings were dominated by internal dispute, especially over Vilankulu, who resigned from CUNIMO at this meeting. The bickering focused on Vilankulu's attempt the previous year to be Renamo Representative in the USA, while still also being a member of CUNIMO, and his suspected embezzlement of funds.[165]

After the failure of this meeting CUNIMO disintegrated as a serious organisation, although a small number of supporters based in West Germany continue to run CUNIMO, with Dr. Antonio Zengazenga as its President. In 1988 CUNIMO was present at the World Congress of the Antibolshevik Bloc of Nations in Washington. In August 1989 it participated in a conference in Lisbon with another splinter group, MONAMO, but seems to have rejected the offer of joining a coalition of splinter groups called UDEMO that was launched at this meeting. In March 1990 it also presented a paper at a CSU conference in Munich. CUNIMO has consistently attempted to represent the middle ground in the conflict in Mozambique, but with little success. All of CUNIMO's activities up to 1988 represented considerable expenditure. The question arises: where did the finance come from, and why?

A major protagonist in CONIMO and its successor, CUNIMO, was Artur Vilankulu, the CAF backed figure in the dispute over Renamo's representative in Washington. It appears that Leo Billinger, the Executive Director of CAF and David Finzer, the Director, after their failure to host Renamo's operations in the USA, decided to fund an alternative group to Renamo.[166] There may lie a deeper meaning to this than American right-wing competition and empire-building. In its approaches to Renamo, CUNIMO attempted to obtain recognition as the civil, moderate wing of Renamo, claiming the middle ground between Renamo and Frelimo. This might explain why CUNIMO appears to have received backing from the West German intelligence and the CAF, in an attempt to break the deadlock between Renamo and the Mozambique government. The plan did not succeed due to the suspicions of Renamo and the embezzlement of its funds by CUNIMO members. Following the Philadelphia meeting, CUNIMO in Lisbon and New York was survived by a foundation, funded by CAF money, known as "Friends of Mozambique". Based in Portugal, it had been a front for CUNIMO, but also offered scholarships to children of Mozambican dissidents to subsidise the costs of secondary education. This in turn has now collapsed due to the suspected embezzlement of its funds by its directors, Jose Massinga and Artur Vilankulu.

UDEMO appears to be in the same mould as CUNIMO. It was launched after the weekend conference (26-27 August, 1989) in Lisbon. As another umbrella group it appears to be a further attempt to provide a third voice in any negotiated settlement. UDEMO's spokesperson, Maximo Dias, described the group as "political, not military". He said that it would lobby for the "immediate withdrawal of foreign forces" from Mozambique at the UN Security Council and that "all Mozambican political forces" must be given a voice in any ongoing negotiations if peace is to be achieved in Mozambique.[167] Khembo Santos and his relaunched MANU in Nairobi are a similar response to the Nairobi talks. With the build-up to direct dialogue between Renamo and the Mozambique government in 1990, Mozambican exiles have attempted again to obtain a place at the negotiating table by holding a two day conference in Cologne in March 1990. The result of this was a document called the "Cologne Manifesto" which demanded that: "the principal armed opponents to include various other national forces — for example, the UNAMO — in their national reconciliation process, who could make a useful contribution to the reconstruction of peace".

At the end of 1986 another splinter group, UNAMO, appeared. This is quite distinct from the others. Its external representation was drawn from the defunct CUNIMO. In contrast to the other splinter groups, it appears to operate within Mozambique, primarily in Zambezia province. Its origins lie in the tension that developed when the remnants of Africa Livre joined Renamo in 1982 (see above) and in the succession and policy disputes within Renamo of the 1980s. UNAMO attacks Renamo's closeness to South Africa and its strongly N'dau biased leadership. It finds itself fighting both Frelimo and Renamo, something it proudly proclaims in its occasional policy statements.

UNAMO's leader is Gimo M'Phiri, the former military chief of Africa Livre. After joining Renamo in 1982 M'Phiri became in 1983 the political number one after Dhlakama on Renamo's National Council. It appears that M'Phiri held considerable influence within Renamo until 1986, having, with Dhlakama, supported Evo Fernandes as the successor to Orlando Cristina as Secretary-General. With the death of Renamo's warlord for the north, General Henrique, in an unsuccessful operation to capture Maganja da Costa in November 1986, it seemed likely that M'Phiri would succeed him. This was not to be. Dhlakama named Calisto Meque to replace Henrique, without consulting Gimo M'Phiri. His aim was to centralise further Gorongosa's control over the north. This decision aroused further tension, especially since Meque, as a N'dau, did not hold the same level of confidence as M'Phiri amongst Renamo's combatants in the northern operation zone. The split finally came about during Renamo's offensive in early 1987 when N'dau combatants in the northern zone suffered far heavier casualties than their Macua, Ghuabo and Maconde counterparts, who knew their terrain better. This fuelled Meque's suspicions of a plot against his authority and drove him to purge non-N'dau commanders from his ranks, even going so far as to have some shot. A spin-off from this confusion was an increase in atrocities against the civilian population in the areas of Zambezia fully dominated by Renamo at the time. Dhlakama was, meanwhile, persuaded to remove Evo Fernandes (a strong supporter of M'Phiri) from the Secretary-Generalship, which further weakened M'Phiri's influence within Renamo. As a result M'Phiri, with 500 supporters, broke with Renamo to form UNAMO.[168]

UNAMO is known to have attacked Renamo bases. There are reports that UNAMO attacked Renamo's headquarters in Zambezia in the spring of 1988 and killed its commander, a national council member, Calisto

Meque (contrary to Frelimo which has claimed, that he was killed, firstly in their operations on August 11 and, secondly, in an operation to retake Gile on September 11). Although uncertainty about these events remains, Frelimo military officials openly admit that UNAMO activity aided their 1988 Zambezia counter-offensive by splitting Renamo's response.

Not surprisingly, Renamo calls UNAMO a Mozambican government orchestrated puppet organisation. It sees Maputo's aim as that of using UNAMO as a proxy force to drive a wedge through Zambezia province in order to split Renamo's operations into two, further denying Renamo access to its Malawian transit and supply routes, especially important to it for obtaining commodities unavailable within Mozambique. Undoubtedly this is partly true. The Mozambican authorities would wish to encourage every internal dissent within Renamo. But the evidence on the ground does suggest that UNAMO is an autonomous rebel group.

UNAMO's areas of influence within Mozambique apppear to be localised to the districts between the Milange and Namuli mountains in Zambezia province. In this area it seems to play on its ethnic ties. But it also has a wider appeal. M'Phiri has been described by one of UNAMO's members, Marcelo Cardoso, as having been the major contact figure between Malawi and Renamo when he was in Renamo. This experience carried over into UNAMO.

As UNAMO does not issue many statements, its objectives are difficult to analyse. A member of UNAMO in Lisbon, Marcelo Cardoso, said in 1987 that Renamo treatment of the local population in central Mozambique had caused the split. He depicted UNAMO as being committed to establishing true "liberated zones" and to achieve social change in Mozambique.[169] UNAMO's Secretary for Foreign Relations, Gilberto Fernandes (otherwise known as Gilberto Magid), has been somewhat more precise, According to Fernandes, UNAMO demands recognition as a legitimate opposition party through free elections.

Frelimo has taken UNAMO more seriously than the other splinter groups. With help from the USA, a meeting was held in Lisbon in November 1988 between the Professor of Law at Eduardo Mondlane University, Dr Emilio Ricardo, and UNAMO's then Portuguese representative, Carlos Reis. This was followed in January 1989, by a meeting, again in Lisbon, between Reis and Frelimo Central Committee Member, Alvaro Casimiro. In January 1989 the wife of Gilberto Fernandes (UNAMO's number two) visited Maputo, returning to Blantyre in Malawi with a further message from Maputo for M'Phiri.[170] These contacts prepared the way for a meeting in April 1990 in Quelimane between Gimo M'Phiri and Mozambican Defence Minister, Alberto Chipande. From this meeting it appears UNAMO has come to an agreement with Maputo by supporting the new constitution with its commitment to political pluralism, and now campaigns freely in Mozambique with Carlos Reis as its Secretary-General.

The Mozambican government has been increasingly keen to woo as many of the splinter groups and dissident exiles as it can into supporting its peace initiative, thereby further exposing Renamo to criticism for continuing to drag its feet over a ceasefire. In Lisbon in April 1990, President Chissano, addressing a meeting of about a thousand Mozambican exiles, made this quite clear, saying: "National reconciliation has to be for all Mozambicans or political groupings: Unamos, Renamos, Monalimos — names don't matter".[171] Since then Maximo Dias, Domingos Arouça and other exiles have been asked by Maputo to contribute to the debate over the new constitution and invited to visit or return to Mozambique.

These approaches have been successful. Long-standing dissidents, such as Artur Vilankulu, who returned to Maputo in May 1990, now support the government's peace initiative. It is, however, unlikely that, with the possible exception of UNAMO, and newly formed parties, such as PALMO, with their internal roots, any of the externally based dissidents or splinter groups will stand much chance of success in the proposed free elections in 1992, having no base or tradition of support inside Mozambique today.

The history of the external representation of Renamo has been one of dispute, murder and intrigue. It is also one which has been dominated by outside interests, be it South African, American or Mozambican intelligence. These dissensions threw Renamo's external representatives in the past into disrepute, highlighting the enormous gap between the Renamo operating within Mozambique and its representatives outside, as the contradictory statements and initiatives taken without consultations with the internal wing have illustrated.

One cause of the bloody disputes within the external wing has been the attempts to put it in order. The deaths of Ataide and Lopes, and the decline of Evo Fernandes and all those close to him are all part of this process. The 1988 Heidelberg meeting, Renamo's "Congress" of June 1989 and the December 1989 Nairobi meeting were significant milestones in the restructuring of the external wing to end the infighting. After the December Nairobi meeting, which removed Luis Serapião from his post and decided to remove Manuel Frank at an opportune time, the reshuffling of the personalities causing contention appears to have been completed for the time being. Renamo hopes that the reshuffling will enable it to cope better with the more high-level diplomatic activities now required to put its point of view across in the on-going search for a peaceful settlement. Renamo also hopes that the changes will attract to it other Mozambican exiles who, in the past, gravitated towards one of the splinter groups because of its wrangling and personality clashes. The Nairobi talks and subsequent events provide a new challenge for Renamo. It remains to be seen how different or effective the re-styled external representation will be.

Although Renamo is now committed towards negotiations, it is unlikely that it will curtail its cross-border raids into Tanzania, Zambia or Zimbabwe. Important for Renamo's operational economy, they are also used as a tactical reminder of the rebels' potential for further destabilization in the whole region. Renamo will only be curtailed in the field by a mixture of political and military action. The improved security of the Nacala, Beira and Maputo corridors are an indication of what can be achieved.

4 THE DOMESTIC DIMENSION

Renamo's activities within Mozambique are far more difficult to assess than those of its external wing. The information available is highly controlled by the Mozambique State. Access to the disputed areas is discouraged by Maputo and visits to them under Renamo auspices are heavily selective in order to ensure favourable reporting. Much of the picture the outside world has of Renamo is moulded by a very successful campaign by AIM, probably the most effective and successful state apparatus in Mozambique. Indeed, because of AIM's rapid and efficient coverage, some reports of Renamo's atrocities have been thought, by a population more used to censorship and inefficiency, to have been government cover-ups of its own troops' excesses.

Since Renamo became a serious preoccupation for the Mozambican Government, the picture of it traditionally painted by Maputo remained basically the same up to 1989 and the Nairobi talks. Within Mozambique the rebels were known as the "Bandidos Armados" (BA's) — Armed bandits.[1] This label remains a popular name for them, although the government has begun to prefer to call them "the so-called Renamo" or the "Renamo bandits", an indication of the progress of the Nairobi talks.

The labels attached to the rebels have also changed in response to developments in Mozambique's relations with the outside world. Up to the N'komati Accord, the rebels were called South African-backed. After N'komati, they were, for a short while, described as Portuguese-backed. When the Vaz diaries confirmed continuing South African support, the South African label returned. With the return of friendlier Mozambican-South African relations after De Klerk succeeded P.W. Botha as President, AIM has become less categoric in attributing Renamo's external support to any particular country.

The basic image AIM disseminated in the 1980's was that of Renamo as a group of South African surrogates, committing atrocities in pursuit of blind acts of terrorism purely for destabilisation, and without any strategic objective, except the hindering of the development of Mozambique and the keeping of Mozambique as a weak and subservient state in face of South African demands. This analysis remained popular, not only in AIM's communiqués themselves, but in world media and within academic analysis of contemporary Mozambique.[2]

AIM and many commentators have also contrasted Renamo with UNITA. UNITA has been depicted as a legitimate rebel movement, with its roots in the pre-independence nationalist struggle. Renamo, in contrast, has been portrayed as a creation of the Rhodesian security forces. It has also been argued that UNITA, unlike Renamo, has popular support amongst sectors of the Angolan peasantry, and that UNITA is led by a both legitimate and charismatic leader, unlike Dhlakama. Although some of these contrasts have been challenged in a recent report by William Minter on UNITA, they continue to be made, not least because of the fear that any direct comparison between Renamo and UNITA would play into the hands of the US right-wing, which has been trying to establish this parallel to justify support for Renamo.[3]

These interpretations were modified in the last years of the past decade. In academic analysis there has been a paradigm shift away from the causality of the Mozambican crisis being South African destabilisation, with the emphasis being shifted to a focus on Frelimo's agrarian policies as the roots of the problem. Within Mozambique the change is less clear-cut. Media analysis has begun to highlight a pattern in Renamo's actions, representing the crisis as more clearly a Mozambican problem.[4] Only with peace, however, will the depth of study needed to understand the current situation in Mozambique come about.

THE MATSANGAISSA MYTH

One clue to the complexities of the domestic dimension to Renamo's activities is a myth that has arisen about Renamo's first leader, Andre Matsangaissa. During a "hearts and minds" campaign encouraged by the Rhodesians in central Mozambique during 1979, captured commodities were redistributed among the local population, generating sufficient support for Renamo to operate without being informed upon.[5] During the same operation, as a tactic, but probably also as a genuine belief, Matsangaissa utilised the services of a respected spirit medium (*mhondoro*) to obtain further standing and support. The significance of this move for the local peasant population is illustrated by the way this event has already become a semi-mythological legend in the oral histories of Gorongosa district. The tale is told that Matsangaissa was given magic powers from the *mhondoro*. These powers protected Matsangaissa and his men from the effects of bullets as long as they remained respectful of the local population. Some Renamo rebels broke this code of conduct by abusing local young women and the magic powers were therefore broken. Matsangaissa did not know this. Believing they were still protected by the magic, Matsangaissa and his men stormed a well-defended government position and were all slaughtered by machine-gun fire.[6] This tale has several variations but its essence remains the same.[7]

Whatever actually happened to Matsangaissa, it is evident that he utilised a very powerful set of symbols for the local population. These symbols are in fact so strong that, in some tales, Matsangaissa is not believed to be dead but still exists as some sort of living dead. Another sign is that in many areas of central Mozambique, and within Zimbabwe, the local population prefers to call Renamo not by its title or by the State's rhetoric label of "bandits", but as the "Andres" or, more commonly, "Matsangas". Matsangaissa has been transformed into becoming part of an oral literary tradition that will eventually become formalised in the way tales of past bandit and warlord figures such as Mapondera (in Zimbabwe) or Gouveia (in Mozambique) have become. Matsangaissa's adoption into such a myth probably grew out of the fact that he died while being airlifted out by the Rhodesians after the serious injuries he sustained from government forces and was never seen again. In central Mozambique the rapid removal of bodies of fallen Renamo combatants after skirmishes by the rebels and their secret burial has helped to encourage the belief that the rebels are bulletproof.[8] This belief also derives from a current theme in folk tales of Sena,

Gaza and other peoples that the N'dau have supernatural powers. As one N'dau member of Renamo commented:[9]

> We N'daus have a reputation, that we can defeat death and have special powers over it. Finding a wife outside our home areas is always difficult, people are frightened of us. You know they even believe that if we were killed we would become revengeful spirits and punish those who did away with us.

Quite clearly such stories facilitate Renamo's operations in central Mozambique, by giving it a psychological advantage.

But the stories do more than this, bringing into focus a range of questions about the domestic side of Renamo's activities. At one level, the Matsangaissa myth both reflects and manipulates peasant attitudes to Renamo, raising questions about how far they are hostile and resentful, how far neutral in their disappointment and disillusion with Frelimo's policies, how far supportive of Renamo's project, how far merely brutalised into submission and acquiescence. These overlap with further questions about the nature of Renamo's ideology, structure, tactics, and civilian management, questions which are discussed in detail in this chapter.

But the myth has broader resonances. It offers, or promulgates, a supernatural explanation for Renamo's apparent successes. It thus brings into play the roles of religion in Mozambique's agony, both as responses to suffering and as a means of mobilising support for Renamo. Renamo has proved itself skilful, if mindlessly ecumenical, in attracting support from every available religious group — building on Catholic links in Portugal and the USA without compromising its support from Protestant fundamentalist churches and organisations, and gaining financial help from the American right-wing without forfeiting support from Islamic fundamentalists. Once again, these dimensions are explored in this chapter.

In the final analysis, however, the Matsangaissa myth is essentially Mozambican. It offers a very localised, neo-traditional explanation of events involving ancestors and the fertility of the land. It raises the final question to be discussed in this chapter, that of how far Mozambique's peasants have themselves been able to mobilise the resources of religion to distance or tame Renamo, enlisting their ancestors to achieve for them what Frelimo has too often been unable to do.

"THE LIBERATED ZONES"

Renamo's publicity describes the territory under its control as "Liberated Zones". It claims to control between 80-85% of the country. Such estimates are meaningless. Boundaries are always changing. Many so-called "liberated" areas are only controlled by one force or another when it passes through.

The so-called "liberated zones" have had some press coverage, especially in the USA. Between 1984 and 1990, US journalists taken into Renamo areas published reports and photographs of Renamo clinics, schools and commerce.[10] One commentator, Andy Elva, reported that in these zones:[11]

> Many cash crops were being grown ... corn, tomatoes, even some tobacco. This was not so a year and a half ago. It was a classic liberated zone ... peasants had become prosperous Farmers could feed themselves and even had surplus for exports. There was also a growing free market, little wooden roadside stands that had sprung up. Coke, Fanta and imported beer was available.

This is an image that Dhlakama and his internal leadership have increasingly adopted to depict the areas they control. In interview in 1989, Dhlakama described Mozambique as:

> Divided into two areas. One is ruled by Renamo the other by Frelimo. Frelimo is represented in the urban areas, we are administering the rural areas. We are building schools, hospitals and even farms. Even Frelimo is calling on the people to make use of them so that parents can send their children to school again, for instance. In the areas that are ruled by Renamo there is a considerably better infrastructure than in those of Frelimo. Frelimo is even conducting trade with us in order to ensure food supply in the cities.[12]

The shallowness of these claims is confirmed by a journalist who attempted to find evidence of Renamo clinics and schools in 1988 from areas recently recaptured from Renamo by the FAM (these were areas that Renamo had claimed as being liberated zones). Except in one case he had difficulty in finding local inhabitants who had seen such services, and could only report one specific example.[13]

The accounts, however far-fetched, make an interesting comparison with the descriptions of visitors to the areas Frelimo dominated during the liberation struggle. As Frelimo did then, Renamo vets its visitors to the areas it controls. Both movements claimed at different periods that they had developed in them an embryonic structure for future government. In both cases, the photography and accounts are based on stage-managed events, or idealised out of ideological commitment. Renamo's statements are evidently modelled on the successful propaganda techniques of Frelimo in its liberation struggle.[14]

IDEOLOGY

Renamo's depiction of itself has also changed, adapting to circumstance. This evolution can be plotted in its external propaganda. The earliest policy statement by Renamo, other than vague anti-communism sentiments mixed with personal abuse on the "Voz da Africa Livre" radio station, is contained within an interview given by Andre Matsangaissa in late June 1979, just before his death. It well illustrates the condition of the movement at the time. Matsangaissa states:[15]

> We are not interested in policy making ... later we will have to work out politics but first communism must go from our country. It is killing us, we have to kill for everything we want. We kill for food, for pills, for guns and ammunition! We have not got enough guns for all our recruits and many are armed with knives, sticks and even bows and arrows. Whenever we can assist the locals with food, seeds or whatever medical supplies we can obtain we do.

Although this was clearly a public relations exercise organised by the CIO in the period of uncertainty before transfer to South African management, it reflects the lack of any long-term vision within Renamo as an insurgent force. It is also a fairly honest account of Renamo's tactics at this time.

The first clear indication of Renamo having a political programme appeared in 1979. Called "Statutes", it was an edited version of Fanuel Mahluza's UDENAMO manifesto. It was followed in late 1981, as part of South Africa's restructuring of the group, by a broadcast on the rebel radio station Voz da Africa Livre[16] calling for a four-point plan. The plan called for:[17]

(i) the extinction of the communist system;
(ii) the formation of a government of "National Reconciliation";
(iii) all nationalisations by Frelimo to be reviewed; and
(iv) the private sector to be the "dynamising sector of the country".

Renamo claims that a more detailed programme was formulated at a secret conference of its leaders in July 1981 in West Germany, and that this was adopted by its National Council on August 17, 1981. The programme consists of seven chapters (politics, economy, justice, constitutional matters, education, public services and international policy). It is said to be the draft for the constitution of a post-Frelimo Mozambique.

The first edited version of this programme appeared in early 1982, bearing the date of August 1981, the date of its adoption by the National Council. In June 1982 a new edition of this "Manifest and Programme" appeared, minus the introductory section. (In spite of the original formation of the National Council in 1981, the publication of the new programme implied that the Council's establishment was a new departure). This 1982 document has been used as the basis for subsequent reissues.[18] Further summaries and translations have emanated from Renamo's offices in Heidelberg, Lisbon, Nairobi and Washington. A summary of the "Manifest and Programme" calls for:[19]

■ The creation of a multi-party and democratic state;
■ A free economy based on private and free enterprise;
■ A state respecting the rights of man and the citizens in which all are equal before the law;
■ The existence of public and private health services and education as the rights of the citizen, helping those who need help including maternity, infancy, old age and providing incentives in education to those deserving them;
■ The state as a guarantor of economic infrastructure, (currency, transport ...) and the submission of the military establishment to the political establishment and the immediate dismantlement of the instruments being used by the current regime in suppressing the rights of the citizen;
■ Respect for international organisations and the implementation of a policy of friendship and cooperation with all peoples in the world based on mutual respect and non-interference;
■ A freely elected assembly which will approve a new constitution based on principles of political and economic democracy and respect for the rights of the citizen, history and a prospective future.

The propaganda outside Mozambique detailing Renamo's proposals for the future is mostly to be found at its external offices, but following its incursions into Zimbabwe, Renamo appears to have felt a need to justify its destabilising activities and has also left leaflets in areas there. Within Mozambique, its leaflets are mainly targetted at army bases and towns, areas that Renamo needs to penetrate to succeed in its objective of forcing change in Mozambique. The leaflets distributed within Mozambique are often pictorial and cartoon-like, a response to the pre-literacy of many Mozambicans.[20] In rural areas Renamo prefers merely to leave posters of Dhlakama, attached to trees and destroyed buildings.

Renamo's attempts to justify its actions amongst its own combatants and the civilian population under its control are even less visible. It seems to hold occasional political meetings amongst its combatants, with rebel leaders addressing the soldiers. The themes appear to be similar to those put on leaflets within Mozambique — vague anti-communism and anti-Frelimoism, with a promise of a better future once the war is won by Renamo. Since 1988 Renamo has, at these occasional rallies, also countered the Government's offer of amnesty by telling its combatants that the Government is lying and that any one leaving Renamo will continue to be shot by Frelimo as a terrorist. Political ideology does not appear to play an important role within internal Renamo.[21]

Renamo has long recognised that, in comparison with the Mozambique government, its propaganda is weak and clumsy. Dhlakama has been particularly concerned to re-open Voz da Africa Livre (closed down at N'Komati), to reach a wider audience. Neither South Africa nor Malawi is however prepared to be embarrassed by having the rebel radio station on its soil.[22]

Renamo's propaganda is targetted at specific audiences. In Lisbon, for example, it emphasises that Renamo's struggle is based on the goals of Eduardo Mondlane's writings which were, they claim, "compromised" by Frelimo's Marxism-Leninism after his assassination. Renamo is depicted as fighting a "second war of liberation", with the rebels being the inheritor of Frelimo's original and worthy nationalist goals. The audience in Lisbon is primarily black Mozambican, including those who took advantage of Portuguese citizenship in 1976-1977. The issues of religious persecution and anti-communism are, on the other hand, emphasised in the US, where the radical elements in Mondlane's thinking, particularly in his later years, would obviously not be well received by the right-wing.[23] The appearance of a fresh Renamo programme in January 1988 under the aegis of the Washington office is an example of this. Unlike the original programme its emphasis was on the very issues of concern to the US right-wing.[24] The document purports to be the outcome of a constitutional meeting of the National Council held from 22-24 May 1982, an event which Renamo had not referred to before. Its Canada based author, Francisco Nota Moises, issued his material under the Washington label from late 1987, because of Canadian hostility towards Renamo. Unlike the original 1981 programme this so-called programme had no authority from inside Mozambique. It became a contributing factor to the replacement of Moises, who had become too autonomous and unaccountable for a Renamo increasingly concerned to establish unity and a more coherent external network of representatives.[25]

As highlighted earlier, Renamo's campaigns to justify itself internationally have met increasing difficulties. Its greatest headache is that the Mozambique Government's policy changes, especially since the 1983 and 1989 conventions, have weakened its main arguments against Maputo, such as those about religious persecution and the lack of free enterprise in the economy. Afonso Dhlakama has himself admitted the problem: "Frelimo has started using all our lines — democracy, freedom of speech, freedom of worship — but only because we are pushing them".[26] This continues to be a major difficulty for Renamo, which continues to claim that its outdated 1981 programme is the basis for future government, a fact endorsed by its so-called First Congress on June 5-9, 1989, which was held within Mozambique.

Although this meeting was described as Renamo's first Congress, past Renamo literature has referred to another first Congress. The original first Congress is said to have been held near Chimoio in Manica province in May 1982. Two councils were said to have been set up then, the Military and the National.[27] The outcome of this congress was reported in the South African press, with Renamo said to be calling for a ceasefire pending free elections and a coalition government between Renamo and Frelimo moderates.[28] Early Renamo propaganda, especially from West Germany and Portugal, refers to this Congress by using a printed symbol "Sede Chimoio".[29] Renamo however now denies that this first Congress took place, and claims it is an example of the "contradictions" that troubled the movement before its restructuring.[30] In fact, this congress did take place, but in South Africa. Its objective was to attract a wider range of black Mozambicans into the leadership: Fanuel Mahluza was recruited at this congress.

The June 1989 "First Congress" of Renamo is, on the other hand, known to have taken place. Independent journalists and observers present confirm the fact. This Congress is important in that it formalised a change of approach by Renamo. Decisions of the Congress altered Renamo's statutes, programme, anthem and flag. Seven resolutions were adopted on National Unity, National Policy (Defence and Security), International Policy, Front-Line States and SADCC, the Group of Five, African Unity and on Peace and Reconciliation. Although these contain little substance they reflect Renamo's continued political dilemma of how to carve out for itself a distinct political profile in the face of Frelimo's reforms. Dhlakama's closing speech at the Congress is more forthcoming. Renamo appears to have reaffirmed its 1981 programme with "commitment to building a market economy, protection of private property, restoration of religious freedom and respect of our traditions" and a confirmation of its post-1986 condemnation of Apartheid in South Africa. Dhlakama also declared that Renamo's statutes would never "consent that military force be used to impose leadership or political options contrary to the will of the people".[31]

The mildness of the Congress's tone must be seen in the context of the negotiating process then under way in the build-up to the Nairobi talks. Nevertheless the commentators who reported on the Congress are wrong to say that it represented a distinct change in Renamo policy. The Congress reaffirmed what was contained in the 1981 Manifest and Programme. It repeated the calls for national reconciliation in a process similar to that which occurred over Mozambique's independence in 1974, with a period of transition, but one to be followed by free elections. What has confused the scene has been the myriad of contradictory oral statements made by Renamo's divided external representation. The one new categoric statement from the Congress was the call for negotiations with only broad preconditions. Dhlakama summarised Renamo's position by saying:[32]

> In conclusion, I ask Frelimo to accept our proposal of genuine negotiation leading to national reconciliation and constitutional reform. Let us come together to form a new Mozambique where our brotherhood is affirmed by debate and concensus, a new Mozambique where armed struggle need never again be the last and only recourse to national unity.
>
> Specifically, we propose the creation of a government of national reconciliation that within two years will institutionalise democracy in Mozambique.

All in all, the most significant aspect of the Congress was its restructuring of Renamo, giving internal Renamo supremacy over its external representation. The outcome reflected the growing desire of Renamo's leadership to obtain political and international respectability, having recognised that the infighting and contradictions of policy in the past were major obstacles in the way of achieving such goals. It would be simplistic to see this desire as having come over-night. The struggles in Renamo over the past decade have much to do with its attempts to break away from its subservience to its foreign backers.

STRUCTURE

Renamo's political structure inside Mozambique is little more than an off-shoot of its military command structure. It was supposedly formalised as the "National Council" within Mozambique at Renamo's now discredited first Congress in May 1982. This Council was described in September 1982 in the Portuguese press as an "Executive Council" comprised of 12 men with specific portfolios.[33] Evo Fernandes, Renamo's then Secretary-General, described in 1985 how Renamo's political organisation operated:[34]

> Renamo's political structure is like this. First, again, there is the President. Then there is the Secretary-General. Below the Secretary-General is the National Council, which is made up of chiefs, military people, civilians and so on. They are proposed by the Secretary-General and then nominated by the President. Then we have external and internal departments. The external departments include foreign relations, finances, information and studies. The studies department is the most important because it examines ideas about the constitution, the economy, social organisation and so on. The internal departments include education, health, economy and administration. Each department has a head who reports to the President.

The National Council, however, was described in early 1984 as a "very basic structure. Members do not have portfolios, but are given specific tasks by the President from time to time".[35] By late 1985, as Fernandes' account illustrates, the National Council was depicted again as a formal structure composed of twelve members with portfolios (it was reduced to ten in 1986 — one representative for each Mozambican province), drawn from both internal and external wings of the group, who were to consult together on policy and administrative matters. There are departments for: Defence; Ideology; General Secretariat (abolished in 1986); External Relations; Internal Administration; Education; Information; Health and Welfare; Agriculture; and Youth.[36] This was changed at the 1989 Congress, with a reduced number of Departments (see Appendix 1). The post of Secretary-General was again declared abolished (another contradiction), with its functions absorbed into the previously unheard of Presidential Cabinet. The reformed National Council is now, with one exception, fully comprised of figures from internal Renamo. Another structure was announced at the Congress — the Commission of Inquiry, which is said to be composed of five members, one each from the military, traditional leaders, women's league, civil population, and religious communities.[37] Another Renamo structure was announced in March 1983 to having been set up following a meeting held in Geneva.[38] This was the "government in exile" otherwise called the "shadow cabinet". This structure was said to be distinct from the

National Council, with Artur Vilankulu, as "Prime Minister", and Evo Fernandes holding the planning portfolio. By 1984, no further mention was made of this cabinet. It may well be that it was only an idea of Orlando Cristina, which, following his murder in April 1983, was quietly forgotten.

These structures are in reality only an aspect of Renamo's depiction of itself to the outside world. The titles and departments continually change, as do the people in charge of the so-called posts. There appears to be little consistency in these structures as the names associated with the posts in question demonstrate (see Appendix 1). The only political structure of any significance in the past has been the National Council. This met, for example, in mid-1983 in South Africa, in an attempt to end the internal struggle over who would succeed Cristina as the new Secretary-General.

Renamo's real organisational force within Mozambique is its military organisation, which is headed by Dhlakama as Commander-in-Chief. Depictions of the military structure have over time become increasingly sophisticated. Until 1981 the highest rank in Renamo was battalion commander, except for the late Andre Matsangaissa and Dhlakama, who both held the title of "Supreme Chief" (until 1981) or "Commander-in-Chief".[39] Provincial commanders were appointed in 1982, from which they were upgraded with some others in 1983 to the rank of general. One of the early detailed descriptions of the military organisation was given by Evo Fernandes in 1985:[40]

> We have the President, Afonso Dhlakama, who is also Commander-in-Chief. Then we have generals. The generals have regional commanders under them. The regional commanders have sector commanders. The sector commmanders are mostly logistical officers. They also have operational activies, but these are their most important functions. Zone commanders are the real fighters, the leaders of tactical units. Then we usually have strategic units in the sector commands that are only to be deployed in the offensive. Zone commanders are essentially guerrilla forces, and strategic units are semi-regular forces. But there are not too many strategic units.

An even more detailed break-down of Renamo's military structure was given in 1987.[41] Renamo's Military Council was said to consist of 15 generals, (3 chiefs of staff — north, centre and south, 10 provincial commanders, and Dhlakama's personal staff). The chiefs of staff were in command in three operational areas: North (from the Rovuma to the Zambezi Rivers); Centre (the Zambezi to Sabi Rivers); and the South (from the Sabi River to the South African border). The 10 generals, each in command of all the forces deployed in any one province, were all technically subordinate to the chiefs of staff in their respective operational areas. Below these levels, the set-up becomes less clear. Under the command of the general responsible for operations in each province, a varying number of regional commmanders are responsible at "brigade" level. The "brigade" level is theoretically then broken down to battalions, containing 250 men, each controlled by a section commander. Below these are company commanders for every 100 men, and platoon commanders responsible for groups of 30 men. There are said to be group leaders for each unit of 10 men.

These descriptions are probably modelled on what was taught during training in South Africa. Paulo Oliveira claims that the division of the headquarters staff into regions happened in December 1983 as part of the move by Renamo headquarters staff from South Africa in preparation for the N'Komati Accord.[42]

The Minter Report confirmed this sophisticated military set-up.[43] Based on interviews with 32 Renamo ex-participants, the report concludes that Renamo's basic operational unit is the company, comprising between 100 and a 150 men. Each company is generally equipped with a communications officer and radio, so as to be in regular contact with the provincial base and, indirectly, with Dhlakama's Gorongosa base. Two or three companies are said to make up a battalion, with some 450 men at full strength. A provincial base may have two or more battalions in its immediate vicinity, sometimes dispersed in several bases within a few hours march of each other. Each province is divided into two or more sectors. Recruits are kept in separate training bases. A company is divided into platoons and sections, as well as "groups" selected for specific operations.

In conjunction with the continuing reports from Mozambique of co-ordinated Renamo attacks against targets, Minter's account has demonstrated that Renamo is not a loose collection of warlords and roving bands. Captured Renamo documents and attacks, such as those on Gurue and Luabo, demonstrate that particular actions are carried out by particular companies named by a title, Lion, Wolf, Thunder, Grupa Limpa and so on.[44] Furthermore Renamo's capability to restrain attacks, as with the Nacala line or Beira's electricity supply and to co-ordinate offensives such as the declaration of war against Zimbabwe and the entry into Cabo Delgado on 25 September 1984 (timed for the 20th anniversary of Frelimo's first attack against the Portuguese), further suggest centralised and co-ordinated decision making. This level of organisation is not, however, maintained consistently throughout Mozambique. Reports from Cabo Delgado suggest that the bands there are small and poorly connected to any centralised structure. The same is true of areas in Niassa and Tete provinces. Although Minter also suggests that much power is held by Dhlakama centrally, visitors to Renamo-held areas have noted that Renamo's provincial commanders (generals in Renamo terms) hold considerable power, like war lords.[45] The dispute with Gimo M'Phiri, and his breaking away from Renamo to form UNAMO, are a further indication of the influence these commanders can hold. M'Phiri was able to break away with around 500 men, which suggests that Renamo's hierarchy is still partly based on ethnicity and personality to ensure that the regional commands continue to be able to attract a stable local core of dedicated supporters.

What enables Renamo's military structure to retain a degree of centralisation is communication by radio. As early as 1981 a British hostage held by Renamo reported that his captors were in daily contact by radio three times a day with a central base.[46] At the end of 1985, Renamo's operations in the Zambezi valley were co-ordinated from Casa Banana, its headquarters in Gorongosa district. Two captured European technicians from Luabo, Patrick O'Connell and William Blakey, confirmed that their Renamo unit, Grupa Limpa, was in frequent radio contact with Casa Banana. Through this network the "Grupa Limpa" was redirected to take O'Connell and Blakey to Malawi, since Casa Banana was under siege by government troops.[47] Documents found at Casa Banana, reporting the capture of Blakey and O'Connell and asking for orders, further confirm this account.[48] Since 1985, Renamo has improved its radio communications within Mozambique to compensate for the reduction in its external backup.

Renamo's radio network is a major contribution to the success of its operations. It uses an advanced British Racal system which shifts frequen-

Figure 4.1 Renamo Structure

cy sixteen times a minute to avoid detection.[49] Through this network Renamo can regularly mass large numbers from its small roving units to attack set targets, and equally rapidly disperse them with orders for strategic retreats. Renamo's radio messages appear to be very brief, containing detailed reports of engagements, with dates, casualty figures, location and any other relevant information. These are received at provincial bases which then broadcast a summary to Dhlakama at his headquarters. Until 1986 messages were spelled out in Portuguese, with a simple word-letter substitution.[50] A syncretic mixture with N'dau has now been developed. Renamo's supplies of radio equipment are nevertheless limited. There continues to be plenty of evidence of messages being carried by motor-bike and runners between outposts and the larger hub bases important enough to have a radio-set.[51]

In addition to the coordination achieved by radio, Renamo has been developing a military lingua franca to cope with the enormous variety of languages within Mozambique. The N'dau dialect has been adopted for this purpose. Renamo has been frequently criticised for being ethnically based on an N'dau élite. This was true originally, but not in simplistic racial terms. The N'dau prominence within Renamo's command arose because central Mozambique was the area targetted by Rhodesia for the creation and encouragement of rebel activity. Rhodesian recruitment of the N'dau, was not, as some commentators have speculated, calculated planning but due to the geographical location of the N'dau along the Rhodesian border. The Rhodesian's choice could not have been better. The N'dau felt no particular love for Frelimo since they were poorly represented in the party. The N'dau are, moreover, historically a martial ethnic group, recognised as such by the Portuguese who recruited them into their colonial army (in the same manner that the British used the Acholi in Uganda). Many N'dau men were therefore professional fighters. For these reasons, Renamo, with its N'dau leadership core, spread as quickly as it did in Manica and Sofala provinces.[52] These early N'dau recruits continue to dominate Renamo's military. But though the splits within Renamo, like that of UNAMO, indicate continued tensions over N'dau predominance, the situation has changed. Renamo's leadership now shows a wider ethnic base. One of the ways to obtain promotion within Renamo is to learn, and then use, N'dau. As one Renamo official stated:[53]

> I went to the congress, and yes the leadership speaks N'dau. But they are not N'dau's. Ululu, Domingos, Lisboa, Almirante, Baza. Shall I name more? I had heard this talked about, but only by being at Gorongosa did I believe. Afonso Dhlakama is clever, many of our people do not speak much Portuguese, he is encouraging unity within Renamo.

Former Renamo officials have admitted that they had problems at Gorongosa if they didn't speak N'dau. Constantino Reis claims this, "Because I didn't speak N'dau, only Shangaan. And when I spoke Portuguese, they said I was showing contempt for national languages".[54] This linguistic preference in Renamo's command has been increasingly noted inside Mozambique. For example Lina Magaia was reported in an interview as saying that Renamo talks "as N'daus but they were not N'daus".[55] This is only true of the leadership and of the radio operators. At rank-and-file level the question of ethnicity and choice of daily language continues to be irrelevant. Only at the higher echelons of the organisation does N'dau become a help to promotion.[56] These are the Shona speaking "veterans" that Minter speaks about,[57] or Geffray's "Mambos".[58] Although it is probably true to say that 80-90% of these commanders speak N'dau, this clearly does not mean that they are N'dau. Peasants, especially in areas neighbouring N'dau territory, have recognised that the dialect spoken is a creole N'dau, and therefore not true N'dau.

This is not to say that there are not some purely N'dau battalions. "The Grupa Limpa" is closely connected to Dhlakama, a kind of praetorian guard. Blakey and O'Connell, who were captured by them, speak of good discipline and a high level of motivation amongst these combatants. They were also in frequent contact with Gorongosa, which controlled their movements. Cyril Pumiyasoma, a Sri Lankan captured by Renamo, and held for over two years until late 1984, also had experience of the "Grupa Limpa". Discussing this he described how he only heard N'dau being spoken throughout his captivity although he was moved to four bases in Manica and Zambezia provinces. He was also told by a proud Renamo commander that the "Grupa Limpa" were the "professionals", given all the tough tasks and rewarded as such.[59] This may not be so far-fetched. The "Grupa Limpa" have been widely credited as having been behind many of Renamo's large massacres in the south. In Zambezia its reputation is well known and feared. Even in the military communiqués which Renamo offices overseas distribute, reports such as:[60]

> The Renamo units carrying out the offensive are the famous "Limpa" group, Renamo's special strike force. Frelimo troops manning the nearby border posts of Villa Nova de Frontana fled their position upon hearing of the Limpa group advance.

indicate the special nature of this particular unit.

As with its external representation, Renamo's conduct in Mozambique has had to change with circumstances. Until the recapture of Casa Banana in 1986 by Zimbabwean armed forces, its internal operations were co-ordinated from there (from December 1983). Other major Renamo bases were in contact with Casa Banana through radio. These were also located in remote areas, structured to remain in place for extended periods of time. Secondary bases reflected the hierarchical set-up of military operations, being regional centres for particular military designated zones. They, in turn, were at the top of a hierarchy of bases which would become smaller, and less permanent, as they were located near contested, or in vulnerable, territory. Casa Banana was, for example, the central core of a whole series of smaller satellite bases, strategically and geographically determined, which in turn launched operations against government targets. Outside these were mobile positions where supplies for more extended operations had been hidden and stockpiled.

Renamo bases in the Gorongosa district became operational by 1979. In 1983 Renamo started to claim that the area contained the "Capital of Free Mozambique". The first capture of Casa Banana in late 1985 provides a valuable glimpse into the set-up of a major Renamo base.[61]

Casa Banana is the most sophisticated base Renamo is known to have constructed in Mozambique to-date. It was located at the top of a foothill in the Gorongosa mountains. Like other bases, it was mainly a dispersed settlement of huts covering several kilometers, under the cover of trees. It had several entrances through paths that were closely guarded by two small huts. In the central area was a series of different structures called the "General Command".

These "Command" buildings were substantially larger than the huts in the rest of the base. In the centre was an even larger building. Rectangular, it was divided into two substantial rooms, with an enclosed kitchen outside and a shrine attached. Unlike the other buildings, it was built of non-perishable materials such as corrugated iron, bricks and prefabricated concrete. The building was also slightly higher than any of the surrounding structures. The "General Command" was separated in its entirety from the surrounding base by a wire fence. It was also serviced by an electricity generator, and linked to the camp's guard posts by a telephone system. Photographs of Dhlakama were placed throughout the base on walls, trees and vehicles.

The social space, size and positions of the "General Command", and the prolific use of photographs of Dhlakama throughout the base, are symbols of autocracy. The segregation of the command area by a wire fence with no defensive function, was clearly meant as a symbolic division between the leadership and its supporters. What was found at Casa Banana contradicts Renamo's claims that "personality cults are discouraged in the movement as they are out of keeping with our belief that they are for autocratic communities".[62]

This type of hierarchy was also noted by Nicholas della Casa during his 18 months captivity with Renamo. He writes:[63]

> On arrival at the chosen site, it would only take one or two days to build new huts of pole and thatch — first for me, then the women guerrillas or the "feminine detachment" which accompanied all senior commanders themselves, then the commanders themselves and lastly ordinary soldiers, who often would not bother too much and disdained the more elaborate dwellings of their superiors.

The extent of Casa Banana's catchment area can be estimated by the origins of the stolen goods found there and by the leaflets found in surrounding areas originating from its printing facilities. Blakey and O'Connell's accounts also speak of three bases on the north side of the Zambezi containing pictures of Dhlakama on trees and huts. Other captured Renamo bases illustrate a similar pattern. A 1985 base at Xighocoxa in Inhambane province was composed of 410 huts, randomly distributed, with an overall capacity for around 500 people.[64] Roughly central to it was a rectangular building which was the residence of the Renamo commander. Garagua base had a similar plan. Located on an interface of desolate and more fertile terrain in Manica province, it was also dispersed. A nucleus of more "sophisticated structures" held the residence of the rebel leadership and its South African advisers.[65]

With the recapture of Casa Banana in 1986, and the decrease in logistical aid reaching Renamo from South Africa, Renamo's tactics changed. After N'Komati Renamo had been encouraged to become more self-sufficient. With the loss of support from Malawi its situation became even more critical as its permanent bases in Mozambique now became more vulnerable. Renamo then decided to concentrate more on smaller, less permanent and more itinerant bases. Nicholas della Casa, for example, records that his base moved eight times in 1988. The change of tactics has also been noted by General Mobote of the FAM. He pointed out that:[66]

Instead of concentrating there (Gorongosa), they opened new fronts, trying to recreate the pattern of the colonial period when separate troops controlled the strategic meeting points of the country which are so important for the trade routes.

What was developing was in fact a return to the Rhodesian plan of cutting Mozambique into uncommunicable segments, with the use of more mobile units with particular orbits. Dhlakama's bases themselves follow this pattern. They have become very itinerant, often situated fairly close to contested areas. This greater mobility also reflects Renamo's now weaker position. A commitment to another Casa Banana would be too vulnerable.

Renamo's vulnerability is also illustrated by its incapacity to hold any of the towns it attacks. Lacking expertise to operate captured ground-to-air missiles, it would find itself dangerously exposed in a set defensive position. This is the main reason why Renamo does not occupy the places it captures, but evacuates the population by force, subsequently destroying most of what was standing.

TACTICS

Renamo's operational targets remain fairly consistent — health posts, schools and any other structure associated with the Mozambique Government. This is not solely mindless violence. It is a type of exorcism, explained to the rural population as a rejection of the government and the government's influence. The destruction of factories and the break-up of the economic infrastructure are also aimed at bringing the government to negotiations — to share power. Luis Serapião has explained that some of these actions are a publicity stunt to gain world attention. He took the example of the Sena bridge, saying:[67]

> Like the great bridge near Sena crossing the Zambezi, it is a symbol of our strength. The once longest bridge in the world blown up by Renamo. What more powerful and lasting symbol could there be of our strength?"

Renamo policy remains the destruction of facilities and property, so as to make government resettlement utterly unattractive, thereby maintaining the vacated areas as purely military zones.

Renamo's tactics have additional coherence. Many of the settlements Renamo occupies or captures are dismembered of everything portable which can be reused or resold. Such booty is an integral part of Renamo's economy. As even those journalists sympathetic to Renamo have witnessed, Renamo completely cleans out the places it takes before destroying whatever is left.[68] Material, such as roofing and vehicle parts, is then transported to Malawi for sale in the markets. Many of the kidnappings following such attacks, including those in Zambia and Zimbabwe, are designed to acquire porters to haul the booty to its destination. O'Connell and Blakey witnessed in 1985 a Landrover being dismantled and carried in parts to Malawi for sale.[69] What impressed them was that several Renamo mechanics were able to reassemble the vehicle in working order before it was taken across the Malawian border. Renamo obtains medicines, bottled beer and luxury items from Malawi in exchange. Apart from what it finds of value for trade outside Mozambique or for subsequent military use, Renamo consumes whatever resources are left in the areas it controls — a pillage economy. An

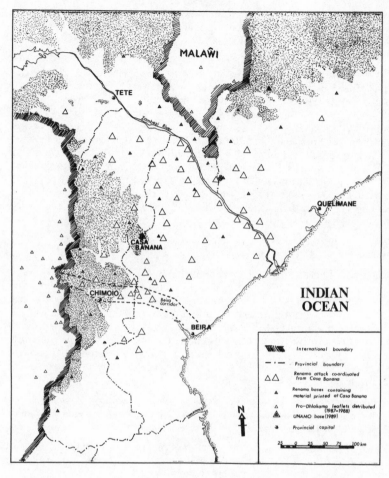

Map 4.1 Casa Banana's catchment area (1985).

old man described it like this to the present writer: "Matsangas, those are the ones that are the locust people. They eat everything, food, clothes and us, until we have no more. Then they go and eat elsewhere".[70]

Another aspect of Renamo's economy has been its involvement in the ivory trade. It has been alleged that Orlando Cristina and Evo Fernandes, in conjunction with South African military officers, were deeply involved in this illicit trade.[71] This trade is not surprising since the Gorongosa national park, Renamo's base, was once famed for its rich wildlife. It is now thought that Renamo has been integrated into the international ivory smuggling network. The seriousness of this trade is suggested by the fact that Renamo bases recaptured by the FAM in 1988 yielded 19,700 elephant tusks, worth some $13 million. Ivory smuggling appears to be an important source of finance or barter for obtaining firearms.[72]

Another consistent policy is the capturing of foreign aid workers, technicians, missionaries and priests. The idea seems to have come from observing the successes of UNITA in obtaining valuable publicity through its policy of capturing foreign workers. It is estimated that over 195 such sequestrations took place between 1980–89, including Americans, British, Chileans, Dutch, Irish, Italians, Pakistanis, Portuguese, Spaniards, Sri Lankans, Swiss, West Germans, Soviets and Eastern Europeans, let alone uncounted African hostages, such as Zimbabwean and Tanzanian soldiers.[73] Targetting foreigners in this way embarrasses Maputo, forces foreign organisations to withdraw from rural areas out of insecurity, and gives worldwide publicity to Renamo. Renamo has consistently tried to use captured foreigners as a bargaining counter for the release of rebel combatants or political detainees in government hands. Renamo attempted in August 1982 to exchange six captured Bulgarian technicians for twenty-eight named political prisoners.[74] The Renamo list contained the well known names of Paulo Gumane, Arcanjo Kambau, Valentino Sithole, Lazero Nkcavandame, Uria Simango, Mateus Gwenjere, Joana Simião, João Unhai, Basilio Banda and Veronica Namiva. The Mozambican government ignored these demands. Renamo has also tried (unsuccessfully until 1989) to gain recognition as a legitimate force by demanding International Red Cross involvement through the latter visiting Renamo areas to collect captured foreigners. Renamo's approaches to foreign governments to negotiate directly with them have not been successful.[75] The case of British journalist, Nicholas della Casa, is an example of their retaining a potential bargaining chip for 18 months in an attempt to obtain some sort of direct contact with British officials, the ICRC, and favourable press coverage. His release was secured by the intervention of Senator Jesse Helms and President Moi of Kenya, whose pleas added welcome publicity to Renamo's cause.[76]

President Chissano has argued that Renamo's attacks on the civilian population are a sign of weakness.[77] He says that Renamo experienced a conventional military defeat in 1986, thwarting its plan to dismember Mozambique. Since then the rebels have changed their tactics to that of terror campaigns in the rural areas in order to survive, military targets being avoided in favour of civilian ones. This is how Chissano interprets the massacres of Homoine, Taninga, Manjacaze, Guija and Moamba. That 1986 marked a distinct shift of gear in the war is unquestionable, but its significance lies in Renamo having lost much of its rear support in Malawi and South Africa, thereby having to carve out for itself many more areas within Mozambique. It was not a response to defeat. Moreover Renamo's tactics did not change radically. Civilians had always been targets, the frequency of attack being due to Renamo now having to survive almost exclusively from "pillage" to maintain its presence. Renamo's attacks on civilians are an important contribution to the movement's military success.

Much media coverage of Renamo originates from its attacks on rural settlements and public transport, especially along the routes from Maputo to Beira, the Beira corridor and from Maputo to South Africa and Swaziland. These attacks are not necessarily sporadic and mindless, as has often been depicted. Traffic into Mozambique's towns and cities is picked off in preference to simple rural traffic because the former offers riches (as for example, what is carried by returning workers from South Africa).[78] Although the majority of passengers are massacred, some are usually left alive to describe what happened. This is part of Renamo's brutal, but effective, psychological warfare, with an eye to media coverage.

A similar pattern is also visible in other Renamo atrocities. Atrocities against the civilian population are seldom perpetrated without show. The dossiers compiled by the South African Council of Churches from refugee accounts speak of peasants being made to watch their kin having their heads crushed with millet grinders and the boiling alive of children of parents who refused to give Renamo information.[79] This type of brutality is well illustrated in Lina Magaia's book *Dumba Nengue*, a compilation of accounts of peasant experience of similar brutalities.[80] The use of anti-personnel mines, targetted at maiming rather than killing, is also a tactic used in these contested areas. The idea seems to have been copied from Angola, where UNITA has used landmines with success. People badly injured by mines are yet another image of Renamo activity, and are an additional burden on the Government's limited medical facilities.

Such gruesome tactics play an important role in Renamo recruitment. The committing of vivid atrocity is often demanded of new recruits as a type of initiation. This is particularly important for Renamo because of heavily forced recruitment. Many coerced combatants will not desert the rebels for fear of a blood price on them for their part in atrocities.

Another reason for brutality is the need for economy of fire power. Renamo documents captured from Musanta base in Manica province (1985) illustrate this:[81]

... when destroying communal villages, a group must by all means not use ammunition. Use fire to burn the village, use knives and axes to cut the throats of Frelimo agents and use fire arms and ammunition in case of enemy counter-action.

The instruction on combat technique reflects the change in Renamo tactics in 1984, when it had to become more self-reliant. This has been confirmed by captured westerners and journalists visiting Renamo bases. Captured arms and equipment have become the major source of supplies, but many of the rebels still have to operate without guns.

There is also a psychological dimension to this tactic. The objective behind many of these atrocities is to make the population compliant to Renamo. The use of maimed people is in a similar mould. Earless, noseless or handless people are a convenient way of transmitting a permanent image of Renamo's activities in areas where their presence remains marginal. It is both a powerful warning and a disincentive to potential Frelimo sympathisers to become active.[82]

Renamo naturally claims that the majority of atrocities on Mozambican civilians are committed by separate "bandits" or by "Frelimo soldiery and their Zimbabwean, Tanzanian, Cuban allies".[83] They claim that it is part of the Frelimo propaganda machine to besmirch their image. Like the Mozambican government, Renamo admits that some atrocities may have happened under the circumstances of war, but they argue that this does not account for the majority of incidents.[84]

Whatever Frelimo may have been accused of, there is no doubt that it has done nothing comparable with Renamo's use of terror. No maimed Renamo supporter has been brought to notice by observers sympathetic to it.

CIVILIAN MANAGEMENT

According to the accounts of Mozambicans who have experienced it, Renamo's administrative set-up within Mozambique can be classified according to geographical, logistical and local political considerations. They have been labelled by Robert Gersony as "Tax areas","Control areas" and "Destruction areas".[85] As with the formal military command structure, the labelling of this admininistrative pattern in any particular area must be taken with a pinch of salt, given the fluidity of the insurgency campaign. The conclusions of the Gersony report apply most realistically to central Mozambique. They should not be regarded as applicable to the whole of the country. In Cabo Delgado province, for example, Renamo operates in smaller bands and does not appear to have set up large camps or treated the local population with the extreme violence it has experienced in other areas.

"Tax areas" are in zones with a scarce, and generally dispersed, population in territory marginal to Renamo interests. As these areas of dispersed population are marginal to its operations, Renamo appears to demand from them a tax on food or labour in return for leaving the population otherwise alone and in peace. The policy appears to be to maintain a presence, symbolised by tax collection. "Tax" areas do not receive any reciprocity from Renamo in the form of aid or alternative services, except the important guarantee of not being violently treated.[86]

"Control areas" are Renamo's main territory and, as such, the basis of what it calls "liberated zones". Their major function is to produce food and services for the organisation. To this end they are run as a type of plantation economy, modelled very much on early Portuguese plantations and 19th century secondary states in central Mozambique, where the population was compelled, out of their inability to meet the heavy taxes imposed on them, to work for very little return. Renamo obtains most of its labour forces from its two other zones, "tax" and "destruction" areas. Its workforce is therefore predominantly captive, detained against its will and forbidden to depart.[87] Renamo exploits those very areas from which its first constituency of support was drawn — rural peasant communities.

Renamo controls its production areas through fear and force. A refugee account, from a peasant farmer, whose village in Niassa province was attacked and burnt by Renamo illustrates this very clearly. The villagers hid in a secluded area but were soon discovered. They were, five hundred in all, force-marched to a camp deep in the bush, called Mussala. They were then incorporated into the alternative system as food producers for the rebels.[88]

The place was a village. The local people were still there working in the fields and preparing food for the bandits who lived among them. We were told that we had to work for the soldiers too .... anyone who refused to work was beaten. They never showed any mercy. Anyone who tried to escape would be killed, they said. No one tried; as well as the soldiers who lived around us, there were sentries all around the place.

In this manner Renamo supervises its control areas, extracting the services of its captive population, within which the work is generally clearly divided between the sexes. Males are used for portering and recruited into the rebels' forces, while females are used in food production. In some areas the captive labourers are allocated their own land to cultivate. Nevertheless a proportion of their produce is commandeered by Renamo. This situation varies between Renamo bases, depending on food availability and the demands of rebel combatants. When food is short, the situation gets worse for the civilians, as the rebel commanders naturally ensure that their combatants receive the best.

Given the extraction of a high level of work for little compensation, these "liberated areas" function only by efficient security and surveillance. As Renamo combatants are involved in operations against the Mozambique Government forces, a second Renamo controlling force operates in these areas, called the "Mujuba", "Majiba" or "Mujeeba" — the equivalent of a Renamo police force. The first public account of the *Mujeeba* came in 1985 in an interview with Renamo's then Secretary-General, the late Evo Fernandes. He said:[89]

The Mujeeba is our representative at the village level. He knows everybody in his village. Nobody can come without being known. Then nobody also can betray us because he surveys the area. He has a weapon not an automatic weapon but a Mauser or something.

The *Mujeeba* is frequently recruited from former tax collectors or petty officials, such as the "regulos" who were appointed by the Portuguese colonial administration. Having been replaced by Frelimo officials after independence, many of these felt themselves marginalised, and became disaffected, joining Renamo. Another source of recruitment to the *Mujeeba* is the local population itself, who sees it as an opportunity of upward mobility in the alternative system. Others will have been coerced into the job. *Mujeeba* are recognised by the population by the fact that they carry cutting instruments (machetes, knives or axes), rather than firearms. Their main task appears to be to ensure that the population produces food for Renamo combatants. The *Mujeeba* are particularly hated by the FAM. After the recapture of Gile in July 1988 from Renamo, at least 50 who failed to turn themselves in were executed.[90]

The manner of this control also varies from district to district. Some Renamo zones completely separate the military bases from the civilian camps. Military bases, especially in central Mozambique, are very mobile and often located away from the civilian population. The pattern that Geffray has noted in Nampula of the rebel base as the core of concentric circles of villages under the watchful eye of Mujeebas and small groups of "Mambos" as an early warning system is a regional variation. Gersony and the conversations that the present writer has had with refugees from Tete and Zambezia suggest that the pattern can be inverted with the main

Renamo bases on the exterior of the coerced civilian population. Other accounts about Zambezia province talk of a more relaxed set-up, with bases being broken up into different wards for particular groups, such as rebel leadership, combatants, visitors and the civilian population (Fig. 4.2). But the basic methods are the same. The *Mujeeba* enforce Renamo control over its population. Escape or dissent is commonly punished by death or mutilation. Refugees' accounts, as above, speak of these methods being an effective and chilling disincentive to those considering escape.

The control areas are clearly very wasteful. Refugee accounts frequently mention the killing of the old, the sick and the disobedient, who are replaced by individuals newly sequestrated during Renamo's operations.

It is difficult to identify much reciprocity on Renamo's part for the demands it makes upon the population in the areas it controls. The only positive compensation appears to be religious tolerance, access to ICRC emergency food aid and the opportunity to remain alive. The use of drugs, especially Dahka, is also encouraged. Any concessions the civilian population get from Renamo are immediately eroded whenever military priorities demand.

Despite the overall picture of Renamo's harsh treatment of the population it encounters, there is another side to its administrative practices. When Renamo enters a district for the first time there is some attempt to win over peasant support. Already in the early 1980's Renamo played in this way on local discontent with Frelimo's achievements, particularly about the lack of consumer goods and villagisation, to obtain sympathy. As part of its campaign, Renamo also selected for attack traders who had cheated the local population, and also corrupt government officials. This was in fact a type of social banditry. When a shop was sacked, some goods were usually redistributed to the local population. For example, when Luabo was first captured in 1985, Renamo used the captured landrovers and tractors to transport some of the booty to surrounding villages for distribution amongst the local population. Renamo is also known to have introduced itself at times to new areas by giving a party, supplying the beer and cooking stolen food and cattle.[91] In Nampula province Renamo appears to refrain from attacking the agricultural marketing network until after the peasants have sold their crops.

Promise of power and land has also been one of the offers Renamo has made in rural areas to obtain support. Even as early as 1979 captured rebels revealed that they had been offered the control of districts, land and even provinces in return for their allegiance.[92] Further confirmation that Renamo was attracting the disgruntled and the power-hungry came in 1982 through research conducted by Frelimo. It showed that many of the rebels in Inhambane province were failed local election candidates from 1978, who saw Renamo as an alternative method to gain power. This was the basis for President Machel's tour of Inhambane province in 1982 and his notable speech in Vilanculos on Renamo in which Machel replied to the crowds' demands for guns to defend themselves against the rebels by pointing out that the rebels were Mozambicans, "they are your children and your brothers", and that many families protected their kin involved with the rebels from the authorities by giving them food and intelligence.[93]

What unites Renamo is the desire for power. Renamo's leadership core is derived of disgruntled or disillusioned Frelimo members who were unable to progress far enough for their ambitions within the party, or were not

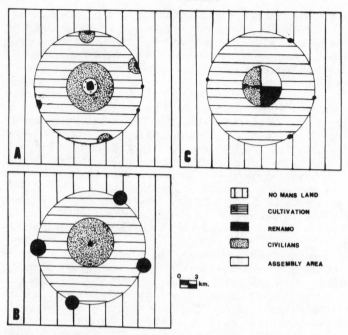

Figure 4.2 Types of Renamo Camps.
Sources: refugee descriptions. A is adapted from Geffray 1989.

important enough to be protected from prosecution for their corrupt activities, as the cases of Matsangaissa and Dhlakama illustrate.[94] This is Renamo's true ideology which continues to motivate its internal leadership. The Pretoria Declaration talks in 1984 and the Nairobi talks (as will be discussed below) show that Renamo is preoccupied with obtaining positions in government, a fact confirmed by President Chissano in a speech at Chokwe in 1989.[95] He revealed that Renamo had recognised him as President but demanded posts as Ministers, Governors or Administrators. Renamo's problem is that although the promise of power and its pillage provide benefits to its leadership and, at times, its combatants, it has very little to offer the peasantry. Mozambique is far too poor a country to produce a surplus of booty for redistribution outside Renamo's leadership and combatants. It relies on its raids for supplies of arms, and labour. If it were to stop such raids, Renamo would collapse as a coherent military force. This is why Renamo very quickly runs out of whatever credit it has obtained from burning down a hated communal village or killing a despised official. It can not provide a better alternative.

The majority of refugees now claim that they fled from Renamo, which suggests they are increasingly unable to accept that Renamo in any way offers a better alternative. This has contributed to the peasantry being ambivalent towards both the government and Renamo. Neither has been able to bring to the rural areas the commodities and services the peasantry desire, while the conflict has only brought violence, death and hardship to their villages. It appears that they now support which ever side will protect them, in order to save their own skin.

The third category of Renamo operational area is the "Destruction Area". These lie at the interface of Renamo dominated areas and those under Government control. Renamo's policy is to devastate them so as to force Government withdrawal, turning them into a no-man's land, even a waste-land, where most of the violence and atrocities take place. The major targets, as already described, are anything that can be associated with the Government, from whole regions to particular settlements or economic establishments. The Homoine and Manjacaze massacres were in a designated destruction area, as are also the incidents recorded by the South African Council of Churches and those in the book *Dumba Nengue*.[96]

Becoming a Renamo combatant offers the recruit the only chance of upward mobility to a better lifestyle under Renamo administration. For some it may well be an easier and more attractive option than remaining a peasant, fleeing as a refugee or working as a porter. Captured westerners, such as Blakey and O'Connell (1985), Kindra Bryan (1987) and Nicholas della Casa (1989), who have first hand experience of Renamo's combatants, speak of them operating with greater motivation and organisation than is usually depicted.[97]

There is nevertheless, plenty of evidence of forced recruitment. As early as 1981, the British Director of the Gorongosa Wildlife Training Centre, John Burlison, who spent 150 days in Renamo captivity, saw young men being captured and kept under surveillance until they participated in their first raids. They were warned that, if they fled, they would be killed by Frelimo as terrorists. He saw many stay for fear of retribution by Maputo if they defected. As mentioned elsewhere in this book, Renamo has also used the threat of spiritual retribution as the penalty for any defection, let alone execution.[98]

Forced recruitment appears wide-spread. There are countless refugee accounts of rebels (and government troops, on occasion) forcibly recruiting young men in villages to join their operations. An eyewitness speaks of reluctant Renamo combatants in training in South Africa at Phalaborwa being put into deep holes and buried up to their necks until they cooperated.[99] This has also been noted within Mozambique where research by Otto Roesch has recorded that kidnapped young men are often put into a "Jaula", a cage or chicken coop, where they are kept for long periods of time and subjected to various forms of deprivation and trauma, in order to break them psychologically before formal military training begins (the use of force, though not as brutal, is also used by FAM, and indeed BMATT has faced severe difficulties over motivation during its training of Mozambicans).[100] Renamo has more recently used children (some as young as 10) to fight. An increasingly large number of refugees tell of this phenomenom in southern Mozambique, something that was virtually unheard of until the late 1980's.[101] Unlike children used by the NRA in Uganda during its guerrilla war against Milton Obote, Renamo's child combatants appear undisciplined and sometimes to be on drugs. They too seem to have been put through psychological trauma and deprivation, such as being hung upside-down from trees until their individualism is broken, and encouraged and rewarded for killing.[102] Some commentators believe that massacres in southern Mozambique are committed by these child combatants, who have been programmed to feel little fear or revulsion for such actions, and thereby carry out these attacks with greater enthusiasm and brutality than adults would. What this really demonstrates is Renamo's increasing difficulty in recruiting in the south. The war is increasingly being fought by those with no memory of the independence struggle or of older policy disputes.

Recruiting is clearly a major preoccupation of Renamo in order to be able to maintain the momentum of operations against the Mozambican government. There can be no doubt that many of its combatants are unwilling victims of the war and that, as already stated, the population is disillusioned with its experience of Renamo. Pressganging of it into Renamo is recorded all over Mozambique. The question then arising is: how does Renamo maintain its forces, if the majority are fighting against their will? What prevents them from escaping or rebelling?

The use of atrocity has already been touched upon. The use of religion will be looked at in greater depth below. A major factor appears to be a realisation that, in the present situation in Mozambique, deserting to Frelimo might, at worst, cause instant execution and, at best, having to fight for Frelimo instead. The options are very limited. Renamo's encouragement of the myth that Renamo soldiers will be executed has remained very convincing since, until the amnesty on offer was widely publicized, many Renamo combatants were executed on capture by local Frelimo commanders.

Another deterrent is the systematic practice of transferring recruits away from their home areas. This is of particular relevance in central Mozambique were there has not been any tradition of migration or travel over large distances. It seems that Renamo posts such recruits to units of mixed ethnic origin in areas in which many find difficulty in communicating in the local dialect.[103]

In the face of these deterrents, the government's amnesty offer has not had much success:[104]

Table 4.1 *Amnesty Figures, 1987-1989*	
Period Amnesty offered	*Number Amnestied.*
December 1987 to December 1988	2,895
December 1988 to December 1989	1,063
Source: *Mozambiquefile*, No.162, January 1990.	

Mozambican government officials now acknowledge officially that, despite the publicity given to the amnesty offer, 1989 was much less successful and that the offer had already earlier attracted many of those who would be tempted by it. For this reason it was not renewed by the People's Assembly in December 1989 for another year.

Are there other factors contributing to the hesitancy to leave Renamo? The answer must lie partly in a continued lack of faith in the Mozambican government, in that the waverers are still not convinced that the government's offer is honest. But perhaps more importantly, Renamo's combatants appear to have a fatalistic acceptance of their present situation. This ambivalence to the government as a better alternative and to Renamo is what is really demonstrated in the Gersony report's break-down of refugee accounts:[105]

Table 4.2		*Break-down of Refugee Accounts*		
	Positive	Very Negative	Somewhat Negative	No Complaint
FRELIMO	11%	7%	10%	72%
RENAMO	1%	91%	5%	3%

Source: *Gersony Report*, April 1988.

"No complaint" is frequently associated with ambivalence, which is the predominant emotional state of many in the refugee camps.

BANDITS

Renamo is not the only contributor to the internal problems of security in Mozambique. Some atrocities and attacks are committed neither by the rebels nor South African special units, nor even by elements of the Mozambique army, but by freelance armed bandits operating opportunely in the chaotic situation in rural areas, where the access to guns and weapons guarantees power. Both Renamo and the Government privately admit this situation, which adds to the difficulties in the attempts to bring peace to Mozambique. The proportion of Renamo-attributed activities which are actually committed by bandit warlords purely for rich pickings is, however, unknown.

These bandit groups do not appear to operate with even the minimum sophistication of Renamo. They seem to function as small bands, marauding and pillaging for their survival in areas not fully dominated by Renamo or the Government. They act without any social element, without trying to redistribute captured booty to the indigenous population. It is, nevertheless, also thought that some of these groups co-exist with Renamo because they increase the insecurity and tension in locations which Renamo have designated as targets for destruction and demoralisation rather than occupation. In Nampula this has taken the form of *Mujeeba* bands, who seem to have organised themselves into autonomous predatory groups, independently of Renamo, improving their poverty-stricken existence through banditry. There is, however, no evidence to date of these bandit groups being disciplined by Renamo for operating in the so-called "liberated zones".

Such banditry is taken seriously in Mozambique. It has been compared with the armed banditry, the so-called "pseudo-terrorists", of the Rhodesian war, who were armed criminals exploiting the confusion and chaos of war. Various plans to deal with this additional problem of independent banditry have been tabled by the government and churches. One idea has been to create "poles of development" around major economic projects, such as the Beira and Nacala corridors. These poles would then serve to attract freelance bandits, eg those who did not belong to Renamo. The aim would be to give them a salaried occupation and encourage them to give up a life of banditry. The scheme would be managed by a new local administrative system involving skilled expatriate Mozambicans who are in contact with Renamo. As a second phase of this experiment, direct dialogue between Renamo and Frelimo would commence, once banditry had been reduced.[106]

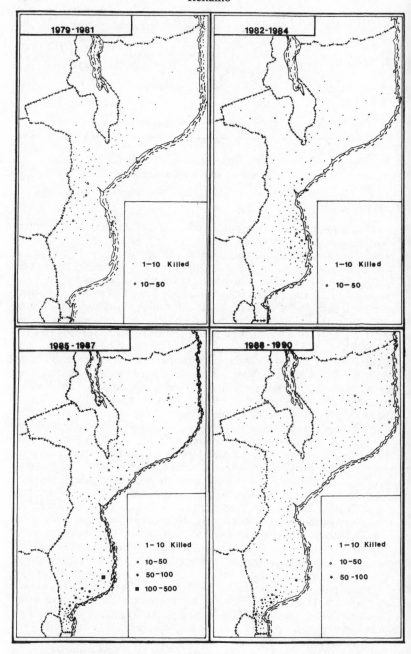

Map 4.2 Distribution of Renamo attributed atrocities
Sources: AIM, Domingo, Noticias, Herald, interviews.

This scheme, although receiving some sympathy in church circles, was generally seen to be incorrectly targetted; dialogue between Renamo and Frelimo was seen by the church as the essential first objective. As Herman Cohen, the US Assistant Secretary of State for African Affairs, stated in an interview in 1989, Renamo is thought to be 75% of the problem.[107]

There is an additional complication in this picture. A pattern was noticed in the vehicles attacked on the roads to South Africa between February 1984 and March 1985, and again, in 1986 and 1987 on the road to Swaziland. The majority of attacks were on vehicles inward-bound into Mozambique, heavily laden with goods. Even more significantly the majority were attacked and burnt-out near FAM and militia checkpoints without counter-action.[108]

These incidents suggest that there is both a selection of targets and connivance. The militia at road blocks have a very drab appearance. They are mostly unsupervised, often disaffected, ill-fed and unpaid. The distinction between Renamo and government forces outside the latter's regular and officered units is, at times, solely one of convenience. This has also been noted in respect of the number of incidents of civilians attacked close to government army camps.[109]

A specific example of this type of incident happened at Inhamizua on the outskirts of Beira in late July 1988, where gunmen attacked a local festival. The government immediately blamed Renamo, but it was latter revealed by both the Zimbabwean *Financial Gazette* and the BBC that the massacre was actually committed by a group of Frelimo soldiers enraged at having to pay an entrance fee.[110] William Finnegan once again records similar occurrences. One involved a co-operante who had just witnessed, and escaped from, a group of soldiers looting a truck, who started shooting at him, once they had spotted him. The other account is of a conversation with a man in Manhica about soldiers ambushing vehicles. Finnegan writes:[111]

> He sneered, and said, "They do it. And they are the most dangerous, because they don't want to leave witnesses, so they kill everyone. The massacre at the Third of February — that was Soldiers." The Third of February was the village near the spot where a big highway massacre had occurred the previous October (1987).

Such sentiments are not uncommon in Mozambique, especially since Renamo is widely accepted as leaving plenty of witnesses, as part of its eye for morbid publicity for the massacres it commits.

Although such tactics by the FAM are unquestionably not Mozambique government official policy, there have been many reports of dirty tactics being used during anti-rebel operations. The locations and times when these have taken place fluctuate with the fronts and offensives of the war. Reports of religious persecution in 1987 (to be cited below) are one example. A report by Karl Maier of a young trooper begging his commander's permission to kill two peasants he had seen, calling them *Mujeebas* (informers), is another.[112] This attitude of government forces towards the local population is widespread in certain areas of Mozambique. Troops seem to suspect every peasant they see as a potential collaborator. In one sense this is logical. In the rural areas that are at an interface between government and Renamo-dominated territory, a peasant would have to collaborate with one group or the other to survive. In these areas the level of violence is at its most extreme, with a violent tug of war taking place. The government at times forces locals into district capitals or accommodation centres (between 1986 and the end of 1988, 466 such centres had been set up), while Renamo tries to force them into its alternative system.[113] The obvious sufferers are the peasantry who make it quite clear they would rather be left alone by everybody. As one peasant farmer from Mabote pointed out recently: "They say as well that they are regrouping us to protect us, but isn't it rather to hide themselves behind us during attacks? So we're afraid of all men we come across".[114]

URBAN AREAS

Although frequently suffering from sabotaged communications and power lines, the towns, with only a few exceptions, have remained in government hands. Those captured by Renamo were generally very small, little more than extended villages. In the mid-1980s Renamo targetted a propaganda campaign against the capital, Maputo, claiming that it would be captured in six months. The aim was to cause a sense of insecurity in the city, which had received many refugees with first-hand knowledge of Renamo's policies in the countryside. The placing of two landmines on the Costa do Sol beach was particularly effective for this purpose, as the beach had become one of the few areas of recreation for Maputo's foreign community.[115]

In the larger cities, like Maputo and Beira, Renamo has been able to penetrate the outlying suburbs, distributing leaflets and harassing government targets and economic installations. Not all attacks of this kind are by Renamo. Large companies, like BP, have found that they have had to pay off corrupt Frelimo officials in order to avoid so-called Renamo attacks. A similar scenario is reported by William Finnegan who was told that many of the attacks around Beira were "social banditry", conducted by the popular militia in order to ameliorate their poverty-stricken existence.[116]

Beira has been under semi-siege since it was surrounded by Renamo activity in 1983. Beira's power supply is something Renamo manipulates as a good demonstration of its capabilities. In honour of the Pope's visit in 1988, Renamo allowed several month's uninterrupted power supply, providing a good example of its units' capacity to respond to central commands. The rumours spread about Renamo in Beira have (if rumour is a valid indicator of popular feeling) tended to show more sympathy towards the rebels than has been apparent when similar rumours circulate in other cities. Finnegan noted, as many before him, that there was serious talk in Beira about workers being prepared to lay down tools and to demonstrate against the government whenever it became apparent that Renamo might be on the verge of an assault.[117] But, all in all, popular support in the cities for the Renamo seems small, at least in the face of effective government control and party discipline over neighbourhood cadres.

Much of the discontent in the towns is reflected in varying degrees of anti-Sovietism. Soviet influence is blamed by many of the non-intellectual circles as a major contributor to Mozambique's problems. Even within the government a growing division has appeared on how the relationship with the Soviet Union should continue, as the document "We the former fighters and founders of this Republic", distributed in government circles in Maputo in 1986, illustrated.

This document, which circulated in the interim period between President Machel's death and the appointment of Joaquim Chissano to replace him, is not only interesting for its anti-Soviet emphasis. It was addressed to four members of Frelimo's Politbureau — Joaquim Chissano, Alberto Chipande, Armando Guebuza and Mariano Matsinhe. Through government channels it later reached the Western diplomatic corps in Maputo. Its main points concern the role of non-blacks in Mozambican society (especially in government) and the war against Renamo. It contains a long discussion on the Renamo problem, arguing that, without talks with the rebels, the war would never cease, giving Uganda and Chad as examples of such a scenario. The document anticipated government arguments against such talks by saying:[118]

> We now fight against puppets, executioners and armed bandits and there are quite a lot of them. Hence it is better to talk directly to the executioners (puppets or armed bandits) for them to stop being used by their bosses.

A similar document circulated in the Mozambican government in June 1987. It was attributed to veteran Frelimo fighters from the north and central provinces, who had fought most of the Independence war. It also argued for greater black Mozambican representation in government, and played on continuing hostility within Mozambique to the enormous presence of the Soviet Union.[119] With the moves towards direct dialogue with Renamo in 1990, Frelimo veterans produced a further document in February 1990. This attacked the Party for corruption and called for a multiparty democracy to be introduced in Mozambique as a measure to end the war. It also defended the military leadership, a response to moves by President Chissano to reshuffle and restructure the military establishment.

A further source of dissatisfaction in the urban areas is the result of the governments forcible transfer of persons from them to the countryside. Its campaign from July to September 1983, called "Operation Production", which aimed at transferring unproductive urban unemployed to the countryside (50,000), was particularly counter-productive, not least because many families were sent to ethnic areas in which they did not belong. Rather than becoming self-sufficient as basic food producers, as the Government had intended, many of those transferred returned to the urban areas. Others joined Renamo as the better of two evils. Evidence from captured Renamo documents shows that the transferred city unemployed were regarded as ripe for recruitment.[120]

The wave of strikes that hit Mozambique in January 1990 has worried the Mozambican authorities.[121] President Chissano's address to a Maputo rally, with proposals for constitutional reform and for the peace process, was timed to calm the city. Chissano admitted that "in Maputo and Matola, there is tension, and provocation; we have this atmosphere; we have discontent, genuine, real, honest discontent".[122]

Renamo has, as in the past, claimed responsiblity for urban discontent. Dhlakama declared that this was the start of an urban war that would soon spread to all of Mozambique's towns.[123] Renamo is still incapable of this, but it is undoubtedly encouraging urban unrest. Leaflets within Mozambique's urban, high-density, suburbs call for demonstrations against the government and for the military to rise up and stage a *coup d'état* against Frelimo to bring about a prompt cessation of the war.[124] These crude leaflets, unlike Renamo's external propaganda, have never stated any objective other than peace.

THE ROLES OF RELIGION

In a report by an observer sympathetic to Renamo, on what is called the "Eyewitness Testimonies of Persecution and Atrocities" of Christians in Mozambique, there occurs the following testimony of three pastors from Angonia district, Tete province:[125]

> The war in Angonia province makes our work very difficult. Most of the villages have been burnt to the ground. All our (livestock) animals have been stolen by the soldiers. All our grain stores have been burnt. Most of our young men have been forced into the army and most of our people have fled as refugees to Malawi. There is always fighting and we do not know the difference between the sides. They all wear the same uniform and carry the same weapons. They all demand food even though we have none ourselves, and they all punish us if we feed the "enemy". The only difference is that at least Renamo does not stop us worshipping God and teaching the Gospel.

The report as a whole, which is addressed to American and South African right-wing protestant groups to solicit funds for Renamo, makes unconvincing reading. The specific testimony of these three pastors, however, rings true and is probably representative of many areas of Mozambique suffering from the conflict. The pastors make the point that Renamo does not interfere with the work of protestant missions.

As will be discussed shortly, this statement needs qualification. But there is evidence of sympathetic relations between Renamo and some elements of the Catholic church as well as with Islam and the neo-traditional religions. This fact is hardly surprising. On the one hand, Renamo has been successful in manipulating an extraordinary collation of religious forces and fundraisers in opposition to Frelimo's materialism. On the other, the representatives and spokesmen of the different religions and denominations have a natural concern for the fates of their congregations and a wish to keep options open.

Even less surprising is the fact that religious belief is so strong and is apparently strengthening among people who have endured what Mozambicans have endured over the past ten years. Religion, whether of the Christian, Muslim or neo-traditional varieties, can offer explanations of disaster which satisfy more than the political and materialist explanations offered by Frelimo. Very occasionally, as we shall see, they offer hope and a measure of security.

CHRISTIANITY

Christianity is the professed faith of only about 20% of Mozambique's population. But Christianity is spreading rapidly in Mozambique, although it does not have anywhere near the influence it has reached in Angola. Nevertheless Christianity has had a disproportionate importance in Mozambique. During colonial rule, the only real opportunity for blacks to receive an education of any standard was through the missions. This encouraged African interest in Christianity, as well as producing an educated black group.[126]

Mission-educated Mozambicans formed the core of several prolonged struggles against colonial legislation and repression during the early decades of this century. One major group was comprised of Catholic educated Africans and Mulattos. They formed a social clique and political lobby called "Gremio Africano". Through their newspaper, they campaigned against the colonial Laws of Exception that had been introduced to curtail black mobility in the face of the growing need to find employment for whites following the increase in Portuguese immigration into Mozambique.[127]

It is particularly relevant that, broadly speaking, this group comprised of two segments. One was Catholic mission educated and Portuguese speaking. The other was Protestant mission educated and spoke in the vernacular dialects. With the increasingly precarious standing of educated Africans in colonial Mozambique, the movement, with some exceptions such as the Swiss mission, which found itself acceptable to both sides, had, by the mid 1930s, split along Protestant-Catholic lines. "Gremio Africano" continued to try to curry favour from the colonial authorities by attacking the Protestant splinter groups who had formed the "Instituto Negrofilo" in the then Lourenço Marques, and its successor, the "Centro Associativo dos Negros de Mozambique". "Gremio Africano" perceived itself as the natural leader of the majority of the population: "civilised people who are morally principled and know how to civilise". As such they claimed they deserved Portuguese recognition. As part of this attempt it also played on Portuguese antagonisms towards its Protestant educated compatriots, claiming that they were less educated and un-Portuguese.[128]

Frelimo inherited this uneasy relationship amongst the mission educated Africans it attracted. Although Mondlane attempted to defuse such tensions, many Catholic educated volunteers were regarded with suspicion and found it difficult to obtain positions of responsibility in what appeared to be a Protestant, mission educated dominated organisation. A major crisis arose over this within the Mozambique Institute in Tanzania in 1966-1967. A dispute developed over the arrival of a black Catholic priest from Beira, Fr. Gwenjere, with around twenty seminarian students. The issues ran along the lines seen in the 1920s between élitist Catholicism, with its Portuguese connections, and Protestant "inferiority". This dispute spread to Mozambican students studying abroad in Portugal, United States and Kenya, with many Catholic mission educated students deciding to break with Frelimo at this stage.[129]

ROMAN CATHOLICISM

Frelimo's suspicion of the Catholic mission educated Mozambicans was not solely due to a conflict within the black élite. It was also an extension of how it saw the Roman Catholic Church generally. The Catholic Church was regarded as particularly suspect (with exceptions like the White and Burgos Father missions) because of its association with the Portuguese colonial state, formalised in 1940 by the Concordat and Missionary Agreement. This agreement had its roots in Vatican frustration over the unsatisfactory results of the 1930 Colonial Act under which Article 14 defined "the Portuguese Catholic missions overseas" as "instruments of civilisation and national influence". This objective was to be achieved through the Portuguese language and Portuguese customs. Finding Portuguese Catholic missionaries for service in Africa proved to be difficult. The missionary agreement was an attempt by the Vatican to improve this situation, opening Mozambique and Angola to non-Portuguese missionary societies.

In return, the Vatican had to agree that all bishops and major ecclesiastical superiors should remain Portuguese, that the government should retain the power of veto over appointments, and that teaching was to continue in the Portuguese style. The government in return payed bishops the same salary as regional governors and supported missionary work financially. In this way the Roman Catholic Church became an instrument for the "Portugalisation" of millions of Africans.[130]

At independence the new Mozambique government was deeply suspicious of the Catholic Church because of its association with the colonial order during the liberation struggle, even although many African catechists, and some bishops and missionary societies (such as the White and Burgos Fathers), had been highly critical of the Portuguese and forced to resign or were expelled or imprisoned during the liberation struggle. Despite such support, much church property was expropriated by the state and the practising of Catholicism was discouraged.

With the appearance of Renamo, the Catholic Church was particularly targetted for criticism as being a focus for support for its cause. Frelimo portrayed the ex-seminarians in the United States as collaborators or integrated members of Renamo, while similar allegations were made within Mozambique, linking the Catholic Church at times with the "Inimigo Interno". Renamo's most serious approaches to the Catholic Church only took place, however, after 1980, with its transfer to South African management and the rise to prominence of Evo Fernandes within the organisation.[131]

Many of Renamo's leadership originated from Catholic missions. Afonso Dhlakama is himself Catholic mission educated. He claims to have wished to have trained to become a catechist, but joined Frelimo instead in the early 1970s. Former major figures in Renamo's external wing are also ex-seminarians, such as Francisco Nota Moises and Luis Serapião. Fernandes, as a devout Catholic, fostered close connections with sympathetic Portuguese Catholic priests in Portugal and Mozambique from whom he obtained information. He organised for Dhlakama, during the latter's visit to Portugal in 1980, a meeting with the Archbishop of Braga, Eurico Nogueira (a former bishop in colonial Mozambique) and his Canon, Eduardo de Melo. Minutes of this meeting found by the FAM in its December 1981 capture of Renamo's Garagua base revealed what happened there. Dhlakama was offered books and money by the diocese for scholarships. Dhlakama asked the Archbishop to send priests to the areas of Mozambique that Renamo dominated "to spread the word of God". He also requested an audience with the Pope. Nogueira responded to this latter request by saying that, although it was not possible, he would send a report to the Vatican on Catholic persecution by Frelimo. The meeting did provide Renamo with some assistance: when Garagua was captured, many religious tracts containing sermons by Nogueira were found.[132]

Fernandes continued to obtain religious literature for distribution in Mozambique. Large quantities, again originating from Portugal, were recovered by the FAM following the capture of Renamo's Casa Banana in 1985. In return for Catholic support Fernandes attempted to give Catholicism a monopoly on Christianity within Renamo-held areas and promised to keep Renamo's operations away from Catholic interests. Nevertheless Catholic missions and personnel have been attacked by Renamo and captured, with some fatalities. Renamo and some church officials have claimed that Mozambican troops were responsible for these, in an attempt to discourage the clergy from giving Renamo support.

Both the style and content of Renamo's external propaganda reflect the influence of its Catholic educated members. Some of the arguments used by Renamo against the Mozambique government are not dissimilar to those made in the 1920s by the Catholic mission educated Africans in their disputes with their Protestant educated counterparts. The following Renamo statement is typical of this type of thinking. "Dhlakama likes educated people, Samora Machel is a mortal and sworn enemy of the educated, particularly men who have had a liberal, western type of education".[133]

Because of Renamo's bias towards it, the Catholic Church has not been blind to its potential as a channel for bringing Frelimo and Renamo together. Some Catholic bishops and priests have shown some sympathy for aspects of Renamo policy, especially where it allegedly stands for the growth of church influence. Some believed that Catholic Church sympathy for Renamo would put pressure on the government which, in its more vulnerable and less dogmatic position of the 1980's, would lead it to moderate its anti-religious sentiments in an attempt to obtain greater public support generally. This line of approach became more formalised in 1987, with the Catholic bishops of Mozambique calling in a Pastoral letter for dialogue and national reconciliation between government and Renamo.[134]

Catholic coolness towards the Mozambican government's stance against negotiations with Renamo was vitriolically attacked by Frelimo. The semi-official newspaper *Noticias* attacked the bishops as being "the Apostles of Treason".[135] This was followed up by President Chissano (Protestant trained) directly criticising the Catholic Church in his 1987 anniversary of independence speech. A spin-off from this was a renewed campaign of hostility towards the Catholic Church encouraged by hardliners such as Politbureau member Jorge Rebelo. This lasted until President Chissano directly intervened when he recognised the potential harm the campaign would do to the government's external image.[136]

Since then Frelimo's relations with the Vatican (the result of growing contacts since 1983) improved to such an extent that the Pope's visit to Mozambique during his southern African tour in 1988 went smoothly and successfully. On its eve the Catholic Archbishop of Beira again reiterated the call for reconciliation, saying that "Mozambique should also take part in calling people to talk about ending the war".[137] There was also a hint from the Archbishop that government policy about talks with the rebels had changed. He stated that "at first the government said they did not agree with the Catholic Church. Now they say they understand (our) position".

The success of the Pope's visit to Mozambique remains an important milestone in the warming of the relationship between Church and State. The enthusiasm and size of the turn-out for the visit has acted as a reminder that the Catholic constituency of 3 million in Mozambique is an important one. With the return of church property expropriated after independence, one main area of Catholic discontent has been removed. Frelimo's pragmatism and liberalisations have also reduced the areas in which the needs of the Catholic Church clash directly with the Maputo government's policies.

In spite of this improving relationship between Maputo and the Catholic Church, older prejudices and suspicions still affect the manner in which Frelimo treats the Catholic community. An example of this is the announcement and commendation in President Chissano's address to the opening of the 10th session of the Frelimo Party Central Committee in December 1988 of the "Peace and Reconciliation Commission", a commission made up of church groups led by the Anglican Bishop of Maputo. Its role was to make contact with Renamo and to encourage the rebels to reintegrate into Mozambique society through the amnesty law, the base line from which the Nairobi talks proceeded. It is noticeable that this commission was initially led by Protestant church groups, rather than the Catholic bishops, who had originally called for dialogue.[138]

The tensions between the Catholic Church and the government had for the most part disappeared by 1989. The Nairobi talks have especially helped in this respect, with the Catholic Church now playing a significant, even central, role in the peace process.

PROTESTANTISM

Protestantism has contributed to one of the most evident contradictions within Renamo's relationships with Christianity. Although Renamo's leadership is largely drawn from people with Catholic sympathies, most of the church-derived external aid it receives comes from Protestant sources. Yet it is the Catholic Church that has suffered most pressures from the government in Mozambique, while the Protestant Churches have in general been left alone.

This has, however, not been true of all Protestant sects. Those that were perceived to be a challenge to Frelimo's authority were at first suppressed. The Jehovah's Witnesses, in particular, suffered in the late 1970s, because they refused to declare their allegiance to Frelimo. The following extract from an article in a late 1975 edition of the Mozambican newspaper *Noticias da Beira* reflects the government response:[139]

> There are found in Mozambique the "Jehovah's Witnesses" and other religious organisations which are allied to imperialism and try, by subversion, to struggle against the ideological line of Frelimo ... We do not tolerate this and it is our concern to pinpoint those agents of the enemy, where they have their bases. We will not accept anyone using religion against us, against our sovereignty ... We did not sacrifice ourselves to establish a religion in Mozambique, nor to create religious arrangements ...We come up against contradictions, when we encounter "Jehovahs" who do not recognise Frelimo.

The response was to harass many of Mozambique's 22,000 strong Jehovah's Witness community, sending them to re-education camps, and later to internal exile in Milange district of Zambezia province. Only in the 1980s did Frelimo become more tolerant.

Moderate Protestantism in Mozambique has nevertheless fared well in general, even in the periods of the government's intolerance, in comparison with the difficulties it encountered under Portuguese colonialism. Its growing stature in Mozambique is in part due to the Mozambique government's increasing awareness of the Protestant Churches' positive contibution in the struggle for majority rule in South Africa. Archbishop Desmond Tutu and Dr Alan Boesak are both treated with the attention given to Heads of State on their visits to Maputo. This is not only an understanding of the positive role the Church can play in the State. It is increasingly recognised that Christianity, especially in the towns, is in a boom period, providing an important constituency of support for Frelimo. Already after N'Komati, the Mozambique government briefed the Protestant Churches so that they could explain the meaning of the Accord to their congregations.[140] The Protestant Churches, unlike the Catholic bishops, have not embarrassed the government by openly calling for negotiations. They have also denounced Renamo in terms similar to those of the Mozambique government.

A reflection of the standing Protestant-based religious groups had *vis-a-vis* the government is the mushrooming of Protestant aid-giving organisations and agencies in Mozambique. World Vision International, the World Council of Churches, Christian Aid and the Lutheran World Federation are all very active in Mozambique. This special relationship is also seen in the Mozambican media, where the Protestant origins of Eduardo Mondlane and Samora Machel are highlighted. The anti-colonial activities of non-Catholic churches during Portuguese rule were also widely publicised. The recognition of the Swiss Mission as a national church is part of this process.[141]

Like the Mozambique government, Renamo has targeted Protestant Christianity for support and recognition. A major increase in the Christian dimension of Renamo appears from around 1985, with the growing influence of the American wing of Renamo. Although initially run by Catholic, mission educated, black Mozambicans, the campaign rapidly became multi-denominational with the return to the United States of the strongly evangelical Tom Schaaf. Schaaf, with his evangelical background and contacts, was able to launch an effective campaign in the US, targetted especially at Protestant organisations and churches. Images such as that of Dhlakama being a devout, god-fearing Christian who always wears a large crucifix around his neck were complemented by descriptions of Renamo's "liberated zones" being the scene of Christian revival in the face of communist aggression. The following description is an example of what was published in church newsletters and depicted in sermons:[142]

> There was an extensive evangelisation programme under way in the liberated zones. 375 churches have been formed in the past year, non-denominational civil-based churches ...

This campaign bore fruit in the form of right-wing support and links with Protestant missionaries and mission societies active in southern Africa: these have become an important source of information and contact for Renamo, as the cases of Ian Grey and the Shekinah Ministries show.[143]

Shekinah has its origins in a split within a white Assemblies of God congregation in Chipinge, a town in the eastern highlands of Zimbabwe, over its work with the black population. Shekinah soon became interested in Mozambique and the possibilities offered there for evangelism. For this reason Rev. Michael Howard, the head of Shekinah, sent a message into Mozambique in January 1985, offering Renamo religious assistance. Receiving a positive response Howard and two assistants, Rodney and Ellie Hein, crossed over to Mozambique and met Renamo military commanders. The result of this meeting was that Shekinah was granted by Renamo "freedom to preach in any area they control".[144]

From mid-1985, Shekinah began to fundraise in South Africa, the USA and elsewhere for its mission work in Renamo areas. Ian Grey was recruited at one of these events in Israel. Shekinah's appeals brought support from several US mission groups. Christ for the Nations Inc (CFNI) in

Dallas, Texas, and Don Ormand Ministries of Melrose, Florida, provided financial support. The End-Time Handmaidens served as Shekinah's US operating base.[145]

With the Zimbabwean authorities becoming aware of pro-Renamo activity amongst church members along the eastern highlands (such as Tom Schaaf), Shekinah decided to base its operations in Mozambique on its Malawian "Blantyre Christian Centre". The pull-out from Zimbabwe came in October 1987, following the reprint in Zimbabwe of an article exposing Shekinah's Renamo links. Ian Grey was arrested while on the final mission to collect left-over possessions in Zimbabwe.

Another Protestant-based group that has been particularly active in supporting Renamo is Frontline Fellowship. Formed by a Cape Town based Baptist pastor, Peter Hammond, its original role was that of a prayer group for South African soldiers who wanted to "take bibles into Angola" during their cross-border raids from Namibia. Since then the Fellowship has grown, and has specialised in recruiting soldiers and ex-military personnel of evangelical persuasion "for aggressive evangelism of 'enemy strongholds'" — the enemy being, according to Frontline Fellowship, "communism, Islam, witchcraft and ...unbiblical heresies like liberation theology in the Christian Church".[146] Interest in Mozambique began in 1985, linked to Shekinah's successful contacts with Renamo. Hammond went into Renamo areas several times in 1985 and 1986, some of these visits being witnessed by Ian Grey. Grey reported that each time he saw him Hammond was leading a group of men that did not strike him as particularly Christian. This has led to speculation that Hammond was closely linked to the SADF and mercenary groups, operating under the disguise of missionary activity.[147]

In 1986, Hammond issued a report based on his experiences the year before in Renamo held areas.[148] The report, entitled "Eyewitness Testimonies of Persecution and Atrocities", was disseminated by the MIO in Washington and by the International Society for Human Rights (ISHR) in Britain and West Germany. It became an important weapon in Renamo's campaigns for external funding in 1986-87. Hammond's report asserted that the Mozambican government was waging a war of "persecution and atrocities" against Christians in the northern provinces of Tete and Zambezia. Much of this report makes unconvincing reading, but as noted above, some of it may be based on real events. Hammond's brief arrest in October 1989, with a group from CERT (as already described), illustrates the continued interest that groups like Frontline Fellowship have in Renamo.

The taking in late 1985 of Renamo's Casa Banana by a joint FAM-ZNA force produced the first conclusive evidence of US evangelical interest in Renamo. Amongst the many captured documents were hundreds of religious tracts, some deriving from Jimmy Swaggart Ministries.[149] The peak of this interest was reached in June 1986 when Renamo organised a religious convention within a day and a half's walk from the Malawian border. Renamo built a camp for the event, with a large church. According to Ian Grey, the meeting attracted over 1,000 Mozambican pastors, catechists and lay preachers, and their wives, from areas as far away as nine days walk. A group of ten American missionaries from various Pentecostal organisations also attended.[150]

The following account by a Mozambican Baptist minister, Rev. Martinho Campos, who was at this convention, provides a different perspective from that provided by Ian Grey:[151]

In June (1986) the bandits demanded to see all the religious leaders in Nauela. There were 120 of us and they forced us to walk to Morrumbala with a guard of 30 men (It is over 300 kms as the crow flies.) We slept on the ground and it took 19 days. We had nothing to eat except leaves or roots. At the end my feet were completely swollen up. In the base at Morrumbala were a group of 20 white Christians, some who were South African and others from the United States among whom was a Portuguese women called Graca who interpreted. The bandits kept questioning me about traders and making threats. They wanted to kill them. Then I and my church colleagues were all questioned by the group of Christians.

I had time to observe what was going on. The camp was divided into three parts. In the first were the captive civilians whose daily work was to find food for the bandits. In the second were the bandits and their leaders and the third part was for whites.

Following the events already described in Chapter 3, which stimulated public criticisms of Renamo in the USA and Malawian action against Renamo, external evangelical support for the rebels has diminished.

Renamo's use of Christian organisations has gone further than fundraising, help for publicity, and back-up for its intelligence and communication network. Renamo's operations reveal a semi-official policy to encourage Christianity as a basis of support. Whilst priests, pastors, catechists and lay preachers have been displaced or sequestrated, they have not suffered the levels of brutality, or even mortality, which other educated groups, such as health workers and teachers, have experienced at the hands of Renamo. In this respect Renamo does not seem to make any particular denominational judgement in its actions.

Further suggestions of Renamo sympathy towards Christianity can be gleaned from accounts of Renamo activities. One report is of particular interest. The congregation of a Seventh Day Adventist church in Zambezia province was at worship when Renamo arrived:

They ordered everybody to move. Then they burned the church with some people whom they called collaborators still inside. Later the bandit chief appeared in the village saying that those who destroyed the church would be shot. They murdered in cold blood 5 people kidnapped in another village, saying they had burnt the church.[152]

The significance of this account is that this particular Renamo group showed, or feigned, remorse in burning the church. The attempt to appease the village indicates a conscious policy. This type of report is not uncommon. Another testimony paints a similar picture of a syncretic mixture of Christianity and brutality. A victim of rebel attack reported the following: "Before stabbing me in the head with a knife, a bandit said a prayer in N'dau. The others kidnapped were ordered to say Amen".[153]

Renamo continues to use Christianity as an instrument from which it can obtain legitimacy and support. When the town of Milange was recaptured by the FAM from Renamo in late 1988, the whole settlement was found razed to the ground, except the church and a house used by priests, suggesting the church had received favourable treatment during Renamo occupation. This pattern has been seen throughout Mozambique.

The Mozambique government has recognised that Christianity has been a source of support for Renamo in rural areas. Reports from Tete and

Zambezia provinces in late 1986 and early 1987 refer to the FAM's activities being targetted at religious establishments in these areas to dissuade them from supporting Renamo. The testimony of 32 people in Chamba district, Zambezia province, illustrates Frelimo's association of Renamo with the church, as well as the continuing hostility of Mozambican government forces in the field towards religion, despite the weakening at that time of the previously hard central government official policy towards the churches: "Frelimo come to our village and ask, 'Why do Renamo like worshipping in church so much? And they burn our churches and destroy our bibles".[154]

ISLAM

Islam is widespread in northern Mozambique amongst the Makua and the Lomwe ethnic groups and among traders in Maputo and the towns. It is also present along the coast in central Mozambique. It can therefore not be ignored as a potential source of support for Renamo. This especially occurred during the anti-religious phase of the government.

In spite of there being over 3 million Islamic believers in Mozambique, there is surpisingly little hard evidence of any large scale support for Renamo amongst it. Renamo appeared to campaign for their sympathies in the mid-1980s, distributing examples of aggressive and tactless actions and statements by Frelimo officials towards the Islamic community in the late seventies.[155] With its historical links with Mozambique, the Omani Sultanate was also targetted externally, as was Saudi Arabia. Within Mozambique, Renamo appears to regard mosques as it does churches. They are left standing whilst the rest of a settlement is destroyed. Renamo has also been reported as having distributed copies of the Koran to Muslim communities in Cabo Delgado as part of its introduction and subsequent campaign for support.

In the post-N'Komati months of uncertainty over who continued to support Renamo, the primarily Muslim Comoros Islands were thought to be a source of aid for Renamo, not least as a South African staging post (as cited above). Similar allegations appeared again in late 1987. It was suggested that the islands were a distribution centre for South African arms to Renamo, transported by dhow to the Mozambique coast. There is however no concrete evidence to support this.

Renamo has approached members of the former Islamic community in Mozambique now resident in Portugal. It has attempted to obtain financial support from them, citing religious intolerance and the case for compensation for their expropriated economic assets in Mozambique as reasons to support Renamo. A press statement by Dr Suleiman Valey Mamede, Director of the Centre for Islamic Studies in Lisbon, reflects the continued ambivalence to Frelimo within this community:

> One-third (sic) of the population of Mozambique is Muslim, but they are not represented in all levels of the community. I openly say that Frelimo continues to treat Muslim Mozambicans as second-class citizens.[156]

It is said that this campaign had little success, having been seen in Lisbon as political opportunism.[157]

NEO-TRADITIONALISM

For the majority of the people of Mozambique, however, the religions that most concern them are their ancestral ones. These involve contact with their ancestors, usually through spirit mediums. They are concerned with rights to land and the means of ensuring the land's fertility, including cults of rain-making. These cults are not necessarily in conflict in people's minds with a degree of commitment to Christianity or Islam. But they draw on, and give coherence to, feelings and needs far deeper than Frelimo's materialism has been able to touch. For these reasons, this survey of the domestic dimension to Renamo's activities must conclude by returning to the myth of Andre Matsangaissa and exploring its broader significance.

One of the most depressing aspects of Mozambique today is the apparent resemblance to the country's situation in the late nineteenth century. After eight decades of wars generated by the Indian Ocean slave trade, Portuguese rule was confined to the coastal enclaves of Lourenço Marques (Maputo), Sofala (south of the present Beira), Quelimane and Mozambique Island, with tiny stockades at Mazaro, Sena and Tete along the Zambezi River. The interior was controlled by independent African chiefs and war lords, some in loose alliance with the Portuguese or with each other, some maintaining armed resistance, but very few of them creating even a temporary stability and even fewer establishing dynasties. They obtained guns and powder by exporting ivory and slaves. They fed themselves through the domestic slave-labour of thousands of captive women or by raiding for food, much of which having previously been imported.

For most of the nineteenth century, Mozambique was a net importer of food. Among the most powerful of these war lords was Manuel de Sousa or Gouveia, a Portuguese ally who ruled from a stockade on Gorongosa mountain and who laid claim to territory along both banks of the Zambezi River. One of the ways in which he, and competing rulers like the Ferrão family at Sena or the Pereiras of Makanga, maintained their power was through the elaboration of ancestral cults, their successors maintaining contact after death through spirit mediums, legitimising their claims to the land they formerly governed.

There have been disturbing echoes of this in the account given in the earlier pages of this chapter. In 1990, Frelimo's power too is largely confined to the coastal enclaves of Maputo, Beira, Quelimane and Nacala, themselves overwhelmed with refugees and reachable only by air. What security exists in the interior is maintained through a system of fortified towns or stockades, often manned by troops from Zimbabwe or Tanzania and themselves attracting refugee populations. Huge numbers of people have, as in the late nineteenth century, fled to Malawi, Zimbabwe and Zambia. Renamo depends for its internal recruitment on something closely akin to the old internal slave-trade while armies of women are forcibly recruited as cultivators or, as in the aftermath of slave-trading, are passed from hand to hand for their sexual services. Food is also obtained by raiding, including the food imports from international aid agencies on which the country depends for survival. Dhlakama maintains on Gorongosa mountain the stockade previously described, and spirit cults have developed around the name of his predecessor, Matsangaissa.

This does not mean, as journalists from the far right to the far left habitually assume, that, with the withdrawal of the Portuguese, Mozambique has simply reverted to its immemorial tribal animosities. Two facts are of paramount importance. The first is that there was nothing timeless or remotely "traditional" about the circumstances in which Mozambicans lived in the late nineteenth century. They were the product of the slave-trade which, from the institution of the British naval patrol off the coast of West Africa in 1807, moved into the south Atlantic and round the Cape to the coast of East Africa. The stockade, the competing war lords, were Mozambique's defensive answer to the demand for slaves and the cycle of insecurity which followed bore little relation to, say, the circumstances in which people had lived in 1750.

Secondly, it would be wrong to make too close an identification between the war lords of the late nineteenth century and individual Renamo leaders. As has been described, Renamo operates most of the time as a disciplined army, made up of separate units but linked by regular radio contacts and able to respond rapidly to fresh instructions. These units do not occupy territory. They move in, they destroy, and they move on to fresh targets. Territorial religious cults are peripheral to such activities. They are, as has been noted, fringe units whose behaviour corresponds more closely with what the Portuguese in the late nineteenth century called "bandits", Frelimo's label for Renamo until recently. But the organisation of the present assault on Mozambique is entirely different in its aims and organisation from nineteenth century political strategies. While the current insecurity may be throwing up patterns of response imitative of the past, the real war lords of the 1980s have been located not in Mozambique but in Pretoria.

There is a good deal of evidence that Renamo has manipulated the religious beliefs of ordinary Mozambicans. Indeed, at this level, its ideological management has been far more sophisticated than anything attempted in its external propaganda. One of Renamo's first actions in areas it enters for the first time has been to embrace whatever religious authority is present. The following scenario is typical:[158]

> In October 1986, when the bandits occupied Gile, they did not destroy the church, and instead invited the townspeople to carry on with their prayers. But this apparent freedom only lasted until the bandits had consumed all the goods they found in the Gile shops. Before attacking the building itself, the bandits began to ambush believers on their way to church. Traditionally Catholics attending church wear their best clothes; the bandits would order them to take these clothes and hand them over. At the same time MNR gangs looted nearby villages and raped young girls in front of their parents.

Another account from a Muslim community at Meloco in the Montpuez region of Cabo Delgado mirror images this scenario. Renamo entered the area with the passive support of its inhabitants, destroyed the communal villages but left the mosques standing. Renamo then tried to build on this base of support by promising that "the whites for whom they worked" would return to Mozambique to rule, bringing sought-after commodities for the people. As Margaret Hall has succintly pointed out, this bears "shades of cargo-cult in conditions of absolute deprivation". As happened at Gile with the passage of time, the situation deteriorated and some people tried to escape. In response, Renamo started killing defectors and began to force popular participation in rituals, calling upon unfamiliar ancestral spirits (at least for the villagers in this area) to kill all Frelimo soldiers or at least change their bullets on firing into water.[159]

Another example of the manipulation of religious beliefs is the widespread employment by Renamo of *feiticeiros* (witchdoctors) and *curandeiros* (healers). An account from central Mozambique of a female witchdoctor, named Maria Nhabele, illustrates how this system can work. Maria supervised religious ceremonies every time a group of rebels departed from base on active service. João Fabião, a former Renamo combatant, describes what she said and did:[160]

> They say our struggle is for the spirits. So when we left on missions the witchdoctor (Maria) carried out a ceremony with a goat. She mixed the goat's blood with medicines and gave it to us to drink. She said "It's so you don't die when you meet the massotcha (soldiers)."

Renamo Commanders were treated differently: "Maria Nhabele recommended to the commanders that they bring her the inner organs of newborn children so that she could make drugs for them".

This distinguishing of ritual between the rank and file and the leadership is significant. Elsewhere in this study similar divisions are shown, be it in ritual, living space or dress. Renamo can be seen in terms of binary oppositions. There are plenty of examples of rebel commanders having resident *feiticeiros* in their bases to strengthen their authority, and to use them as a supernatural guarantee for success in their raids.

As captured documents from Garagua base suggest, Dhlakama also used important territorial spirit mediums to strengthen his position after the death of Matsangaissa. It may well be that access to such spiritual guidance is used by Dhlakama and his senior commanders as a symbol of their power.[161] There are examples of this too in southern Mozambique. A captured rebel base in Gaza province illustrates this well. The base was controlled by a former Frelimo officer who had married his daughter to a *feiticeiro*. With this legitimacy he was able to "recruit many people".[162] In another incident, the depth of superstition amongst the rebels is shown. A captured Renamo operational register noted that a wounded rebel died "due to diabolic spirits which were in a 500 metical note he stole".[163] Dhlakama, too, is known to have told his combatants that the "spirits" of Renamo will pursue and kill anyone who defects.[164]

A conversation on Inhaca Island, however, suggests a different perspective on some of this evidence:[165]

> Antonio: "I came back from Joni at the beginning of 1984. We have since had big storms, a hunger that kills, no work. I cannot find a wife. I need to pay lobolo. You know what that is? Times are hard. They (Frelimo) have angered the ancestors, eh, we must make them pleased again".
> Intwr: "How can you do this?"
> Antonio: "Frelimo will be shown in the wrong".

This view is not unique. It clearly indicates one area of potential co-existence with, if not positive support for, Renamo, the disasters which have overtaken Mozambique being blamed not on Renamo as human agents but on Renamo as the expressions of the ancestors' united anger over Frelimo's policies.

Frelimo's agrarian policy, and, in particular, its policy of villagisation have increasingly been a topic of academic research and debate on the extent to which they may have contributed to Renamo's successes in rural Mozambique.[166] This shift in academic interest reflects the developing understanding that Renamo's growth in the early 1980s can not be explained in the purely one-dimensional terms of South African destabilisation, although this probably remains the most important single contribution.

Collectivism is, in theory, a logical and practical response to one of the major problems Frelimo faced in newly independent Mozambique. The young government had hoped that the setting up of communal villages would be an efficient method of managing its redistribution to the peasantry of scarce resources and services, such as marketing services, health care and education, by communalising peasants rather than allowing them to stay in highly dispersed traditional family units. Communal farming was also believed to be far more productive than individual cash cropping. This is why the basic economic policy decided at Frelimo's Third Party Congress in 1977 was targetted at transforming the rural sector into communal villages functioning as co-operatives.

As in Tanzania this was not the only attraction villagisation had for the authorities. It also appeared to be the easiest method for bringing the peasantry (90%) under direct state control. In many areas of Mozambique this would be the first experience of a modern centralised State, Portuguese colonialism having remained a remote experience for many. In many areas of Niassa province it was, for example, only in the late 1960s that a Portuguese presence was felt and that cash began to be used for transactions in trade and barter.

Villagisation was also an attractive response to internal insecurity. As early as 1975, Frelimo was already talking about setting up collective farms as a way of protecting the population from rebel incursions from Malawi, the incursions of what became Africa Livre. In spite of these attempts to separate the local population from Africa Livre by putting them into communal farms, it would appear that Africa Livre grew in strength and size until its external support was cut off. It is an early and important example of a pattern repeated with Renamo in the 1980s.[167]

Villagisation began as an optional policy, except, as the above example illustrates, in areas where the government felt particularly insecure. Large-scale forced villagisation only began in the early 1980s in part response to a Renamo rearmed and refurbished by South Africa. The academic debate has recently focused on whether villagisation, before it became a crude, forced and hasty response to rebel insurgency, was a universally unpopular programme amongst the peasantry providing Renamo with a campaigning base from which to recruit.

The answer seems to be that this is true for some areas, but not at all for others. The issue that really lies at the heart of the villagisation policies is that they needed to be implemented with sensitivity, especially in respect of geographical, regional and traditional structures and variations. Experiments were successful in the south amongst the Gaza-Nguni, who had historical experience of living in larger village units. Although there was some opposition in the Limpopo valley to the setting-up of communal villages following the 1977 floods, this was mostly over their poor location and, later on, in 1983, over the poor protection given against Renamo's attempts to dominate the area. This region is Frelimo's heartland. It has produced all three of its Presidents — Eduardo Mondlane, Samora Machel and Joaquim Chissano. It has also witnessed some of the most disgusting massacres of the war so far, several of which stylistically can only be Renamo's doing. Their experience of atrocities and the widespread use of child combatants in the area explain further the reluctance of the local population to join Renamo. For this very reason Renamo has designated the region a destruction zone.[168]

This is not the case in other areas of Mozambique. Villagisation has actively encouraged the peasantry to support Renamo. The response to Africa Livre is an early example of a pattern which Margaret Hall has compared to a "cancerous growth, in which abnormal cells proliferate and spread throughout an already debilitated system".[169]

The debilitated system is the result of the government's policies, in particular its Soviet-style control over land and other national resources as decided at the Third Congress. This created an over-centralised economy which displayed all the worst features of Portuguese bureaucracy and Eastern European central planning. While it is fair to say that programmes in health and education were dramatically successful, the economic policies were ill-suited to a basically peasant society. The State farms were marred by misjudgement, misuse and squandering of the large amount of investment put into them. The basic agricultural needs of the peasantry were meanwhile generally ignored. At Frelimo's Fourth Congress this policy was recognised to have failed and decisions were taken designed to reverse the process. But sadly, due to the expanded war, it has not been possible to implement these reforms widely.

Over-centralisation, preoccupation with the "cement cities", unreasonable State regulation of prices, the additional collapse of industrial production of consumer goods, and the lack of surplus foreign exchange to purchase goods abroad — all these factors increased the lack of incentive under an increasingly worthless local currency, which, in any case, found little worthwhile in exchange on the shelves. All this contributed to discontent amongst the peasantry, especially among those who were now obliged to sell at set rates to the State stores and only in Mozambique itself. In return for very little, many peasant farmers saw themselves as being impoverished even further to feed distant and seemingly irrelevant towns. They therefore stopped attempting to produce a surplus. Where they could they returned to a subsistence economy, which in turn created greater hardships in the urban areas which relied on peasant production for their needs.

Because of economic degeneration the policy of villagisation was intensified in an attempt to increase the productivity of the ailing state sector. Government encouragement of rapid villagisation brought about peasant discontent and resistance, when it became obvious that the Government had little to offer in return. Zealous officials enforced the policy in order to gain praise and promotion, with an iron-fisted response to resistance, such as denying food aid or even burning down the property of recalcitrant peasants who refused to move. In such areas, Renamo has found a peasantry with no great desire to inform on them, even an active welcome.

What makes the analogy of villagisation and Renamo with a "cancerous growth" so real is that as rebel activity increased and spread so the Government's position hardened. A rapid expansion of the villagisation policy occurred. It has been estimated that betwen 1981 and 1985 villagisation increased in Nampula province by around 400%.[170] The authorities' response to Renamo of bringing the peasantry into protected villages now only antagonised the situation further. Villagisation has brought no more security to the Mozambique government than it did to the Portuguese with their *aldeamentos*, or to the Rhodesians with their PVs (protected villages).

Various academic case studies have now looked at peasant response to villagisation in Mozambique. It is clear from these that, in Cabo Delgado and Nampula provinces, the villagisation process itself contributed to the conditions under which Renamo found little hostility, and indeed, some support.

It appears that the villagisation process itself can create or exploit social tensions already present within the peasantry affected. Such tensions are thought to be why communities that had no knowledge of Renamo until the late 1980's, like some in the far north of Mozambique, welcomed the rebels on initial contact.

It seems that in some cases a particular clan or lineage on whose land the communal village was constructed obtained from the status *de facto* political and economic hegemony over the other lineages or clans that had been forced to settle at the village. In this way the dominant group was able to command any leadership position existing in the new village — be it the presidency of the consumers' co-operative or head of the local party apparatus. These lineage or clan segments take advantage of the situation by sharing any privileges they have obtained only with their matrimonial allies and blood kin. Tensions arise in the village on this account. There are reports of communal villages splitting down lineage lines over such issues, and resolving them by each lineage setting up its own village, only to have the authorities force all these new settlements back into the original communal village, because of the challenge to State policy and ideology.[171]

This unforeseen social stratification of the communal villages is clearly a weakness which Renamo can exploit to obtain support. Its tactic of first killing the village secretary or whoever carries a symbol of authority linked to Frelimo is, therefore, not only part of its campaign against the State. It is also responding to lineage politics of rural Mozambique as an additional way in which to obtain support. This combination is at its most dangerous for the government when one of the leaders of an underprivileged lineage is a popular ex-chief who has suffered humiliation from Frelimo. Other disenchanted social strata — the young in particular, who have been unable to obtain secondary school education or upward mobility in the village structure because it has fallen into the hands of the dominant lineage's elders — probably find life with Renamo offering the only alternative, providing some excitement and the potential of authority denied to them in their villages — albeit by the barrel of a gun. Some villagers have also attempted to avoid conflict in what Renamo would designate "tax" zones by establishing symbolic non-functional communal villages (often with the knowledge of local Frelimo officials), while still living on their ancestral lands. In this way the villagers hoped to placate both Renamo and Frelimo.[172]

Equally important, however, has been Frelimo's gift to Renamo at the level of religious protest. Ancestral cults, as was noted earlier, involve communications with the ancestors, often through *mhondoro* or spirit mediums but overlapping with the roles of *feiticeiros* and *curandeiros*. They deal with such matters as physical and spiritual health, and crucially with rights to land and the land's fertility, including cults of rain-making. In the wake of Frelimo's villagisation policies, Renamo's promotion of the roles of *mhondoro* and *feiticeiro* had renewed relevance. As the Governor of Manica province (in a surprisingly open statement for the Mozambique government at the time) stated in 1981:[173]

> All peasants are individualistic. At first sight they think that all collective life must be bad. The resistance movement has built on this, encouraging people to live in the traditional way. It promotes tribal differences and the power of *mhondoro*. In rural areas many families have at least one member fighting for MNR.

Yet the evidence is mounting of a different way of interpreting this testimony. From the mid-nineteenth century onwards, one of the ways in which dispossessed peasantries in the region have tried to secure their rights has been through their assertion of the authority of the ancestors over invading armies. In the Shire valley in the 1860s for example, the invading Massingiri who destroyed the rain shrine of Mbona found they had provoked a drought which was only broken when they rebuilt the shrine and made appropriate reparations. The despoilers had to come to terms with the spirits of the land before they could rule. Communication with these spirits was made in the local language through the local spirit medium, in this instance the wife of Mbona, the python god of the Shire valley. Such stories were repeated throughout Mozambique as the Portuguese imposed colonial rule and their policies of forced labour, the language and cults of ancestral religions being used not in collaboration with invading armies but in an effort to control them. It seems increasingly probable that the neo-traditional religious aspect to Renamo's activities springs less from Renamo's manipulative propaganda than from partially successful attempts by ordinary people to secure for themselves some personal security and continued access to land while the war brought by Renamo rages around them.

This is certainly the conclusion to be drawn from the remarkable account by Karl Maier of the spirit of Mongoi (Mungoi) and his dealings with the Matsangas:[174]

> For two years, the legend has filtered out of Manjacaze in southern Mozambique: the story of a pocket of territory known as Mongoi, no bigger than 15 square miles, mysteriously untouched by the massacres and battles which have swirled all around during the long war between the Frelimo government and the Renamo rebels.
>
> "Nothing can happen in the land of Mongoi", Carlos Tchlene, a local Frelimo official, told me. "The bandits can come, eat and leave and Frelimo troops can come, eat and leave, they just pass each other."
>
> "The story began on 22 December 1987, when Renamo, known here as the Matsanga, attacked the village, looting huts and kidnapping women and children. Mongoi said he appeared later that day and found his nephew, Armando, preparing to flee with the rest of the people. "I asked: "What is happening in the land of Mongoi?" and my nephew told me: "There is war here now". I asked what this war was about and he did not know. So I told Armando to call a meeting with the Matsanga.
>
> "When the group arrived, all of them sat down except their commander. I asked him why he would not sit down and he said he did not want to. So I told him: "You know, I am not like you; I am already dead and a spirit cannot die twice". Then the commander dropped his gun and sat down. "I asked him why there was war. "I heard that you want to attack the government but is Mongoi

part of the government?" His answer was no. "Why do you take away children, the women and the old people?" I asked. "Do women and children make war with you in the bush?" Again his answer was no. I told him I was physically dead, but I had the powers to defend my children in the land of Mongoi. The commander asked forgiveness and he would tell the others not to attack the land of Mongoi."

Medicine men have long influenced Renamo leaders, sharing a common enemy in Frelimo, which tried to suppress "reactionary" ways. Frelimo itself is split on Mongoi. Officials in Xai Xai, capital of Gaza province, are said to have advocated eliminating him by whatever means. Local officials, however, show great respect and some even join in Mongoi's religious ceremonies. "The party can do nothing here," said Mr Tchlene, the Frelimo man. "We have no alternative but to respect the people's belief in Mongoi".

His view appears to be shared by Joaquim Chissano, Mozambique's President, who has ordered that Mongoi be left in peace. Mongoi said his method was simple: "When the Matsanga commanders have a problem, they call their *curandeiros* [medicine men] for advice. I appear in one of the *curandeiros*, because Mongoi can appear in any person. I tell them the solution to their problem is to let the women and children go.

The appearance of Mongoi is by no means unique. In 1987 reports drifted out of Renamo's heartland of Gorongosa that a spirit medium called Samantanje had established a "neutral zone" on one of the Gorongosa mountains by convincing Renamo commanders that any abuse of the people in his "neutral zone" would be met by spiritual retribution through death from a cobra or a lion.[175] From the isolated town of Alto Molocue, some 1000 km north of the "land" of Mongoi, have also come reports of a variation to similar attempts by Mozambicans to create an island of tranquillity for themselves: this time in war-torn Zambezia. Drawing inspiration from Manuel Antonio, a 28-year-old traditional healer, the community formed a volunteer army called *Naprama*, a Macua word meaning "irresistible force". Manuel Antonio claimed to have died of measles, to have spent six days in a grave, and to have been revived by God and told to free people held by Renamo against their will. He then ascended into local mountains to commune with the spirits.[176] David Beresford describes what followed:[177]

For three months they taught him the magical properties of roots and herbs, and then *Naprama* came down from the mountain to lead the crusade.

He approached the local Frelimo commanders to get their permission, and called for volunteers whom he inducted into his army at a magical ceremony. He would place an AK47 assault rifle on the ground and stand on it — to symbolise triumph over the gun — and, one by one, his recruits would present themselves to be cut on the arms and chest with a razor blade, special *muti* (magic potion) being rubbed into the wounds.

The effect of the *muti* was to render them invisible to bullets, provided certain taboos were respected. The magic was negated if one ate the flesh of a certain type of deer, stepped over a log from a particular tree, left a wooden spoon standing in a pot, made love to a women and, above all, if one killed another person. The movement is pacifist, their aim to drive the bandits off, their weapons to frighten, not to kill.

Naprama is said to be successful, attracting hundreds of supporters.

Reports since March 1990 describe its warriors as being dressed in loin cloths, wielding spears or machetes with red ribbons pinned to them (the symbol of loyalty to *Naprama*) and rattling tin cans as they advanced through the bush into rebel occupied territory. In this way many Renamo camps were captured and hundreds of Mozambicans freed, the rebels having fled convinced that it was futile to fight against the spiritual protection given to *Naprama's* followers through vaccination with the magical *muti*.

These are clear cases of ancestral spirits being used against Renamo to achieve a local peace. But these accounts are also moving from another perspective. They are examples of how, if there is a solution to Mozambique's problems, it will be found by drawing deeply on the skills, resources and sensibilities of Mozambique's own culture.

5 PEACE AND NATIONAL RECONCILIATION

The Mozambican authorities recognised as early as 1984 that Renamo's 20,000 strong rebel force could not be defeated by military means only. President Machel's decision that Mozambique would participate in the proximity talks in Pretoria in that year is a reflection of such thinking. Although these talks collapsed, the Mozambique government continued to pursue a dual strategy of military and diplomatic initiatives in the search for a cessation of the war.

The Mozambican churches have made an important contribution to this process. The Mozambican Christian Council (CCM), the umbrella body uniting 17 of the country's Protestant churches, became involved in 1984, believing that "dialogue is the way forward for peace in any dispute". The CCM approached President Machel, and obtained his go-ahead for a low-key and confidential dialogue with Renamo.[1]

Government hostility towards the Catholic Church continued until 1988. While this denied it any official backing for its independent contacts with Renamo, the fact that its relations with the government were seen to be cool gave the Catholic Church an access to Renamo denied to the Protestant churches. This was particularly noticeable in 1985 and 1986 when the influence of Fernandes and Correia in Renamo was at its height. Both were devout Catholics. Although they announced that Renamo no longer recognised Machel as a "valid interlocutor" (and therefore refused to negotiate with the Mozambique government) a Catholic lay organisation, the International Centre for Peace, engaged in trying to bring about a round-table meeting between the rebels and the government, continued to be in contact with Renamo.[2]

The Catholic Church in Mozambique began, for its part, to call openly from 1984 for dialogue between the Government and Renamo.[3] By 1987, as the war spread further, the Church became even more vocal in its calls for dialogue. An episcopal letter circulated in April 1987 particularly upset the government. This pastoral letter of the Catholic Bishops in Mozambique, published by the Archdiocese of Maputo, and entitled "A Paz que O Povo Quer" (The Peace that the People Want), implied in its call for dialogue that the Government and Renamo enjoyed equal legitimacy.[4] In late 1987, President Chissano told a visiting Church delegation that the Government's problems with the Catholic Church derived from their basic approach of condemning everybody's violence: "They also condemn anyone who gives aid to any of the parties. By that they are putting South Africa, Tanzania and Zimbabwe on the same level". Chissano added that certain "pastoral letters" and Sunday preachings almost constituted political rallies, but that "I am in constant conversations with the Roman Catholic hierarchy in the country and explain with great patience to them

that some of their utterances can be construed as illegal and subversive".[5]
Dialogue between the Catholic hierarchy and President Chissano was also
facilitated by a cousin to the President, Joaquim Mabuianga, a Catholic
priest.

The peace initiatives of the Churches got underway seriously in late
1987 when six members of the CCM approached President Chissano for re-
confirmation that they might make contact with Renamo. Chissano later
confirmed to an official delegation from the World Council of Churches
(WCC) in December 1987 that he had encouraged the Churches to talk to
Renamo, as long as they followed the following guidelines:[6]

(i) Churches — Both locally and ecumenically, such as through AACC and
WCC — not only should feel free but are encouraged to contact "the other
side" (the Bandits) with clear understanding that these contacts are not construed as paving the way for any negotiations with them as a political entity.

(ii) The main purpose of such contacts would be to pursuade the "other side"
to stop assassinating their own people and devastating their own country.

(iii) In case of future positive developments, churches locally may have to help
with the reintegration of the rebels into Mozambican society.

With Chissano's further "green light" to the Mozambican churches, preparations got underway for them to make contact with Renamo. The AACC
and WCC promised to provide funds to cover the costs for Mozambican
church leaders to visit the USA and Kenya for meetings with Renamo representatives.[7]

The CCM's first contact with Renamo was made in February 1988 in
Washington, D.C. while a delegation was visiting the USA on invitation from
the National Council of Churches of Christ. This first meeting was regarded
by the church leaders as disappointing. They found the Renamo delegate
out of touch and out of tune with the situation inside Mozambique.[8]

This visit to the USA marked the joining of the Protestant forces with the
Catholic Church. Tensions between the Mozambican government and the
Catholic Church (as already described above) had made the CCM hesitant
to be seen too close to the latter. With improving relations between the
Catholic Church and the Mozambique government in early 1988, the CCM
felt it appropriate to invite the Catholic Archbishop of Maputo (now
Cardinal), Alexandre dos Santos, to be a member of the delegation "with
the same rights as a leader of a member church".[9]

In May and October 1988, two CCM and two Catholic representatives
made contact with the Kenyan authorities, seeking assistance and facilities
for the holding in Nairobi of a meeting between the churchmen and
Renamo. A group of church leaders once more met President Chissano in
August, this time to report on their preliminary findings. They were
encouraged by the President to pursue their conclusion that only a meeting with Renamo's internal leadership, rather than its external representatives, was likely to bear fruit.[10]

The Churches' initiative to bring about dialogue between Renamo and
the Government became public in November 1988. Details of their objectives were revealed at a press conference given by the Rev Sigue Banze, a
Methodist minister and Secretary-General of the CCM. Rev. Banze
announced that a "Peace and Reconciliation Commission", headed by the
Anglican Bishop of Maputo, Dinis Sengulane, would attempt to meet
Renamo leaders and convince them to accept the government's amnesty.

As a preliminary to direct talks the Commission would send a letter to Renamo outlining its objectives.[11]

A first meeting was held in Nairobi in December 1988. Only the CCM was represented. A request to meet President Dhlakama of Renamo "in order to talk about peace" was made. In February, 1989, both the CCM and the Catholic representatives met three internal Renamo officials, sent by Dhlakama. The Commission again requested a meeting with Dhlakama himself but this did not take place until August. Kenyan officials were present at both these meetings.[12]

These meetings convinced the Peace and Reconciliation Commission that Renamo, although still extremely hostile to the Mozambique government, was serious about wanting to end the war. Other objectives of the Commission, such as obtaining a guarantee that Renamo would not continue to commit further atrocities, were unfulfilled, with Renamo consistently denying its involvement in them.

The Commission hoped to meet Dhlakama and his delegation in Nairobi, first in March, then in April, and then in three dates in July. Each time Renamo was unable to oblige, for political and logistical reasons. Meanwhile the Mozambique government drew up a document on the basic principles with which the Churches and Kenyan officials could, in their view, hold a dialogue with Renamo. This document (Frelimo's 12 Principles for Dialogue) was approved by the Frelimo Central Committee and circulated to specific embassies in Maputo in June 1989, as well as leaked to the press (an earlier draft had circulated in Maputo in 1988).[13]

Renamo held its so-called First Congress in June 1989 also, timed to capitalise on the build-up to serious talks in Nairobi. For this reason Renamo's language at the Congress was far more conciliatory than is usual in its propaganda against the Mozambique government.

The pace quickened on July 9. Chissano met President Mugabe in Beira to discuss the on-going attempts to bring about talks in Nairobi and a possible ceasefire with Renamo. It was also later revealed that President Chissano had asked President Mugabe to act as a mediator at this meeting. On July 17, President Chissano gave a press conference and issued a statement on the progress of the Churches' initiative. At this conference what has now been called Frelimo's "12 Principles" for peace was officially unveiled. It was described by the Mozambique Government as a "nonpaper" or as an "aide-memoire" (Appendix 3). Chissano also revealed that he had invited President Moi to visit Maputo to discuss the progress of the talks with Renamo, and that the Church leaders were that very day waiting in Nairobi for Renamo to turn up for the talks, but that there had been no sign of the rebel delegation so far.[14]

The reason why Renamo did not reach Nairobi for the talks is that on July 12, on the eve of the Renamo delegation's departure, an offensive within Gorongosa district by a joint ZNA-FAM force narrowly missed capturing Dhlakama and his assembled delegation. The light aircraft chartered to take them to Kenya was shot up and damaged. It had to abort its mission to collect the rebels to take them to Nairobi. Renamo denounced the attack as "Frelimo radicals trying to sabotage the Nairobi meeting".[15] President Chissano admitted that the offensive had taken place and that an aircraft was intercepted and attacked. But he denied that it was timed to affect the talks, saying that the offensive was planned in accordance with the normal calendar of operations, and that the armed forces and the bishops were not informed of each other's plans.[16]

At the end of President Moi's two-day visit to Maputo, Chissano announced that President Moi had agreed to join President Mugabe as mediators in the conflict.[17] The two Presidents were to be, depending on how talks with the rebels progressed, the core of a possibly larger mediating group of African Heads of State. The decision to invite President Moi to become a mediator was warmly welcomed by Renamo. Dhlakama's response, made in a statement issued by Renamo's Lisbon office on July 25, confirmed that there was no objection to Zimbabwean participation in the talks and that he was waiting to hear from President Moi so that he could begin peace negotiations.[18] The statement was timed to coincide with the opening of Frelimo's Fifth Party Congress, whose central theme was expected to be the party's attempts to achieve peace. The initiatives of the Mozambican government on the peace progress were further endorsed on July 30 at the Fifth Congress. The Congress decided that the efforts to speak with Renamo should continue, but that it should be made clear that "we are speaking of people who have broken laws, and who are therefore criminals".[19] At a rally in Maputo marking the end of the Congress, Chissano addressed a large crowd summarising it, and putting the talks with Renamo into context, by saying: "We want peace, but only the peace that strengthens and consolidates our independence, the peace that eliminates discrimination".[20]

The endorsement of the peace initiative by the Party Congress was important for Frelimo. Although party traditionalists such as Marcelino dos Santos and Jorge Rebelo continued to advocate a purely military response to Renamo, the party's moderate wing continued to dominate. This tactically more flexible group — the Transport Minister, Armando Guebuza, the Security Minister, Mariano Matsinhe, the Foreign Minister, Pascoal Mocumbi, and the State Inspector, Raimundo Pachinupa — supported dialogue with Renamo. What has been uncertain is what offer should be made to the rebels in addition to amnesty, the latter being accepted as not having been succesful on its own.[21]

At the end of July, Presidents Moi and Mugabe met at the OAU in Addis Ababa, to plan their mediation role. On August 4, President Chissano visited Harare to discuss the talks with President Mugabe and to brief him on the Mozambican government's position before the scheduled talks between the Church leaders and Renamo commenced on August 8 in Nairobi.[22] In a final diplomatic flurry before the talks, President Mugabe flew to Nairobi on August 7 to review and endorse with President Moi the guidelines for the meeting between the Churches' representatives and the Renamo delegation. The meeting lasted five hours, with the Presidents issuing a joint communiqué stating that "the two Presidents are greatly encouraged by the spirit and willingness of the two sides to the conflict to undertake serious discussion to find a peaceful solution to the conflict". Remaining in Nairobi to be available for any consultations that might arise from the talks were Mozambique's Transport and Communications Minister, Armando Guebuza, and its Minister of Information, Teodato Hunguana.[23]

The Renamo delegation had been in Nairobi since August 3 preparing for the talks. Led by Dhlakama, it was also comprised of five senior officials, Vincente Ululu, João Almirante, Raul Domingos, Faustino Adriano and Cristovão Soares. The Church delegation was comprised of Anglican

Bishop Dinis Sengulane, the Roman Catholic Bishop of Maputo, Cardinal Alexandre dos Santos, the Roman Catholic Bishop of Beira, Jaime Gonçalves, and the Chairman of the CCM, Pastor Osias Mucache.[24] Talks in earnest began on August 8, with the leader of the Church delegation, Cardinal dos Santos, presenting to the Renamo delegation the Mozambique government's "12 Principles" for dialogue. Although the content of these talks has not been made public, Cardinal dos Santos described them as "open and frank", adding that "Renamo says it wants peace, and will work for peace ... So does the Mozambican government. But there will be difficulties in reaching agreement on several points".[25] The nature of these points became public on August 15 when Renamo produced its reply to the Mozambique government's 12 points with its "16 Point Declaration" (see Appendix 2), the day after having given them to the Church delegation. The first round of Nairobi talks ended on August 14, with an agreement to meet again when President Moi saw fit. The church leaders returned to Maputo and briefed President Chissano the following day.

The differences between Frelimo's "12 Principles" and Renamo's "16 Points" have now become clear. Issues such as the demand for the withdrawal of all foreign troops from Mozambique as a prerequisite for a ceasefire could be flexibly negotiated, in spite of contradictory statements made in Lisbon by Manuel Frank after the talks ended. Renamo was also prepared to drop its outright demands for multi-party elections by conceding instead the adoption of "a principle sanctifying the people's right of suffrage and the cessation of armed struggle". Its declaration that "it is not Renamo's intention to change the existing order in Mozambique through armed force" was aimed at being conciliatory. The major stumbling point was, however, Renamo's point five which stated that:

> Renamo is an active political force in Mozambique's political arena. Any peace solution must take into consideration this reality as well as traditions, culture, present stage of development and other present realities.

This challenged the fundamental base of the Mozambique government's initiative which had been in place ever since its launching in late 1987. As individuals, through the amnesty law or even through any negotiated agreement to end the war, Renamo cadre members might be allowed to participate freely in elections. What the Mozambique government found utterly unacceptable was recognition of Renamo as a political party. President Chissano and the Mozambique government consistently argued that Renamo had only obtained support through violence, fear and external backing and that its origins and tactics demonstrated that it did not have a legitimate political base. This is why Chissano described Renamo's 16 Points as "meaningless", when asked by the press for his opinion of the document.[26]

Meanwhile, Renamo in Nairobi was enjoying its newly found attention, with a series of meetings with diplomatic officials from the US, USSR, West Germany, Portugal, France and Italy. Renamo also continued to keep up the pressure for concessions on Maputo. It announced on August 18 that they "would allow the Nacala corridor to function normally without interferences". As already stated above, this declaration was probably the culmination of other independent negotiations, although the timing was calculated for maximum effect, rather than being the result of the "fruitful talks" under Kenyan chairmanship that it had announced as having been achieved.[27]

President Chissano's response to Renamo's "16 Points" as being "mean-ingless" and as having "no significance at all", marked Renamo's return to a harder line. In a radio interview, broadcast on August 29 in Lisbon, Dhlakama reacted strongly to Chissano's statement, claiming that Frelimo "is not ready to talk to Renamo about true peace in Mozambique". Dhlakama also reiterated his demand that "Frelimo must recognise Renamo as a political party", but stated that unconditional talks could continue. Dhlakama also revealed that Renamo had backtracked on one of its earlier concessions in which it had accepted the "existing order" in Mozambique. He now stated that the Mozambican people should be "able to vote for the political system of their choice".[28]

There was another reason why both sides hardened positions after their initial flexibility. This was the developments in Angola following the late June (Gabodolite) agreement in Zaire, at which 17 Heads of State and Government ratified a cease-fire and agreement to begin peace talks between the Angolan government and the UNITA rebels. What initially seemed a model process for Mozambique began to fall apart. UNITA chal-lenged the interpretation of the agreement, which was followed by the breakdown of the ceasefire. These events contributed to the Mozambique government's return to a more cautious assesment of what the peace pro-cess could give Mozambique. The same is true of Renamo, which had been watching the developments in Angola with keen interest. It is interesting to note that these distinctions have now become blurred, with Mozambique being regarded as ripe for a peaceful cessation of its war as Angola.

President Moi attempted to keep the dialogue going by organising a sec-ond round of talks in Nairobi on August 29. It was hoped that a compro-mise set of principles drawn up by Kenyan officials would revive the dia-logue. But these further talks were not a success. The Churchmen returned to Mozambique on 1 September.[29] Renamo had refused to compromise and to be flexible over the four main points, namely:

(i) national reconciliation and cease-fire,

(ii) Renamo's participation in a government for national salvation,

(iii) the creation of a constituent assembly, and

(iv) general elections.

In late September, with Dhlakama threatening to return to Mozambique unless further progress was made, dialogue recommenced in a new frame-work in which Kenyan and Zimbabwean officials took over from the clergy-men as negotiators with Renamo. In October there were two meetings, the first, in early October, between Dhlakama and the Zimbabwean Permanent Secretary at the Foreign Ministry, Elleck Mashingaidze and, the second, in mid-October, with Mashingaidze's Kenyan counterpart, Bethwell Abdu Kiplaget. As before, a small Mozambican government delegation stayed on the sidelines to monitor the talks and to clarify the government's standpoint to the mediators. These meetings again attempted to break the rigidity of Renamo's demands but made no progress from the earlier attempts.[30] South Africa also became involved at this time, responding to a request by the joint mediators. In mid-October, Neil van Heerden, Director-General of the South African Foreign Ministry, met Dhlakama in Nairobi. Van Heerden's man-date was to tell Dhlakama in no uncertain terms that he should become more cooperative in the negotiations. This contact was preceded by a rather humiliating incident for the South African. Van Heerden was kept waiting for some six hours before Dhlakama consented to see him, a further example of the negative feelings towards the South African government present in Renamo's leadership.[31]

On this note, Dhlakama left Nairobi in late October to return to Mozambique, leaving Vincente Ululu and João Almirante in Nairobi to continue lobbying for Renamo's positions. The Mozambique government indirectly criticised President Moi for this failure, suggesting that he had been too accommodating in his approach towards Renamo. It seemed that the peace initiatives had now run out of steam. Renamo utterly rejected Chissano's offer that they could participate as individuals in the 1991 general elections. It continued to demand recognition as a political movement and direct talks between equals, while the Mozambican authorities continued to insist that Renamo should recognise the Frelimo government as legitimate. On 7 December, Ed Fugit, US *Chargé d'affaires* in Harare, had a second meeting with Dhlakama to try and break the deadlock. He brought with him a 7-point peace proposal (see Appendix 4) for Renamo-Frelimo talks, copies of which were given simultaneously to Presidents Moi and Mugabe. The meeting initially got nowhere, Dhlakama rejecting the document because of point six, which calls for recognition of "the legitimacy of the Republic of Mozambique". The next day, on December 8, President Mugabe flew to Nairobi to join President Moi in a desperate attempt to break the deadlock and to revive dialogue, holding four hours of consultations reviewing the situation. The outcome was to herald a new stage in the peace process. The two Presidents proposed direct talks between the Mozambique government and Renamo, a call made in a confidential joint-letter, based on the US peace plan, to both President Chissano and Dhlakama following the meeting.[32] It stated:

This is the third time in Nairobi to consider the best way to start the necessary process of peace and reconciliation. Directly and indirectly-held meetings of our own representatives have conducted intensive preliminary soundings ...

The conclusion was the necessity: "to effect changes to some aspects of both the constitutional and political order they disagree with." and to progress to: "meaningful direct talks. These talks would have to take into account the historical and present political realities of Mozambique and the reality of the African political experience, and aim at building up a united Mozambican nation".

Dhlakama, in Nairobi at the time, welcomed the proposal for direct talks. He claimed this as a victory, because it was now being suggested that Renamo should be treated on equal terms with Frelimo, and that this therefore meant recognition. As Dhlakama said in interview "You can't forget that Mugabe is one of the pillars holding up Frelimo ... If Mugabe says there is no need to have to have recognition, that these negotiations should take place, I am very satisfied". Dhlakama also hinted that the issue of creating a multi-party system was negotiable.[33]

Although President Chissano at first responded cautiously to these proposals, the Mozambique government was in fact prepared to negotiate with Renamo. The Mozambique government intended to use its new draft constitution as the basis for discussion with the rebels. The one pre-condition placed on such talks continued to be Renamo's demand that it should negotiate with the Frelimo Party, Renamo insisting that it did not recognise the Mozambique government, but that it would talk to Frelimo.

The call by President Moi and Mugabe for direct talks was taken serious-ly in Maputo, as President Chissano's important speech in Maputo on January 9 1990 announcing proposals for constitutional reform, demon-strated.[34] The government had prepared a revised, more liberal constitu-tion in preparation for free elections in 1991. The only outstanding area of divergence from Renamo's demands was the central theme of a multi-party system, over which Dhlakama now appeared prepared to negotiate.

In his January 1990 speech President Chissano reviewed the progress over possible dialogue with Renamo. Presidents Moi and Mugabe's pro-posals were mentioned, as was Renamo's demand to talk to Frelimo and not to the Mozambique government. Chissano added that: "The People's Republic of Mozambique has replied saying that we accept direct dialogue but on the basis of principles. It must be a dialogue with the People's Republic of Mozambique".

This final hurdle in the way of direct talks between the Mozambique government and Renamo was surmounted, following very active US and South African pressure on Renamo to be flexible over recognition of the Mozambique government (point 6 of the US peace plan). This is why President Chissano was able to announce during his visit to Washington and London in March 1990 that the Mozambique "government (is) to enter into a direct dialogue with Renamo as soon as possible".[35] By April, Chissano was even more concrete, announcing that "our timetable for talks is now. We have a commission working full-time on the question". Initial attempts by Maputo to set up a meeting between Renamo and the Mozambique government in Malawi on April 16 had been rejected by Renamo on the grounds that it was not neutral territory, since Malawian troops assist government forces within Mozambique, while Renamo's choice of Lisbon as the venue was in turn rejected by Maputo because of its colonial overtones. Munich in West Germany was also suggested as a suit-able location for talks but rejected on technicalities. Renamo continued to favour Nairobi as the location for talks, with Dhlakama spending much time there between February and July.

Mid-1990 produced intense diplomatic activity from the Mozambican government in preparing its platform for dialogue. During President Chissano's visit to Lisbon in April, Mozambican government officials approached various splinter groups and exile clubs such as Jose Massinga's newly formed Mozambique Civic Association, a student group called Pro-Civic and individuals such as Domingos Arouça to discuss the contents of the draft constitution, to seek their views on how to bring about peace.[36]

Portugal was also active in trying to bring both sides together. The head of SIM, General Xito Rodrigues, visited Malawi in February to see if Dhlakama would be ready to talk to President Chissano in Lisbon. This initiative failed due to Chissano ruling-out Lisbon as a venue. During the President's visit to Lisbon, the Portuguese government made their position clear, stating that "Portugal is interested in the peace process in Mozambique and prepared to help both sides in the conflict, without being the official mediator".

In June it seemed that direct talks would take place. Malawi, Kenya and Lonhro had been in frequent contact with Renamo, and appeared to have obtained an undertaking from Dhlakama that he would drop his demand that for "security" reasons no talks could be held in a neighbouring coun-try to Mozambique. On June 11 Dhlakama, Domingos and another

Renamo official, together with Betwell Abdu Kiplagat, Kenya's Permanent Secretary for Foreign Affairs, were flown by a Lonhro aircraft from Nairobi to Blantyre. The Malawian authorities, believing that this was the preliminary to direct talks, had contacted the Zimbabwean, Mozambican and Kenyan governments several days before to invite them to send delegations to Blantyre for talks on the 12th. However, following discussions with President Banda and his officials on the 11th, Dhlakama seems to have developed cold feet over the prospect of talks at this time, demanding agreement on three pre-conditions, namely:

(a) that Malawi should ensure that the activities of Mozambican intelligence in Malawi should be curtailed during the talks.

(b) that transit facilities to the FAM should be denied and that FAM operations in central Mozambique should cease during the talks.

(c) that as long as Zimbabwe has troops involved in Mozambique it would be unacceptable as a mediator.

Dhlakama announced that Malawi would be unacceptable as a venue unless these pre-conditions could be guaranteed. In spite of Malawian attempts to persuade the Renamo delegation to change its mind, Dhlakama and his leading officials left, crossing into Mozambique that evening, while leaving several officials behind to monitor the results of his action. Meanwhile the main Mozambican and Zimbabwean delegations arrived in Blantyre to find that Dhlakama had left and that Renamo was refusing to talk. They were briefed by Malawian officials the following day who afterwards issued a press statement stating that direct talks had been planned but had been postponed because of "apparent difficulties experienced by the Renamo and Kenyan delegations".[37]

Although Renamo publicly denies that it ever gave an undertaking to negotiate in Malawi, having consistently rejected the location because of "insecurity", events suggest otherwise. What probably happened is that Dhlakama lost his nerve over talks, although the Malawian authorities, with Mozambican government blessing have given him accommodation when required and have guaranteed his safety. Ever since his near-escape from capture in July 1989, Dhlakama has been pre-occupied with security. It also seems likely that he is well aware that his position will become more vulnerable to being undermined by the wheeling-and-dealing that will take place with his other officials once the peace process takes root. His reliance on the advice of Kiplagat reflects this. Dhlakama has a history of becoming reliant on advisers, probably in compensation for his lack of formal education. His past reliance on, and subservience to, Cristina, Fernandes (especially in the Pretoria Declaration talks) and van Niekerk among others, attest to this weakness.

Direct talks between Renamo and the Mozambique government finally took place in Rome on the 8th-10th July at the head quarters of the Vatican-linked charity, the Santo Egideo Community.[38] This meeting had been set-up through contacts of the Mozambican bishops and through the Vatican. The Mozambique government delegation was led by Armando Guebuza, Transport Minister. Renamo sent Raul Domingos, Vincente Ululu and Joao Almirante. Observers from the Santo Egideo Community and the Italian government attended, as well as the Catholic Archbishop of Beira, Jaime Gonçalves. A joint statement at the end of the meeting said:[39]

the two teams expressed the superior interest and willingness in making every effort to implement a constructive search for lasting peace in the country and for the Mozambican people. Taking into account the superior interests of the Mozambican nation, the two sides agreed on the need to set aside sources of division and look for areas of consensus, so that they can create a common working basis that will enhance a spirit of understanding and allow differences to be discussed. The two teams expressed their readiness to become deeply committed to the search for a working platform to end the war and to create political conditions permitting the normalisation of the lives of all Mozambican people. They agreed this should be done in a spirit of mutual respect and understanding.

The Mozambican government appeared pleased with the results of this first meeting. It appeared that serious talks on bringing about a ceasefire and eventual reconciliation could take place now that the ice had been broken. President Chissano announced that mediation with Renamo would no longer be required and could be replaced by direct talks. The Zimbabwean and Kenyan governments were informed.

Direct talks took place (again in Rome) between the 11 and 14 August, Mozambican and Renamo officials having remained there to continue to liaise with Church representatives. This second meeting was not succesful. Renamo insisted that they would not continue to negotiate without Kenyan mediation. President Chissano called this demand "delaying tactics".[40] Renamo's reliance on Kenya and Dhlakama's insecurity have already been described above. Its worries have probably been increased by Frelimo's ability to erode Renamo's campaigning demands through showing flexibility over democratic and other reforms. While the second round of talks in Rome was taking place, Frelimo's Central Committee met to take decisions on the months of earlier national debate over a new draft constitution and on the advice from the 12-member Political Bureau of the party that the one-party state should be discarded. The Central Committee's decision came the day after the Rome talks closed, with an unanimous vote to abandon Frelimo's monopoly of political power and to adopt a multi-party system for the country. In any case President Chissano had himself indicated even earlier that Renamo could take part in any 1992 General Election as a political party, it being expected only to respect the laws and the constitution and to refrain from violence.[41]

A third round of peace talks due to take place in Rome in late September 1990 failed to take place. Renamo announced that it was boycotting the talks because of the government's bad faith shown by its launching of an assault with Zimbabwean troops against Renamo's heartland of Gorongosa and a general offensive in three other provinces: Tete, Manica and Zambezia at this time. The Mozambique government, in turn, accused Renamo of again using delaying tactics.

The third round of direct talks between the government and Renamo eventually resumed on 10 November in Rome. Following very active Italian government mediation, with trips by Mario Rafaeli (Africa consultant to the Italian government) to Nairobi and Maputo, a compromise formula for talks was agreed upon. Rafaeli, two members from the Santo Egideo community and Jaime Gonçalves, Archbishop of Beira, would act as official mediators while Kiplagat would remain as a consultant to Renamo.[42]

This arrangement appeared to find acceptance. During this three-week round of talks Dhlakama himself travelled from Nairobi to visit Geneva for discussions with the ICRC, continuing on to Rome for discussions with the mediators. During his visit to Rome Dhlakama was received informally by Italian government figures, including the Prime Minister, Guilio Andreotti.

On December 1, with Mozambique's new pluralist constitution coming into effect, Renamo signed a partial cease-fire with the Mozambique government in Rome. The timing was no doubt intended to counter the positive publicity obtained by Maputo for its abolition of the one-party state and its commitment to multi-party elections in 1992. Under this agreement, Zimbabwean troops inside Mozambique were to be withdrawn to the Beira and Limpopo corridors and limited to 1.8 miles on either side of the railway lines. In return Renamo guaranteed that it would not attack these "corridors of peace".[43]

To ensure that the cease-fire was implemented correctly, both sides agreed that an international commission should monitor it (Joint Verification Commission). Three Renamo military officials arrived in Maputo in late December as part of this commission. It was also announced that Renamo and the Mozambique government would from that date allow the ICRC a free hand in its relief operations inside Mozambique.[44]

The partial cease-fire represented the first step towards a general cease-fire once mutual confidence over the partial agreement was established. A fourth round of talks commenced in Rome on January 27 (having been postponed for the festive period on December 18) in the expectation of further progress. This round was short lived. By January 30 the talks had ended without further agreement. Although further rounds of talks are planned for 1991, a return to military action meanwhile seems inevitable.

Many worries remain whether Renamo is really committed to peace. It continues to reject the government's new constitution, on the grounds that it was not freely debated, and is reoccupying positions in central Mozambique vacated by withdrawing Zimbabwean troops. It also appears to have violated the 1 December cease-fire, with attacks on both the Beira and Limpopo corridors. In early January Renamo also attacked the Nacala corridor for the first time since August 1989. The attacks on the Nacala corridor may well be linked to Malawi failing to pay the protection money which appears to have been part of an agreement with Renamo in August 1989. This would also explain the increased Renamo action along the Tete corridor in January 1991, in which transit traffic is now having to circumnavigate through Zambia. Secret talks between Renamo and the Malawian authorities are said to have taken place to resolve this crisis.

January 1991 is therefore marked by Renamo returning to military action, which has in turn, attracted government counter-action. Renamo has also increased its political campaigning in central Mozambique, reminding the peasantry that "we, the matsangas, are the ones to bring true peace". The threat of inflicting more hardship through further war may yet provide Renamo with more votes in any election.

But the peace process continues. The pressures within war-weary Mozambique for dialogue are far too great. The popular ambivalence to the war and, indeed, even to the government's draft new constitution unveiled in early 1990 is illustrative of a people who, having had their hopes for peace raised several times, first at Zimbabwean independence, then after N'Komati, then after Songo and now, more recently, at the Rome Agreement, do not want further disappointment. The government, recognising that many have shown little enthusiasm for its new constitution, has begun to explain in the vernacular dialects the significance of these reforms. The majority of Mozambicans are naturally preoccupied with peace. If Frelimo is to regain popular enthusiasum for its mandate to govern, the key for success lies in this. Frelimo has recognised this and hopes that its reforms and search for peace will mean that it will retain the support of the electorate in any general elections.

The Mozambique government's dual strategy of diplomatic and military initiatives remains the only approach likely to bring about a solution to the Mozambique war. Renamo will not be defeated by military means alone. As this book has demonstrated, it has become a successful military force in its own right. Its terror tactics have contributed more to this success than to its failures. With its 20,000 combatants, it has the capacity, as it itself boasts, to carry on the war for another decade. But it does not have the strength to win the war by taking over the towns.

Nor is Renamo a coherent political force. Although its external wing has, in the past, formalised a political agenda, the Renamo set-up inside Mozambique has been little concerned with the wider issues of politics, conceptualising them within a localised rural context. The one issue uniting Renamo has been the search for a share of power with Frelimo. The central issue at the Pretoria Declaration talks, it became a stumbling block at the preliminary talks in Nairobi in 1989. It has again become clear that Renamo's leadership wants major portfolios in government. It is rumoured that, although Frelimo was prepared to offer Renamo leaders on an individual basis portfolios in the social field — education, culture, health and justice — this was rejected by Renamo who continued to demand major positions, such as the defence ministry.

This suggests that, if Renamo were offered sufficiently attractive positions in government, its leadership would end the war. Renamo's efforts to portray itself as a political movement, instead of the fundamentally military organisation that it is, are designed to give its bid for power-sharing some sense of reality. But its political demands, overtaken by Frelimo's reforms, are already outdated. The insistence on sharing power therefore reflects its realisation that its leaders must obtain safeguards for whatever posts they gain in a settlement with Frelimo. To avoid losing ground thereafter, they must win from Frelimo positions of such authority and patronage that they could only be dislodged from them with difficulty.

Renamo is now in a very difficult situation. It now has no justification for continuing the war, yet competing in general elections is likely to bring defeat. Although Renamo has some popular support in Mozambique,this is not enough to win it positions of power. However much ambivalence to Frelimo there is in the rural areas, and hostility to it in the towns, Renamo will not win popular support. Groups such as UNAMO and PALMO with their very local ethnic strengths might even make a serious challenge in some constituencies. It remains difficult to see any other party than Frelimo winning in a 1991 election, given the lack of creditable alternatives.

By accepting the new constitution and competing in general elections Renamo would create the conditions by which true peace and reconciliation could grow within a devastated Mozambique. That Renamo can deliver a significant reduction of disorder should not be doubted. This book has attempted to show that Renamo is based on a central leadership. But it would be simplistic and naive to believe that a signed agreement would end the war in Mozambique overnight. Renamo has become for many the way to make a living. The plundering and attacking of settlements and convoys is now designed as much for replenishment of supplies and generation of booty as a reward for its combatants as for economic disruption for political ends. As long as the government is unable to offer services and commodities in the rural areas to challenge this way of life, groups of Renamo combatants, and indeed of freelance bandits, are unlikely to cease to operate within Mozambique.

Although it is true that most of Renamo's combatants were forced to join the rebels, evidence has shown that many are deeply traumatised by their experiences, and have accepted terrorism and banditry as a way of life. Many of these indoctrinated fighters who have not been tempted to respond in some part to the government's amnesty may feel that continuing fighting is their only option. Moreover, as the example of UNAMO demonstrates and as the South African military found after N'Komati, much of Renamo's power lies in the hands of its regional commanders. Those who are unhappy about a settlement, or become dissatisfied with what they are offered, are likely to continue to stay in the bush with their followers.

It does not need more than several thousand rebels, remaining as small and highly mobile rebel bands, to cause real problems. The chilling remarks of a Renamo commander to survivors of a Renamo attack on a train near Ressano Garcia in February 1990 hint at these potential complications. He said: "We don't like the nonsense that your President has been saying (Chissano on peace). So we're going to carry on the war to liberate the country".[45] This all suggests, that, although agreement with Renamo's leadership would improve the security situation, peace and reconstruction for the whole country will take far longer to achieve.

Peace is, nevertheless, what the majority of Mozambicans, whether in the government, Renamo, or the refugee camps, desire. The next stage is a crucial step forward, if Mozambique, and indeed all those who wish for peace and reconciliation, is not to be deeply disappointed. As one Mozambican refugee told this present writer: "Why do those Matsangas (Renamo) and the Massotcha (Soldiers) not leave us to grow old with our ancestors? We want peace, when will they hear our cries?"[46]

NOTES

Introduction

1 Hanlon, J. (1984), *Mozambique: The Revolution Under Fire*; Knight, K. (1988), *Mozambique Caught in the Trap*; Urdang, S. (1988), *And Still They Dance, Women, War and the Struggle for Change in Mozambique*; Egerö, B. (1987), *Mozambique: A Dream Undone*.

2 *Die Welt* (FRG), 6 January 1989.

3 *The Herald* (ZIM), 31 March 1989.

4 CENE & DPCCN. (1988), *Rising to the Challenge. Dealing with the Emergency in Mozambique. An Inside View.*

5 Mondlane, E. (1983), *The Struggle for Mozambique* p. 101.

1 A Backcloth to Disorder

1 *Tempo* (MOZ), No. 322, December 1976.

2 Created Insurgency

1 For a critical study of Frelimo's origins see Opello, W. (1975), *Pluralism and Elite Conflict in an Independence Movement: Frelimo in the 1960s*, pp. 66–83.

2 Christie, I. (1989), *Samora Machel: A Biography*, pp. 35–36.

3 A detailed account of this dispute is in Munslow, B. (1977), "Leadership in the Front for the Liberation of Mozambique, Part 1" pp. 156–161.

4 Fauvet, P. (1984), *Roots of Counter–Revolution: The Mozambique National Resistance*, p. 111.

5 Munslow, B. (1983), *Mozambique: the Revolution and its Origins*, p. 128.

6 Hanlon, J. (1986), *Beggar Your Neighbours*, p. 136.

7 Personal communication from Landeg White, Centre for Southern African Studies, University of York, who drove down to Beira in this period.

8 Hodges, T. (1979), *The Politics of Liberation*, pp. 57–93.

9 *Africa Research Bulletin* (political), 1980, p. 5908c; *To The Point International* (Brussels), 5 March 1976.

10 *To The Point International* (Brussels), 5 March 1976.

11 Middlemas, K. (1979), *Mozambique: Two years of Independence*, p. 104.

12 Voz da Africa Livre, Rhodesia, 19 December 1976.

13 *The Star* (RSA), 7 May 1977; *Africa Research Bulletin*, 1977 (political), p. 4428b.

14 *To The Point International* (Brussels), 29 August 1977.

15 There is considerable confusion over these early groups. Hodges, T. (1979), *Mozambique: The Politics of Liberation*, speaks of an amalgamation of the MNRA and FUMO in mid-1977. Although the MNRA might have existed, it is more probable that it originates from the South African propaganda campaign in 1977 in support of insurgency within Mozambique. This was clearly revealed by Gordon Winter, a former South African Intelligence sponsored journalist, who wrote fictitious articles on rebels in Mozambique from mid-1977 in the South African press. See Winter, G. (1981), *Inside Boss* pp. 545–552.

16 The best published sources on Renamo's Rhodesian origins are; Cole, B. (1984), *The Elite: The story of the Rhodesian Special Services*; Martin, D & Johnson, P.

(1986), *Mozambique: To N'Komati and Beyond*, Ch. 1, pp. 1–17; Flower, K. (1987), *Serving Secretly*.

17 Martin, D & Johnson, P. (1986), Ch. 1, pp. 7–8.

18 These titles arose from the need to portray the rebel as an autonomous group. In every press account and intelligence report, the group is only called the "Mozambique National Resistance" (MNR or RNM) in 1977. Renamo's former Secretary-General claimed that this name was chosen at a secret meeting in Salisbury, Rhodesia in 1977 between, Fernandes, Cristina, Matsangaissa, Dhlakama, Khembo dos Santos and Leo Milas (Martin & Johnson 1986, p. 7). The title Renamo, the Portuguese acronym of "Resistencia Nacional Mocambicana" is said to have been introduced and encouraged by Evo Fernandes as part of his Portugalisation of the rebels (Cain 1985, p. 66).

19 Martin, D. & Johnson, P. (1986), Ch. 1, p. 11.

20 *Africa Confidential* (UK), Vol. 23, No. 15, 21 July 1982.

21 Ibid. Legum, C. (1988), p. 248.

22 *Africa Confidential* (UK), Vol. 23, No. 15, 21 July 1982.

23 Hanlon, J. (1984), Ch. 21, p. 221.

24 *Africa Confidential* (UK), Vol. 29, No. 5, 4 March 1988.

25 Gersony, R. (1988), "Mozambique Refugee Accounts of Principally Conflict-Related Experiences in Mozambique".

26 Middlemas, K. (1979), p. 100.

27 Frelimo (1987), *Mozambique Briefing: The roots of Armed Banditry* pp. 11–13.

28 Interview with Commander Michael Evans, formerly lecturer in War Studies, University of Zimbabwe, York, July 1987.

29 Martin, D. & Johnson, P. (1986), Ch. 1, p. 13.

30 Flower, K. (1987), p. 262.

31 *Africa Confidential* (UK), Vol. 23, No. 15, 21 July 1982.

32 Martin, D. & Johnson, P. (1986), Ch. 1, p. 16.

33 *Africa Confidential* (UK), Vol. 28, No. 24, 2 December 1987.

34 Cole, B. (1984), p. 249.

35 *Africa Confidential* (UK), Vol. 23, No. 15, 21 July 1982.

36 Martin, D. & Johnson, P. (1986), Ch. 1, p. 19.

37 *Africa Confidential* (UK), Vol. 23, No. 15, 21 July 1982.

38 Ibid.

39 For examples of such activity in Mozambique, see, Martin, D. & Johnson, P. (1986), Ch. 1, pp. 22–23.

40 Martin, D. & Johnson, P. (1986), Ch. 1, pp. 25–27.

41 For the main provisions of the N'Komati Accord, see Appendix 6 in Hanlon, J. (1984).

42 Interview with Luis Serapião, Renamo delegate, USA. Washington, D. C. June, 1988. It is also interesting to note that the South African authorities attempted to hush up the murder by claiming Cristina was in a Pretoria flat, not at a training camp and simultaneously issuing to the Press Editors a "D" notice, banning any mention of the circumstances of his death. *The Economist* (UK), 16–22 July 1983 p. 20.

43 Thomashausen, A. (1987), *The Mozambique National Resistance*, p. 42.

44 Cain, E. (1985), p. 55.

45 *Press Trust of South Africa* 17 May 1983.

46 Further details of this struggle were revealed by João Santa Rita, a former Moçambican journalist who had joined Renamo, but left in these disputes. *The Star* (RSA), 18 March 1985.

47 Cain, E. (1985), p. 66.

48 Martin, D. & Johnson, P. (1986), Ch. 1, p. 32.

49 Legum, C. (1988), p. 356. For the best account, see Davies, R. (1985), pp. 27–32.

50 Legum, C. (1988), p. 357. The Renamo delegation was led by Evo Fernandes and included Dhlakama, its secretary, J. Vaz and two commanders, M. Ngonhamo and J. Horacio.

51 Diplomatic source Maputo, January 1985. For Evo Fernandes' account of the

Pretoria talks, see JODD (1985), Interview with Fernandes, *Journal of Defense and Diplomacy*, Vol. 3, No. 9, September 1985, p. 47.

52 Legum, C. (1988), p. 357.

53 Interview with Fernando Honwana, Mozambican Official, September, 1985. Renamo also denied that it had recognised President Machel, other than as a co-equal. See *A Luta Continua, Orgão Official da Renamo*, Dezembro 84/Março 85, No. 4, 3rd series, pp. 4–6. (Lisbon).

54 Legum, C. (1988), p. 358. Davies, R. (1985), p. 30.

55 Legum, C. (1988), p. 361.

56 The Vaz diaries comprised of a desk diary for most of 1984 and two note books. They were kept by Afonso Dhlakama's secretary as log books that recorded the comings and goings at Casa Banana. They have been published in facsimile in two volumes by the Ministry of Information, Maputo in 1985 as *The Gorongosa Documents*.

57 Oliveira, cited in Minter, W. (1989), *The Mozambican National Resistance (Renamo), as Described by Ex-participants*, p. 11.

58 Interview with Malcolm Blakey & Patrick O'Connell, former Renamo hostages, Maputo, September 1985.

59 *South Africa Report* (RSA), 1 April 1988.

60 *The Indian Ocean Newsletter* (FRA), No. 413, 13 January 1990.

61 Interview with Professor H. Howe, Georgetown University, Washington, D.C., 9 January 1990.

62 Legum, C. (1988), p. 300.

63 Ibid. p. 361.

64 These measures were, (i), Radar to be installed to detect illegal flights, (ii), All Mozambicans in the SADF to be removed from the border area and no more recruited, and (iii), A private security firm to be established to guard key installations in Mozambique.

65 *South African Press Association* 18 September 1985.

66 Interview with South African Defence Attaché formerly involved in Renamo, May 1987.

67 Martin, D. & Johnson, P. (1986), Ch. 1, pp. 39–40.

68 *Informafrica* (PORT), Vol. 1, No. 7, March 1988, p. 10; *Africa Confidential* (UK), Vol. 29, No. 18, 9 September 1988, p. 1.

69 Legum, C. (1988), p. 397.

70 Knight, D. (1988), Ch. 3, p. 35.

71 *Scope* (RSA), 18 February 1983, part 2, p. 29. Containing an interview with defecting Head of Mozambican Security, Jorge Da Costa.

72 Botha, P. (1985), House of Assembly Debates (Hansard), 25 March to 10 May, Vol. 3, Cols. 4214–4215.

73 *Southern Africa Political & Economy Monthly* (Zim), June 1989, p. 9.

74 *The Wall Street Journal* (USA), 14 June 1988.

75 *New York Times* (USA), 13 September 1988.

76 *Revista de Sudafrica Panorama* No. 151, October 1988, pp. 16–19.

77 Renamo press release "The Future of Cabora Bassa", 29 June 1988, Washington, D.C.

78 AIM (MOZ), *Mozambiquefile*, No. 151, February 1989.

79 *The Independent* (UK), 14 February 1989; AIM (MOZ), *Mozambiquefile*, No. 152, March 1989.

80 *The New York Times* (USA), 17 December 1989.

81 *The Guardian* (UK), 4 October 1985.

82 *Noticias* (MOZ), 26 January 1989.

83 Minter, W. (1989).

84 US Diplomatic source, Harare, April 1989.

85 Interview with South African Defence Attaché formerly involved with Renamo, May 1987.

86 *The Weekly Mail* (RSA), Vol. 6, No. 9, 9–22 March 1990; The Southern Africa

Quaker Peace Initiative report cited in this article does not actually provide evidence
to support such a theory.

3 The International Dimension

1 Associacão de Naturais e Ex-Residentes de Moçambique.

2 Associacão de Empresarios e Propitarios de Moçambique.

3 Movimento Nacional de Fraternidade Ultramarina. An equivalent group is the
Liga das Communidades da Lingua Portuguese (Lusofona).

4 Movimento Independente de Reconstrucão Nacional.

5 The Indian Ocean Newsletter (FRA), No. 425, 7 April 1990.

6 Movemento Nacionalista Moçambicana, Frente de Salvacão de Mocambique.
For more details see Torres, E. (1983), "Moçambique entre dois fogos a URSS e a
Africa do Sul", pp. 114–115.

7 Arouça, D. (1974), *Discursos Politicos*.

8 Frente Unida Democratica de Moçambique; *Journal Novo* (Port), 13 July 1976;
Voz da Africa Livre, Rhodesia 19 December 1976.

9 Martin, D & Johnson, P. (1986), Ch. 1, p. 8.

10 *Daily Telegraph* (UK), 30 May 1977. Further details given by Arouça in an
interview in Martin, D. & Johnson, P. (1986), Ch. 1, Footnote 16, p. 343.

11 *Africa Confidential* (UK), Vol. 23, No. 15, 21 July 1982. According to the
Garagua Documents, Dhlakama took this challenge seriously and welcomed an
attempted car bombing of Arouça in Lisbon in 1980 as the "Spirit's Vengeance". See
Fauvet, P. & Gomes, A. (1982), *The Mozambique National Resistance*.

12 Torres, E. (1983), pp. 114–115, for a discussion on FUMO.

13 *Africa confidencial* (PORT), No. 16, April 1987.

14 Martin, D. & Johnson, P. (1986), Ch. 1, p. 34.

15 The Gorongosa Documents (1985), Vol. 2.

16 Martin, D & Johnson, P. (1986), Ch. 1, p. 34.

17 Ibid.

18 Hanlon, J. (1986), *Beggar Your Neighbours* Ch. 12, p. 147.

19 *SA Report* (RSA), 1 April 1988.

20 *The Indian Ocean Newsletter* (FRA), No. 413, 13 January 1990.

21 Legum, C. (1988), p. 358.

22 Martin, D & Johnson, P. (1986), Ch. 1, p. 35.

23 See Fauvet, P. (1984), *Roots of Counter-Revolution: The Mozambique National
Resistance*.

24 *O Diario* (PORT), 14 August 1986; *Africa Confidential* (UK), Vol. 28, No. 6, 18
March 1987.

25 *Africa confidencial* (PORT), No. 15, February 1987.

26 *Africa confidencial* (PORT), No. 16, April 1987; *Africa Confidential* (UK), Vol. 28,
No. 6, 18 March 1987.

27 Interview with Luis Serapião, Renamo Delegate, Washington, D. C. June 1988.

28 *The Independent* (UK), 24 March 1988; *SA Report* (RSA), 1 April 1988.

29 *Informafrica* (PORT), Vol. 1, No. 5, December 1987; Interview with Luis Serapião, Renamo Delegate, Washington, D. C. June 1988.

30 *Africa Confidential* (UK), Vol. 29, No. 1, 8 January 1988.

31 *SA Report* (RSA), 1 April 1988.

32 *The Independent* (UK), 2 December 1988.

33 *SA Report* (RSA), 1 April 1988.

34 *Informafrica* (PORT), Vol. 1, No. 8, April 1988.

35 Interview with Antonio Rocha, Director of Research, Mozambique Research
Centre, Washington, D. C. June 1988.

36 Interview with Jose Ramos-Hoita, Director of Press & Public Affairs, Mozambican Embassy, Washington, D. C. June 1988.

37 For details of Portuguese police investigations see *Informafrica* (PORT), Vol. 1,
No. 9, June 1988. Further developments of the case are covered in the weekly

Expresso (PORT), 7 January 1989. The best summary of the different angles in the case is found in *Fim de Semana*, 18 March 1989 (PORT). For the trial see *Informafrica* (PORT), Vol. 1, No. 5, 27 May 1989, and *Southscan* (UK), 28 July 1989. For Chagas' final account of why he killed Fernandes, see *Sabado* (PORT), 1 July 1989.

38 *Southscan* (UK), 28 July 1989.

39 *Southern Africa Political & Economic Monthly* (ZIM), June 1989, p. 8.

40 *Noticias* (MOZ), 14 March 1989.

41 *The Indian Ocean Newsletter* (FRA), No. 397, 28 October 1989.

42 For a rather imbalanced but more detailed account of Renamo's activities in the FRG see Nilsson, A. (1990), *Unmasking the Bandits: the true face of the MNR*. Chapter 4, section 2.

43 SA Report (RSA), 1 April 1989.

44 *Africa Confidential* (UK), Vol. 29, No. 15, 29 July 1988.

45 This was not a National Council meeting, as claimed in Minter, W. (1989), p. 124. Only Fonseca, Lisboa, Moises and Dhlakama were National Council members.

46 For example, *The Washington Times* (USA), 17 August 1988.

47 *Tempo* (MOZ), No. 322, December 1976.

48 *The New York Times* (USA), 27 March 1984.

49 See the Heritage Foundation's "National Security Record. A Report on the Congress and National Security Affairs", No. 92, June 1986.

50 Renamo newsletter on the history of Mozambique, dated 2 April 1986. From Renamo Office Heidelberg.

51 *The Freedom Fighter* (USA), Vol. 1, No. 4, September 1985.

52 Organisations that have in the past shown sympathy for Renamo in the USA not named in the text include: About My Father's Business, Inc, KY; American Enterprise Institute, DC; Americans Freedom International, DC; Americans for Tax Reform, DC; Bashore International, DC; Citizens for America, DC; Coalitions for America, DC; Cuban American National Foundation, FL; Free Congress and Education Foundation, DC; Fund for Africa's Future, DC; Good News Communications, GA; High Frontier, DC; Open Doors Mission, Restore A More Benevolent Order Coalition (RAMBOC), CA; RUFFPAC, DC; Selous Foundation, DC; The Believers Church, CA; The Freedom League, DC; United States Global Strategy Council, DC; Vigeries Association, DC; World Missionary Assistance Plan (World MAP), CA.

53 Ibid. Senators Malcolm Wallop, Gordon Humphrey, Paul Tribble and Congressmen Dan Burton, Robert Dornan participated in this pro-Renamo rally.

54 *The Freedom Fighter* (USA), Vol. 1, No. 17 November 1986.

55 Letter brought out of Mozambique by Thomas Schaaf, dated 19 October 1986. Vilankulu claimed that his credentials were vouched for by Franz Josef Strauss, John Singlaub, Mahluza and Khembo dos Santos. See *Washington Times* (USA), 8 September 1986.

56 Interview with Thomas Schaaf, Washington, D. C, 8 January 1990. *Africa Confidential* (UK), Vol. 29, No. 18, 9 September 1988.

57 *Washington Times, Washington Post, Newsweek & Soldier of Fortune*.

58 *The New York Times* (USA), 22 May 1988.

59 *International Herald Tribune* (USA), 12 November 1987.

60 Interview with Thomas Schaaf, Executive-Director of Mozambique Research Centre, June 1988.

61 Interview with Jose Ramos-Hoita, Director of Press & Public Affairs, Mozambique Embassy, Washington, D. C. June 1988. It has also been reported that American sympathisers attempted to bring Dhlakama to the USA in April 1988. The visit was stopped by State Department pressure on the South African authorities. See Cline, S. (1990).

62 *The New York Times* (USA), 22 May 1988.

63 *Africa Confidential* (UK), Vol. 29, No. 18, 9 September 1988. His latest visit into Renamo areas in mid 1989, is described by his wife, Sibyl Cline, in *Soldier of Fortune* (USA), January 1990. For a more detailed account, including interview transcripts with Renamo officials at Gorongosa, see Cline, S. (1989), *Renamo. Anti-communist Insurgents in Mozambique: The Fight goes On*.

64 For details of the mission see Jordon, B. (1988), *Mission Mozambique: SOF Escorts Missionaries out of Combat zone.*

65 *Africa Confidential* (UK), Vol. 29, No. 18, 9 September 1988.

66 *Newsweek* (International), 8 August 1988; *The New York Times* (USA), 31 July 1988; *The Washington Post* (USA), 31 July 1988.

67 Interviews with Thomas Schaaf, Executive-Director Mozambique Research Centre, Washington, D. C., September 1988 & January 1990.

68 *The New York Times* (USA), 22 May 1988.

69 Diplomatic Source Harare, April 1988.

70 *Africa Report* (USA), September-October 1989 & *Indian Ocean Newsletter* (FRA), No. 406, 18 November 1989.

71 *Africa News* (USA), November 1989.

72 Askin, S. (1989), p. 64.

73 Ibid., pp. 81–82.

74 CERT Press Release, 5 November 1989. *Weekly Mail* (RSA), 17 November 1989.

75 The accounts of his visit are in *Soldier of Fortune* (USA), Part I, February 1986 & Part II, March 1986. Also in *Reason* magazine (USA), December 1985.

76 *The New York Times* (USA), 22 May 1988.

77 Source wishes to remain undisclosed. Interview with Prexy Nesbitt, London, December 1990.

78 Senators Pete Wilson, James McClure, Malcolm Wallop, Don Nicholas, Gordan Humphrey, Steve Symms and Jesse Helms; Congressmen Dan Burton and Mark Wander. *Africa confidencial* (PORT), No. 11, September 1986.

79 *Informafrica* (PORT), Vol. 1, No. 6, January 1988.

80 *Africa Report* (USA), September-October 1987; *The Wall Street Journal* (USA), 11 May 1987.

81 *The Washington Times* (USA), 23 October 1989.

82 *Africa Confidential* (UK), Vol. 29, No. 18, 9 October 1988.

83 Interview with US State Department Mozambique Desk Officer, Randy le Coque, December 1989.

84 *The Independent* (UK), 8 August 1989.

85 *The Herald* (ZIM), 31 March 1989.

86 Diplomatic source, Nairobi, May 1988.

87 *The Independent* (UK), 25 November 1989. DSL Ltd began operating in Mozambique in August 1986. By May 1987 it had set up a training programme in Cuamba in Niassa province. This programme is targetted at training Mozambican conscripts to become "Special Force" units whose role is to defend convoys to the tea estates in Niassa and Zambezia, and to keep the Nacala corridor open. Both these objectives are linked to Lonhro's economic concerns. There is also a similar training programme run by DSL Ltd in Maputo.

88 *Financial Mail* (RSA), 15 February & 10 May 1985.

89 *Southscan* (UK), 22 September 1989.

90 *The Sunday Telegraph* (UK), 7 August 1988. His account is to be found in *Janes Defence Weekly* (UK), 12 July 1986. Renamo's first publicity in Britain was over their capture of John Burlison in 1981. They telexed the Foreign Office in 1982 with the statement of Renamo's aims and principles which they demanded published in the British press as the condition for his release. In 1985 Renamo approached the British Embassy in Lisbon, to lobby and explain its actions.

91 *The Observer* (UK), 9 October 1988.

92 Ibid.

93 Interview with Thomas Schaaf, Executive-Director of the Mozambique Research Centre, Washington, D. C., January 1990.

94 *The Observer* (UK), 13 November 1988.

95 *The Times* (UK), 25 November 1987; *The Salisbury Review*, 6, 2, December 1987.

96 Hoile, D. (1989), *Mozambique: a Nation in Crisis*; Interview with D. Hoile, London, December 1990.

97 As attested by President Machel's visit to Malawi in October 1984. He visited

the locations of former Frelimo safe houses and transit camps.

98 Swift, K. (1974), *Mozambique and the Future*, Appendix 4.

99 Paul, J. (1975), *Mozambique: Memoires of a Revolution*, p. 207.

100 Martin, D. & Johnson, P. (1986), Ch. 1, pp. 7–8.

101 Martin, D. & Johnson, P. (1986), Ch. 1, pp. 23–24.

102 Ibid.

103 Fanuel Mahluza, for example. See Thomashausen, A. (1983), "The National Resistance of Mozambique".

104 Interview with Landeg White, Director, Centre for Southern African Studies, University of York (UK), September 1988. He was in this area at the time and saw Africa Livre operate.

105 Martin, D. & Johnson, P. (1986), Ch. 1, footnote 18, p. 344.

106 Interview with Landeg White, Director, CSAS, September 1988. Speaks of the radio broacasts being a focus of entertainment amongst the rural population with access to radios in these areas.

107 Hanlon, J. (1984), Ch. 21, pp. 226–227.

108 *Africa Confidential* (UK), Vol. 23, No. 15, 21 July 1982. J. Jardim died in 1982 in Libreville (Gabon).

109 *The Indian Ocean Newsletter* (FRA), No. 371, 25 February 1989.

110 *Africa Confidential* (UK), Vol. 23, No. 15, 21 July 1982.

111 Diplomatic source, Maputo, September 1985.

112 *AIM* (MOZ), No. 123, October 1986.

113 *The Observer* (UK), 24 August 1986; *Africa Report* (USA), November-December 1986.

114 *AIM* (MOZ), No. 123, October 1986; *Africa Contemporary Record* Vol. 30, 1986–87, B676–77.

115 Norval, M. (1988), *Red Star Over Southern Africa*, p. 195. One estimate is that 4,000 Renamo combatants were pushed into Mozambique; see Legum, C. (1988), p. 413.

116 *Africa confidencial* (PORT), No. 11, September 1986.

117 *The Washington Post* (USA), 12 September 1988; *The Independent* (UK), 9 October 1987; Hanlon, J. (1986), Ch. 18, footnote 2, p. 338.

118 *Southern African Review of Books* (UK), Vol. 1, No. 2, p. 26.

119 Ibid.

120 The details for this pact were drawn up at a Joint Security Commission meeting held in Nampula, a week earlier. Initially 300 Malawian troops were to be deployed along the Nacala line. *Africa Research Bulletin* Vol. 23, No. 12, 18 January 1987, 8326–B.

121 Ibid.

122 *Africa Confidential* (UK), Vol. 29, No. 10, 13 May 1988.

123 Ibid. But the report is wrong, Tembo was not named.

124 BBC World Service "Focus on Africa", 15 November 1989 17. 20 GMT.

125 Askin, S. (1989), p. 81.

126 Interview with Thomas Schaaf, Executive-Director, Mozambique Research Centre, Washington, D. C. September 1988.

127 *Informafrica* Vol. 1, No. 10, 2 December 1989; Munslow, B. (1983), *Mozambique: the Revolution and its Origins* Ch. 9, pp. 79–80.

128 *Africa Confidential* (UK), Vol. 31, No. 11, 7 June 1990.

129 *The Independent* (UK), 28 August 1990.

130 For example *Daily Nation* (KEN), 16 August 1989.

131 *Africa Confidential* (UK), Vol. 31, No. 11, 7 June 1990.

132 *The Independent* (UK), 28 August 1990.

133 Cain, E. (1985), p. 66.

134 Hanlon, J. (1986), Ch. 10, pp. 97–98.

135 Interview with Commander Michael Evans, formerly lecturer in War Studies, University of Zimbabwe, York, September 1987.

136 Diplomatic source, Harare, September 1989.

137 Ibid.

138 Zimbabwean official, Harare, September 1989.

139 Interview with Commander Michael Evans, formerly lecturer in War Studies, University of Zimbabwe, York, September 1987.

140 *The Herald* (ZIM), 28 February 1989.

141 Conversation with a ZUM official, Harare, May, 1989.

142 Sithole has sent open letters to President Mugabe, from his Zimbabwe African Research Centre in Washington, D. C. on 4 August 1987; 31 May 1989; 1 November 1989.

143 Interview with Ndabaningi Sithole, December 1989, Washington, D. C.

144 *The Herald* (ZIM), 8 May 1989. The "friendship and co-operation agreement" states that: "We, the leaders of our respective parties representing our two countries, solemnly agree that our two parties shall strictly adhere to the following principles. . . " Then follows a list of 10 points, including regular free and fair elections and an independent judiciary. It was signed on behalf of Dhlakama, by Artur de Fonseca, Jorge Correia and Luis Serapião on 17 August 1986. It appears that the Heritage Foundation encouraged this alliance (see the *Aida Parker Newsletter* No. 93 October 19 1986, for publicity for such an alliance). Although the Foundation has now distanced itself from Renamo it continues to support Sithole's Zimbabwe African Research Centre.

145 Interviews with Luis Serapião and Thomas Schaaf, Washington, D. C., December 1989.

146 An example of this propaganda is published in Ellert, H. (1989); *The Herald* (ZIM), 15 April 1989.

147 *The Herald* (ZIM), 19 September 1989; *Sunday Mail* (ZIM), 26 March 1989; *Moto Magazine* (ZIM), No. 85, February 1990.

148 *Africa Confidential* (UK), Vol. 30, No. 12, 9 June 1989; *The Herald* (ZIM), 14 April 1989.

149 *The Herald* (ZIM), 28 September 1989.

150 *Africa Confidential* (UK), Vol. 30, No. 12, 9 June 1989.

151 *Informafrica* (PORT), Vol. 1, No. 5, 27 May 1989.

152 Interview with Pleasant Mahende, Masvingo, August 1989.

153 Johnson, P. & Martin, D. (1989), Ch. 3, pp. 83–88 & Ch. 4, pp. 154–156.

154 Martin, D. & Johnson, P. (1986), Ch. 1, p. 347, footnote, 41.

155 *The Herald* (ZIM), 27 September 1989.

156 Partido Democratico de Liberacão de Moçambique. *Africa confidencial* (PORT), No. 8, May 1986.

157 Comite Nacional Independiente Moçambicana. *Africa Confidential* (UK), Vol. 28, No. 6, March 1986.

158 "A Reuniao da Colonia e a sua Resolucão" CUNIMO, West Germany, 16 June 1986.

159 Comite para a União Moçambicana.

160 *Daily Times* (MALAWI), 5 May 1988.

161 *Southscan* (UK), 8 September 1989.

162 *El Nuevo Lunes* (SP), 18–24 April 1983; *O Pais* (PORT), 7 July 1983.

163 CUNIMO Newsletter "A Liberacão de Moçambique depende de nos Moçambicanos", Lisbon 5 October 1986.

164 *Africa confidencial* (PORT), No. 9, June 1986.

165 Anonymous source.

166 Howard Stontoms of the CAF was directly involved. *Africa confidencial* (PORT), No. 6, March 1986.

167 *Southscan* (UK), 8 September 1989.

168 *The Indian Ocean Newsletter* (FRA), No. 371, 25 February 1989.

169 Interview by Landeg White with Marcelo Cardoso, Lisbon, August 1987.

170 *The Indian Ocean Newsletter* (FRA), No. 366, 21 January 1989.

171 AIM (MOZ), *Mozambiquefile*, No. 166, May 1990.

4 The Domestic Dimension

1 Frelimo (1987), *Mozambique Briefing No. 5. The Roots of Armed Banditry* (1987).

2 For example Metz, S. (1986), *The Mozambique National Resistance and South African Foreign Policy*.

3 Minter, W. (1990).

4 *Tempo* (MOZ), No. 973, 4 June 1989; Young, T. (1990).

5 *Africa Confidential* (UK), Vol. 23, No. 15, July 1982.

6 Interview with Fernando Honwana, Government Official, Maputo, September 1985.

7 Variations of this theme are found in Martin, D. & Johnson, P. (1986), Ch. 1, p. 345, footnote, 21; *Africa Report* (USA), November-December 1982, pp. 5–7; Finnegan, W. (1989), Part 1, p. 70.

8 Finnegan, W. (1989), Part 1, p. 70.

9 Interview with Antonio Rocha, Director of Research, Mozambique Research Centre, Washington, D. C., July 1987.

10 *The Washington Times* (USA), 16 December 1986. For a recent account see *Soldier of Fortune* (USA), January 1990.

11 *Human Events* (USA), 8 November 1986.

12 *Die Welt* (FRG), 6 January 1989; Cline, S. (1989), contains further interviews with Dhlakama and officials Anselmo, Alfainho, Baza, Soares & Ululu.

13 Finnegan, W. (1989), "A Reporter At Large" (Mozambique, Part 1), p. 72.

14 Henrikson, T. (1983), *Revolution and Counter Revolution. Mozambique's War of Independence 1964–1974*, p. 149.

15 *The Daily Telegraph* (UK), 5 July 1979.

16 "Voz da Africa Livre" derived its name from the CIA's "Radio Free Europe". It was labelled by the Mozambican authorities as "Radio Quizumba", meaning Radio Hyena. In Mozambique the hyena is commonly the symbol of evil and treachery. It is another example of the rebels being denied any sort of legitimacy in government inspired language. The radio station was set up by the Rhodesians in response to pro-Nationalist "The Voice of Zimbabwe" broadcasts from Maputo. It started broadcasting a daily five minute address to Mozambique on the 5 July 1976. These were soon extended to hour-long broadcasts in both Portuguese and vernacular dialects. The early broadcasts were crude, full of colonialist nostalgia, admiration for Rhodesia, and personal abuse of Mozambican government figures. By 1979, the broadcasts had become more sophisticated eg. depicting Renamo as the inheritor of Mondlane's ideas. Litle attempt was made to disguise the origin of the broadcasts until 1979. The address was once given as PO Box 444, Highlands, Salisbury. With the Lancaster House Agreement, the radio station was transferred, with the rest of Renamo, to the north Transvaal. From then on it gave its postal address as Evo Fernandes' flat in Cascais, Portugal. It went off the air between 12 May & 23 June 1983, a sign of the succession dispute within Renamo after the murder of Orlando Cristina. When it came back on the air it had changed its name to "Voz de Renamo", which functioned until it was closed down just before the signing of the N'Komati Accord.

17 *Africa Research Bulletin* (political), 1981, p. 6185b.

18 The summarised political programme and economic manifesto are published in Hoile, D. (1989), Appendices, 1 & 2. Examples of the original full programme and the "Manifest and Programme" are on file at the CSAS (York), archive.

19 Renamo leaflet further summarising the Programme, no date, but distributed in 1984 and more recently in Lisbon in June 1989.

20 *AIM* (MOZ), 11 September 1989; *Mozambiquefile* No. 150, January 1989. Renamo does occasionally seem to hold political meetings after its massacres to justify its actions. Such a meeting took place after the attack of a train in February 1990 near Ressano Garcia. *The Guardian* (UK), 20 February 1990.

21 Minter, W. (1989), pp. 107–108.

22 Interview with Thomas Schaaf, Washington, D. C., September 1988.

23 *A Luta Continua, Orgão de Informaçao de Renamo* No. 3 3rd Series, October/ November 1984 & No. 4, 3rd Series December 1984/March 1985.

24 "President Afonso Dhlakama's message to the United States" read by Luis Serapião at a press conference on 28 October 1986, Dirksen Senate Office Building, Senate Foreign Relations Committee room, Washington, D. C.

25 "Political programme", January 1988; Renamo Department of Information, Washington — Renamo Bulletin & Newsletter No. 14. Moises did not go to Canada as part of an organised move by Renamo as has been claimed (Nesbitt 1988, p. 121). His move to Canada was as an economic migrant from Kenya. The move was unpopular with internal Renamo because they had not been consulted and because it made Moises even more autonomous. These tensions contributed to his hostile reception at Renamo's "First Congress" in June 1989 and the decision to dismiss him.

26 *Newsweek* (International), No. 32, 8 August 1988.

27 Cain, E. (1985), p. 65; *The Star* (RSA), 6 September 1982.

28 Ibid.

29 For example Renamo Bulletin No. 4, 31 August 1986.

30 Interview with Thomas Schaaf, Washington, D. C., January 1990. The Congress was attended by Moises, Khembo Santos, Muhluza, Ululu, Fernandes Cristina, Cabrito, Dhaklama.

31 "Summary of Resolutions of the First National Congress of Renamo: Renamo Carta Aberta A Comunidade Moçambicana" (Lisbon), 29 July 1989.

32 Closing speech of the first Congress of Renamo by Afonso Dhlakama, 10 June 1989.

33 Fauvet, P. (1984), *Roots of Counter-Revolution: The Mozambique National Resistance*, p. 119.

34 *Journal of Defense & Diplomacy* (USA), Vol. 3, No. 9, September 1985, p. 49.

35 Cain, E. (1985), p. 65.

36 *Africa confidencial* (PORT), No. 10, August 1986.

37 "Summary of Resolutions of the First National Congress of Renamo".

38 Fauvet, P. (1984), p. 120.

39 Minter, W. (1989), p. 118; Fauvet, P. (1984), p. 117.

40 *Journal of Defence & Diplomacy* (USA), Vol. 3, No. 9, September 1985, p. 49.

41 Thomashausen, A. (1987), *The Mozambique National Resistance*, pp. 44–45.

42 Minter, W. (1989), p. 118.

43 Ibid.

44 *Africa Report* (USA), March-April 1989, p. 15.

45 Wheller, J. (1986); Blakey & O'Connell in interview, Maputo, September 1985. See also *Sunday Times* (RSA), November 30 1986.

46 *The Rand Daily Mail* (RSA), 29 May 1982; *The Star* (RSA), 4 June 1982.

47 Interview with Malcolm Blakey & Patrick O'Connell, Maputo, September 1985.

48 *AIM* (MOZ), 10 September 1985.

49 Interview with Zimbabwean military official, Harare, September 1989.

50 Minter, W. (1989), pp. 119–120.

51 Jordan, B. (1988), *Mission Mozambique: SOF Escorts Missionaries out of Combat Zone*.

52 Geffray, C. (1989), *Erati en Guerre*, p. 141, footnote 96.

53 Interview with Luis Serapião, Renamo Head of Higher Education, Washington, D. C. January 1990.

54 *AIM* (MOZ), No. 102, January 1985 Supplement.

55 *Race and Class* No. 30, p. 4.

56 Minter, W. (1989), pp. 120–121.

57 Ibid.

58 Geffray, C. (1989), pp. 135–147.

59 Diplomatic source, Maputo, September 1985.

60 Renamo Military Communiqué, 27 October 1986. Issued by Washington Office.

61 *AIM* (MOZ), 10 September 1985.

62 "Renamo History of Mozambique", dated 2 April 1986 by Francisco Nota Moises. Issued in Heidelberg.

63 *New African* (UK), No. 260, May 1989.

64 *AIM* (MOZ), 18 December 1985.

65 *Africa* (UK), No. 127, March 1982, p. 38.

66 *Africa Reseach Bulletin* (political), 1986, p. 81556c.

67 Interview with Luis Serapião, Renamo delegate, Washington, June 1988.

68 Finnegan, W. (1989), Part 1, p. 48; Script for German TV documentary by Dittman Hack on Renamo, June 1989.

69 Interview with Malcolm Blakey & Patrick O'Connell, Maputo, September 1985.

70 Mozambican refugee in Zimbabwe, April 1988.

71 *AIM* (MOZ), No. 102, January 1985 Supplement; *AIM* (MOZ), No. 142, May 1988.

72 *The Guardian* (UK), 14 February 1989.

73 Sources are *Tempo, Noticias*, international press.

74 Fauvet, P. (1984), p. 119.

75 The International Red Cross (ICRC), has been particularly targetted by Renamo for lobbying and threats (eg. *The Times* (UK), 9 January 1988), in its attempts to obtain external recognition. Already in 1983, ICRC operations were attacked to increase pressure on it to seek recognition from the Mozambican authorities as a "neutral" agency operating in contested areas. This was firmly rejected by Maputo who saw such a move as giving international recognition to Renamo's insurgency. With the escalating conflict and human suffering since 1983 in the country, the ICRC has had to walk a political tight-rope in its attempt to distribute relief aid to civilians in rebel areas. This has led to several cessations of operations due to threats from the rebels and also confrontations with the Mozambican authorities. A crisis of relations in 1988 was only resolved by a visit of the ICRC President to Maputo. It appears that during this visit he obtained the reluctant permission of Maputo for the ICRC to fly relief by scheduled flights along predetermined routes to recognised airstrips within Renamo dominated territory. The fragile nature of this understanding is illustrated by attacks on such airstrips by the Mozambican and Zimbabwean airforces in 1988 and 1989.

76 SABC Radio broadcast (in English), 15:00 gmt, 14 December 1988.

77 Glaser, T. (1989), "Country Reports — Mozambique", pp. 30–31.

78 Pattern noted by author on these routes, April 1984 to September 1985. Recent example is that of an incoming train attacked and 55 killed near Ressano Garcia. *The Times* (UK), 15 February 1990.

79 *The Star* (RSA), 26 December 1986.

80 Magaia, L. (1988), *Dumba Nengue: Run For Your Life*.

81 *The Star* (RSA), 26 December 1986.

82 There have been several reports of decapitated heads of Government supporters being impaled on stakes and placed at roadsides as a sign of Renamo's presence. *Africa Research Bulletin* (political), 1980, p. 5908c; *Soldier of Fortune* (USA), Part 1, February 1986.

83 *The Washington Post* (USA), 31 July 1988.

84 Interviews with Jose Ramos-Hoita, Director of Press and Public Affairs, Mozambique Embassy, Washington, D. C. June 1988 & with Luis Serapião, Renamo delegate, Washington, D. C. June 1988.

85 Gersony, R. (1988), "Summary of Mozambican Refugee Accounts of Principally Conflict-Related Experience in Mozambique".

86 Ibid.

87 Ibid.

88 Interview of Rosario Muterume, *The Times* (UK), 23 February 1987.

89 *Journal of Defense & Diplomacy*, Vol. 3, No. 9, September 1985, p. 49.

90 *Africa Report* (USA), March-April 1989, p. 15.

91 Hanlon, J. (1984), Ch. 21, pp. 228–230.

92 *AIM* (MOZ), No. 31, January 1979.

93 *AIM* (MOZ), No. 68, February 1982.

94 *Africa Confidential* (UK), Vol. 23, No. 15, 21 July 1982.

95 AIM (MOZ), *Mozambiquefile*, No. 154, May 1989.

96 In this massacre 424 people were slaughtered on the 17 July 1987. An American agronomist attached to the Mennonite Church was present when the massacre happened. For his account see Knight, D. (1988), Ch. 1, pp. 6–7. Renamo deny responsibility. For an example of their propaganda distributed in Maputo in late 1987, see CSAS archive.

97 *The Washington Post* (USA), 22 August 1987; *The Houston Post* (USA), 30 August 1987; *New African* (UK), No. 260, May 1989.

98 *The Rand Daily Mail* (RSA), 29 May 1982; *The Star* (RSA), 4 June 1982.

99 Informant wishes to remain anonymous.

100 Letter by O. Roesch in *Southern African Review of Books*, December 1989/January 1990.

101 Duffy, B. (1989), "An American doctor in the schools of hell" pp. 32–35; *Politiken* (DEN), 4 March 1990.

102 *Politiken* (DEN), 4 March 1990.

103 Minter, W. (1989), pp. 104–105.

104 AIM *Mozambiquefile*, No. 162, January 1990.

105 Gersony, R. (1988), p. 23.

106 *The Indian Ocean Newsletter* (FRA), No. 387, 17 June 1989.

107 *Africa Report* (USA), September–October 1989, p. 18.

108 Observation made by author on these roads during this period.

109 Ibid.

110 BBC "Focus on Africa" 17:22 gmt 28 July 1988.

111 Finnegan, W. (1989), Part 2, pp. 93–94.

112 *The Independent* (UK), 24 November 1987.

113 *Southern African Review of Books* August/September 1989, p. 27.

114 *The Guardian* (UK), 17 March 1990.

115 *The Herald* (ZIM), 4 March 1986.

116 Finnegan, W. (1989), Part 2, p. 70.

117 Ibid., p. 72; For background to these tensions in Beira see Christie, I. (1989), pp. 156–159.

118 *Africa confidencial* (PORT), No. 15, February 1987. The document consisted of 12 pages plus a 7 page addendum.

119 *New African* (UK), September 1987.

120 Interview with Fernando Honwana, Mozambican official Maputo, September 1985.

121 *The Independent* (UK), 8 January 1990.

122 BBC Summary of World Broadcasts, "Mozambique: President's Address to Maputo Rally on Proposals for Constitutional Reform". Radio Mozambique, Maputo, in Portuguese 08:22gmt 9 Jan 90 in 12 Jan 90, ME/0660 B/1.

123 BBC Summary of World Broadcasts, "MNR leader pledges to extend strikes". Radiodifusão Portuguesa, Lisbon 19:00gmt 11 Jan 90 in 16 Jan 90, ME/0660 B/1.

124 Examples in Renamo archive, CSAS, University of York.

125 Hammond, P. (1986), p. 4.

126 Kaplan, I. (1977), *Area Handbook for Mozambique* p. xi.

127 Penvenne, J. (1989), "We are all Portuguese: Challenging the Political Economy of Assimilation: Lourenço Marques, 1870 to 1933".

128 Cited by Penvenne, J. (1989), from *O Africano*, 1 March 1909.

129 For a background on the uneasy relations between Frelimo and the Mozambican ex-seminarians, see Mondlane's "White Paper to Mozambique Students" & the students' reply "The Mozambican Revolution Betrayed" in Wheller, D. (1969), "A Document for the History of African Nationalism" *African Historical Studies* II, 2,

pp. 319–332 and III, 1, pp. 169–81.

130 Hastings, A. (1974), *Wiriyamu. My Lai in Mozambique*, pp. 18–19.

131 *Africa Confidential* (UK), Vol. 23, No. 15, 21 July 1982; *The Washington Times* (USA), 17 December 1986. Fernandes' pro-Catholic leaning is reflected in the JODD (1985), interview in *Journal of Defense and Diplomacy*.

132 *AIM* (MOZ), No. 66, December 1981.

133 "Renamo History of Mozambique", by Francisco N. Moises, 2 April 1986, p. 13. Heidelberg Office.

134 *Africa confidencial* (PORT), No. 9, June 1986. Special on "As Igrejas Cristas em Moçambique".

135 *The Guardian* (UK), 30 June 1987.

136 *Informafrica* (PORT), Vol. 1, No. 3, September 1987.

137 *The Independent* (UK), 9 September 1988.

138 The situation between Catholic Church and the Government has improved so much that articles sympathetic to the Catholic Church such as "A Igreja Ante O Racismo" in *Tempo* (MOZ), No. 965, 9 April 1989, pp. 32–35., can now be published.

139 *Jehovah's Witnesses in Africa*, Minority Rights Group Report No. 29, January 1985; *Weekly Mail* (RSA), 15 September 1988.

140 Author was present at an Anglican church service after the Accord.

141 Knight, D. (1988), pp. 71–72.

142 *The Washington Times* (USA), 17 December 1986; *Human Events* (USA), 8 November 1986.

143 Askin, S. (1989), "Militarism and Religion" pp. 61–82.

144 Ibid. p. 63.

145 Ibid. p. 64.

146 "Constitution of the Frontline Fellowship" in the *Frontline Fellowship Story* pp. 1–4.

147 AIM (MOZ), *Mozambiquefile*, No. 160, November 1989.

148 Hammond, P. (1986).

149 Diplomatic source, Maputo, September 1985.

150 Askin, S. (1989), p. 78.

151 Knight, D. (1988), pp. 23–24.

152 *Mozambique Information Bulletin* (UK), No. 93, November 1986, p. 26.

153 *AIM* (MOZ), 12 May 1985.

154 Hammond, P. (1986), p. 2.

155 Some of these tales originate in Jardim, J. (1976), *Terra Quemada*, p. 587.

156 *Africa Events*, May 1987.

157 Interview with A. Karim Vakil, Islamic "retornado", London, October 1988.

158 *The Herald* (ZIM), 27 February 1989.

159 Hall, M. (1990), "The Mozambican National Resistance Movement (Renamo); A Study in Destabilisation of an African State".

160 *The Herald* (ZIM), 27 February 1989.

161 *Africa* (UK), No. 127, March 1982, p. 38.

162 *AIM* (MOZ), 12 April 1986.

163 Ibid.

164 For a discussion on spirit belief amongst Renamo's leadership see, Fauvet, P. & Gomes, A. (1982), *The Mozambique National Resistance*.

165 Interview with Antonio, unemployed, Inhaca, Maputo province, January 1985.

166 Clarence-Smith, G. (1989), "The Roots of the Mozambican Counter-Revolution". See letters on the article in *Southern African Review of Books* (1989), June/July, August/September, December 1989/January 1990; Geffray, C. & Pedersen, M. (1986), "Sobre a guerra na Provincia de Nampula e consequencias socio-economicas locais".

167 *Tempo* (MOZ), No. 275, 10 January 1975 & No. 359, 21 August 1977.

168 *Southern African Review of Books* (1989), August/September; Vail, L. & White, L. (1980), *Capitalism and Colonialism in Mozambique*, Ch. 9, p. 399.

169 Hall, M. (1990).

170 Geffray, C. & Pedersen, M. (1986).

171 Ibid. Colin Darch's claim that Renamo in its propaganda and ideology was little concerned with communal villages and that this further illustrates its South Africa-centric axis is incorrect (Darch 1989, p. 54). The first "Manifest and Programme" (1981), attacks them saying: "The broad peasant masses of Manica and Sofala, dissatisfied with the forced labour the government introduced in the so-called "communal farms" also join the forces of the second struggle of National Liberation and so do those who for traditional reasons refuse to live integrated in communal villages ..." (1981, archive CSAS, York). Fernandes in his JODD (1985), interview also discusses this issue as does Renamo's 1989 Congress statutes.

172 Geffray, C. *La Cause des Armes au Mozambique. Anthropologie d'une guerre civile.*

173 Interview with Governor Manual Antonio *The Guardian* (UK), 16 July 1981.

174 *The Independent on Sunday* (UK), 25 February 1990 & *Domingo* (MOZ), 9 September 1990.

175 *Domingo* (MOZ), 9 September 1990. The editorial to this spread on Mungoi entitled "Spiritual Phenomenon: another revolution in the countryside" is illustrative of how Frelimo is now attempting to obtain the support of the traditional authorities for its mandate to govern.

176 *The Independent* (UK), 27 July 1990.

177 *The Guardian* (UK), 31 August 1990.

5 Peace and National Reconciliation

1 AIM (MOZ), *Mozambiquefile*, No. 160, November 1989.

2 Legum, C. (1988), p. 398.

3 *African Concord* (USA), 16 July 1987.

4 "Carta Pastoral dos Bispos Catolicos de Moçambique, 30 April 1987". The cited excerpts in Hoile, D. (1989), pp. 45–46 are incorrect, derived from a biased translation of the MRC, Washington, D. C.

5 LAD-WCC-CICARWS report entitled "Mozambique" dated November 1988.

6 Ibid., p. 18.

7 Ibid., p. 21.

8 Interview with official involved in this visit.

9 AIM (MOZ), *Mozambiquefile*, No. 160, November 1989.

10 *The Independent* (UK), 25 November 1988.

11 Ibid. ; *Buenos Aires Herald* (ARG), 23 November 1988.

12 AIM (MOZ), *Mozambiquefile*, No. 160, November 1989.

13 The Guardian (UK), 24 June 1989.

14 AIM (MOZ), *Mozambiquefile*, No. 157, August 1989, pp. 3–4.

15 *Diario Popular* (PORT), 20 July 1989.

16 AIM (MOZ), *Mozambiquefile*, No. 157, August 1989, p. 5.

17 Ibid.

18 *The Washington Post* (USA), 27 July 1989.

19 AIM (MOZ), *Mozambiquefile*, August 1989, pp. 7–8.

20 Ibid.

21 Diplomatic Source, Harare, September 1989.

22 *The Herald* (ZIM), 8 August 1989; *The Independent* (UK), 8 August 1989.

23 Ibid.

24 Government & Renamo sources.

25 AIM (MOZ), *Mozambiquefile*, No. 158, September 1989, pp. 4–5.

26 Ibid.

27 *Kenya Times* (KEN), 21 August 1989.

28 *Southscan* (UK), 8 September 1989.

29 *The Indian Ocean Newsletter* (FRA), 2 September 1989.

30 *The Independent* (UK), 16 September 1989.

31 *Informafrica* (PORT), No. 10, 2 December 1989.

32 *The Independent* (UK), 9 December 1989.

33 *The Independent* (UK), 18 December 1989.

34 Radio Mozambique, Maputo in Portuguese 08:22 gmt 9 January 1990. *Summary of World Broadcasts* (BBC), Third Series ME/0659ii in ME/0660 B/1, ME/0662 B/1 & ME/0663 B/1.

35 "Mozambican President in the United States: Departure statement by H. E. President Joaquim Alberto Chissano", The White House, Washington, D. C., 13 March 1990; *The Guardian* (UK), 13 April 1990.

36 *The Indian Ocean Newsletter* (FRA), No. 426, April 14 1990.

37 Radio Mozambique, Maputo, in Portuguese 18:00 gmt, 17 June 1990. *Summary of World Broadcasts* (BBC), Third Series ME/0795 B/1-4. The Mozambican delegation was Foreign Minister Pascoal Mocumbi, Transport Minister, Armando Guebuza and Rafael Maguni, Chief of Debate Over New Constitution. Two Zimbabwean Ministers were present.

38 Radio Mozambique, Maputo, in Portuguese, 11 July 1990. *Summary of World Broadcasts* (BBC), Third Series ME/0814.

39 Ibid. The government delegation also included Labour Minister, Aguiar Mazula; Information Minister, Teodato Hunguana, and the diplomatic adviser in President Chissano's office, Fransico Madeira.

40 *Domingo* (MOZ), 19 August 1990.

41 *The Guardian* (UK), 17 August 1990.

42 The Renamo and government delegations remained the same.

43 Text of the Accord is published in *Domingo* (MOZ), 2 December 1990. This formula for a cease-fire had already been discussed with President Chissano, and encouraged by Mrs Thatcher during his visit to London in March 1990 (Mozambican diplomatic source, London, December 1990).

44 The agreement with the ICRC was a partial result out of Mozambique's energy crisis in 1990. With the end of Soviet barter deals and the Gulf Crisis, the Mozambique government has found it increasingly difficult to provide essential aviation fuel for relief work and its war effort. Given that much of Mozambique relies on airborne relief, due to the war this has become a major concern.

45 *The Guardian* (UK), 20 February 1990.

46 Mozambican Refugee in Zimbabwe, August 1989.

APPENDIX 1 *List of figures associated with Renamo and its splinter groups.*

Name	Position and date when last heard of
Faustino Adriano	Chief of Staff (1989-)
Jose Agosto	Head of the Office of the President (1989), European Rep. (1990-)
Antonio Alfainho	Secretary for Education & Culture Dept. & NC. member (1988-89), Cabinet (1989)
Bernardo Alfuai	Renamo Rep., Malawi (1984), UNAMO (89)
João Almirante	Cabinet (1989), Portugal Rep. (1990)
Carlos Anselmo	CUNIMO (1986)
Victor Anselmo	Dept. of Ideology (1989)
Domingos Arouça	President of FUMO (1976-80), Hon. President of FUMO (1980-)
João da Silva Ataide	European Delegate for Propaganda & Inform. (1986), Lisbon Rep. (87), D. 87
Paris Raul Baza	Agricultural Minister (1988-)
Latifa Grao Bene	Women's League (1989)
Commandant Bokema	Commissioner for National Politics (1982)
Adriano Bomba	Head of Information & Youth (JUNO), (1982), Secretary-General (83), D. 83
Bonaventura Bomba	National Politics Commissioner (1982-83), D. 83
Pedro Buccellato	Renamo (1985)
Zeca Caliate	Renamo (1977-80), FRESAMO (1981-84), CONIMO (85), CUNIMO (86), Renamo (86), FRESAMO (87-89), UDEMO (89), MONALIMO (1990-)
Marcelò Cardoso	FRESAMO (1983), CUNIMO (86), UNAMO (87)

Vincente Chambuli	Head of Dept. of Inform. (1986)
Augustus Chanico	Head of Dept. of Agric. (1986)
Anibal Chilenge	CUNIMO (1986)
Euesebio Coelho	CUNIMO (1986)
Jorge Correia	Lisbon Rep. (1983), Western Europe, Rep. (86), Lisbon Rep. (87), Exp. 87
Jorge de Costa	Intelligence Officer (1983)
João Rajabo da Costa	West German Rep. (1983-85), CUNIMO (1986)
Orlando Cristina	Renamo (1977-1980), Secretary-General (1981-83), D. 83
Maximo Dias	Renamo (1978), MONAMO (1979-85), CONIMO (85), Renamo (87), UDEMO (89), MONAMO (1990-)
Comandante Dick	Commander Northern Zone (1986)
Afonso Dhlakama	Commander (1977-79), President & Commander-in-Chief (1980-)
Raul Manuel Domingos	Chief of Defence & Security & Dhlakama's Chief Secretary & In Charge of Finance (1982), Commander Southern Zone (86), Chief of Staff (1988), Secretary for Foreign Affairs (1989-)
Albino Ducuza	Cabinet (1989-)
Luis Ereneu Emilio	CUNIMO (1986)
Edna Enoch	NC. (1989-)
Albino Faife	Head of Dept. of Internal Administration (1986).
Evo Fernandes	FUMO (1976-77), Renamo (77-80), Lisbon Rep. (1980-82), Co-ordinator of Political & Foreign Dept. (82), European spokesperson (83), Minister for Planning, Secretary-General, (1983-86), Head of Studies Dept. (86-88), Exp. from NC. (87), D.88
Gilberto Fernandes	UNAMO Secretary for Foreign Affairs

Gilberto Fernandes	UNAMO Secretary for Foreign Affairs (alias Gilberto Magid) (1988-)
Artur de Fonseca	Secretary for Foreign Relations (1984-89)
Jose Francisco	Renamo (1988-)
Manuel Frank	Lisbon Rep. (1987-)
Asencio de Freitas	Lisbon Rep. (1987-88), Dept. of Studies (1989-)
Mario Gonzaga	Head of Department of Youth (1986–90)
Priscilla Gumane	CUNIMO (1986)
J. Henrique	Northern General (1986), D. 87
João Horacio	Commander (1985)
Comandante Ismail	Commander Central Zone (1986)
Chanjunja Chivaca João	Chief of Dept. of Organisation & Mobilisation (1988), Def. 88
Antonio Juliane	Chief of Education and Social Affairs (1982)
João Khan	President of FUMO (1983)
Artur Lemane	USA Rep. (1983-85), Renamo (86)
Horacio Leven	Assistant Rep. West Germany (1984), Rep. West Germany (1985-)
Manual Lisboa	Kenya Rep. (1987-9), NC. (1989-)
Mateus Lopes (alias Jose de Costa)	Special Envoy of Dhlakama (1987), D. 87
Guideon Macheluze	Head of Finance Dept. (1986), PADE-LIMO (86)
Mario Macuacua	NC. (89-)
Gilberto Magid (cf. Gilberto Fernandes)	Renamo (1986), UNAMO (1987)
Fanuel Mahuluza	Africa Livre (1977-80), Head of Dept.

	of Political & External Relations (1983-4), PADELIMO (86), CUNIMO (86)
Comandante Marquez	Chief of Dept. of Operations (82)
Jose Francisco Masarenhas	Assistant Rep. Lisbon (1987)
Jose Massinga	CUNIMO (1986), Friends of Mozambique (88), Pro-Civic (1990-)
Faustino Mateus	Nairobi Rep. (1990-)
Andre Matsangaissa	President & Commander-in-Chief (1977-79), D. 79
Carlos Mbwere	CUNIMO (1986)
Calisto Meque	Commandant & NC. (1985-87), D. 87
Leo Milas	Renamo (1977), Assistant Africa Rep. (1984), Nairobi Rep., (1984-86)
Francisco Nota Moises	Swaziland Rep. (1984), Secretary for Information (1985-89)
Casimiro Monteiro	Liaison with MID (1980)
Agostinho Morrial	Secretary for Education & Culture Dep., NC. (1989-)
Zeca Mublanga	CUNIMO (1986)
Lucas Mu'langa	Commander (1977-79), D. 79
Jose Fata Munhlanga	Renamo (1988-)
Valeriano Nicame	NC. (1989-)
Mateus Ngonhamo	Commander (1985), Chief of Renamo Security (1987), General (1989).
Henriques Nhancale	Assistant Rep. USA (1990-).
Antonio Nunez	CUNIMO (1986)
Paulo Oliveira	Editor of "A Luta Continua!" (1986) European spokesperson (1986-87), Def. 88.
General Antonio Pedro	Department of Defence and Security (1989).

Jimo (Gimo) (M')Phiri	Africa Livre (1977-80), Commander (80-87), President of UNAMO (1987-)
Carlos Reis	FRESAMO (1983), CUNIMO (86), UNAMO (87-)
Antonio Rocha	Director of Research, MRC. (1988-)
Khembo dos Santos	FUMO (1977), Renamo (1977-81), NC. (81- 82), Adjutant for External Relations (83), Nairobi Rep. (84), PADELIMO (86), CUNIMO (86), MANU (89-)
Julius Seffu	Rep. in USA (1989-)
Luis Serapião	Rep. in USA (1986-89), Director of Higher Education (89-)
Simao Serapião	Renamo (87-)
Thomas Schaaf	Executive-Director, MRC. (1986-)
Cristavo Felpe Soares	Head of Department of Health & Welfare (1986), Department of Health & Social Affairs (1989)
Ernesto Tembo	CUNIMO (1986)
Sebastião Temporario	Renamo (1988-), Dept. of Finance (1989)
Vincente Ululu	Adjutant to the Chief of the Dept. of Politics, responsible for International Affairs (1982), Nairobi Rep. (1984), Dept. of Education (1986), Minister for Home Affairs (1987), Minister for Civilian Affairs (88-89), Secretary for Information (89-), NC. (86-)
Jose Fransico Vaz	Secretary (1985), Renamo (88-)
Anselmo Victor	Chief Civilian Administrator (1986), Political Ideology Minister (88).
Artur Vilanculos (Vilankulu)	Prime Minister (1983), Secretary for Foreign Relations (1983), Exp. (83), CONIMO (85), PADELIMO (86), CUNIMO (86-87), Friends of Mozambique (88)

Paulo Zamba	CUNIMO (1986)
Comandante Zeco	Chief of Security (1982)
Antonio Disse Zengazenga	CUNIMO (1986). President of CUNI-MO (1987-)

D.— Died; Exp. — Expelled; Def. — Defected; NC.— National Council

RENAMO NATIONAL COUNCIL		Regional Origin
Zambezia	Manuel Lisboa	Sena
Maputo	Edna C. Enoch	Ronga
Inhambane	Agostinho Murrial	Chope
Cabo Delgado	Vincente Z. Ululu	Makonde
Tete	Raul M. Domingos	Sena
Nampula	Ossufo F. Momad	Lomwe
Manica	Albino F. Ducuza	N'dau
Niassa	Valeriano J. Nicame	Makonde
Gaza	Mario Macuacua	Chope
Sofala	Samuel Simango	N'dau

RENAMO STRUCTURE

President	Afonso Marceta	
	Macacho Dhlakama	N'dau
Cabinet	Jose Agosto	N'dau
	João Almirante	N'dau
	Albino Ducuza	?
	Antonio Alfainho	?

Department Heads

External Relations	Raul Domingos	Sena
Information	Vincente Ululu	Makonde
Education	Agostinho Murrial	?
Agriculture	Paris Baza	Shangaan
Health	Cristovão Soares	Tsonga
Political Affairs	Anselmo Victor	N'dau
General Staff	Faustinho Adriano	Mamganja

(Adapted from the summary of Resolutions of the First National Congress of Renamo (1989))

Renamo Generals in order of Seniority (1990)

1. Afonso Dhlakama   2. Antonio Pedro
3. Mateus Ngonhano   4. Paulo Gomes

APPENDIX 2 *Renamo's 16 Point Declaration*

1. Since 1964, the people of Mozambique are dying daily, the victims of war.

2. It is imperative therefore, that all true nationalists and peacelovers, affiliated or not with any political organisation should make all efforts to mobilize the effective means at their disposal in order to find a genuine Mozambican and African solution conducive to lasting peace and stability.

3. The people of Mozambique need freedom. It is Freedom that precedes stability, prosperity, and respect for individual traditions.

4. We believe it is a prevailing principle that the people are sovereign and have inalterable (sic) rights to elect their leader that will serve their expectations and essential traditions.

5. Renamo is an active political force in Mozambique's political arena. Any peace solution must take into consideration this reality as well as traditions, culture, present stage of development and other present realities.

6. It is not Renamo's intention to change the existing order in Mozambique through armed struggle.

7. Renamo will never consent that military force be utilized in order to impose leadership or political options contrary to the will of the people.

8. None of the involved parties in this conflict has anything to gain with the continuance of this war. Only the people's suffering is aggravated every day.

9. Verbal attacks should be avoided by those who are fighting as well as by those who are directly interested in our country and the region. We should emphasize the future and not the past.

10. Propaganda against Renamo will not change the political and military reality in Mozambique.

11. The presence of the foreign forces brought by Frelimo did not bring peace or well-being for our people. We in Renamo see this presence as an obstacle to peace. Additionally, it signifies an outrage to our dignity and loss of our sovereignty and independence.

12. For the resolution of the present conflict, Renamo takes into consideration the neighbouring and regional interests and states.

13. Renamo has committed itself to continuing the present peace initiative. Renamo will make all efforts to continue the process.

14. Renamo stands for the population of Mozambique and is against any massacre or violation of the population. Renamo is a people's force. Its strength lies with the people.

15. Renamo is a guerrilla force, whose survival depends on the people and therefore is by nature against massacres or violations of the people. Renamo's reason for existence is the people.

16. Renamo wants a genuine negotiation conducive to national reconciliation without victors or vanquished and without recrimination followed by constitutional reform; to unite efforts in order to form a new Mozambique where brotherhood will be affirmed by free debate of ideas and decision of consensus; a new Mozambique where armed struggle need never be the last and only resort for the solution of our problem.

Taken from Renamo's Press Release "In Search for Peace: Renamo's Reply to Frelimo's Proposals", Nairobi, 15 August 1989.

APPENDIX 3 *Mozambique Government's "12 Principles" for Peace.*

1. We are faced with an operation of destabilisation which should not be confused with a struggle between two parties.

2. The operation has been mounted through brutal acts of terrorism which provoke immense suffering falling, above all, on the population and their property. Hundreds of thousands of people have already died. Many economic and social infrastructures in the country have been destroyed or paralysed, impeding the normal life of citizens and turning millions of people into displaced persons.

3. The aim is to put an end to this inhuman situation. The first action should be to stop all terrorist and bandit actions.

4. Afterwards, conditions should be created for all Mozambican citizens to lead normal lives in such a way that they can participate on the one hand in the political, economic, social and cultural life of the country, and on the other in the discussion and definition of the policies which will guide the country in each of these aspects (political, economic, social and cultural).

5. These policies are established by national consensus, formulated through a process of consultation and debate with the people or social groups involved. The principal laws relating to land, health and education were approved after consultation with the people. The on-going revision of the constitution has been taking place through a debate which aims at introducing factors of democratic participation in the working of the State. Religious institutions are being consulted in the process of the preparation of legislation on religious liberties.

6. Dialogue will aim at clarifying these positions and giving guarantees of participation in it to all individuals, including those who until then had been involved in violent actions of destabilisation.

7. This participation and enjoyment of rights applies immediately to the processes which are already underway regarding the affirmation of the principles defined in the Constitution in relation to: the protection of individual and collective liberties; the protection of human rights; the protection of democratic rights.

8. Individual and social liberties, such as freedom of worship, freedom of expression and freedom of assembly, are guaranteed. They should not be used against the general interests of the nation. They should be not used to destroy national unity, national independence and the integrity of persons and property. They should not be used to propagate tribalism, racism, regionalism or any form of divisionism or sectarianism. They should not be used for the preparation or perpetration of acts punishable by law, such as robbery, assassination or aggression. They cannot be used for the preparation or perpetration of violent acts against the State and the Constitution, such as secessionist movements or coups d'état.

9. Policy or constitutional changes or revisions, or changes or revisions to the principal laws of the country, where in many cases debate or consultation with citizens has already occurred or is in process, can be brought and should be brought about only through the ample participation of all citizens.

10. It is unacceptable for a group to use intimidation or violence to impose themselves on the whole society. It is anti-democratic to alter the

constitution and principal laws of the country through the violence of a group.

11. The normalisation of life and the integration of those until now involved in violent actions of destabilisation implies, in a general way, their participation in economic and social life through suitable ways agreed by them, and guaranteed by the government.

12. The acceptance of these principles could lead to a dialogue about the modalities for ending violence, establishing peace and normalising life for all in the country.

Taken from Statement made by President Chissano in Maputo, on 17 July 1989;
published by Informacão Publica.

APPENDIX 4 *The US Peace Plan.*

1. There must be a peaceful solution to the conflict and a cessation of all attacks on civilians.

2. Democracy in Mozambique is based on freedom of expression, association and economic opportunity.

3. All Mozambican citizens have the right to participate in the political, social, cultural and economic life of the nation and in the determination of national policies.

4. The people are sovereign and have the right to make decisions involving their governance.

5. National reconciliation and unity shall be the guiding principles in the peace process.

6. All parties shall recognise the legitimacy of the Republic of Mozambique and its constitution, institutions, and the fundamental laws emanating from them.

7. Fundamental changes in the existing order within the Republic of Mozambique are to be brought about peacefully and democratically.

Text of US 7-Point Peace Proposals. Presented to Afonso Dhlakama by Ed Fugit in Nairobi on 7 December 1989.

BIBLIOGRAPHY

Arouca, D. (1974) *Discursos Politicos*. Atica, Lisboa.

Askin, S. (1989) "Militarism and Religion — A Global Connection (Including: Interview with Ian Grey)", in EDICESA (ed) *Religion and Oppression. The Misuse of Religion for Social, Political and Economic Subjugation in Eastern and Southern Africa. Documentation 1989*. Ecumenical Documentation and Information Centre (EDICESA), Harare.

(1990) "Mission Improbable: Here come the "missionaries" — again!" *Africa South* No. 3, January/February 1990.

Beach, D. (1986) "The uses of the Colonial Military History of Mozambique", *Cahiers d'Etudes Africaines*, 104, xxvi-4.

Becker, J. (1987) "Graveyard Mozambique and How Britain Sponsors It", *The Salisbury Review*, December 1987.

Botha, P. (1985) "Reply on Mozambique", *SA House of Assembly Debates (Hansard) 25 March to 10 May*, Volume 3. Government Printer, Pretoria.

Cain, E. (1985) "Mozambique's Hidden War", in Mosser, C. (ed) *Combat on Communist Territory*. Free Congress Foundation, Washington, D. C.

CENE. & DPCCN (1988) *Rising To The Challenge: Dealing with the DPCCN. Emergency in Mozambique*. CENE & DPCCN, Maputo.

Christie, I. (1989) *Machel of Mozambique: A Biography*. Panaf, London.

Clarence-Smith, G. (1989) "The Roots of the Mozambican Counter-Revolution", *Southern African Review of Books* April/May 1989.

Cline, S. (1989) *RENAMO. Anti-communist Insurgents in Mozambique: The Fight Goes On*. United States Global Strategy Council, Washington, D. C.

(1990) "Forgotten Freedom Fighters: Mozambique's RENAMO lost in Maelstrom of Misinformation", *Soldier of Fortune* January 1990.

Cole, B. (1984) *The Elite: The Story of the Rhodesian Special Services*. Three Knights Publishing, Amanzimoti, Transkei.

Darch, C. (1989) "Are there Warlords in Provincial Mozambique? Questions of the Social Base of MNR Banditry", *Review of African Political Economy* No. 45/46, winter 1989.

Davies, R. (1985) *Research Report no. 73 South African Strategy Towards Mozambique in the Post-N'komati Period. A Critical Analysis of Effects and Implications*. Scandinavian Institute of African Studies, Uppsala.

Duffy, B. (1989) "An American doctor in the schools of hell", *U. S. News & World Report*, 16 January 1989.

Egerö, B. (1987) *Mozambique: A Dream Undone. The Political Economy of Democracy, 1975-84*. Scandinavian Institute of African Studies, Uppsala.

Ellert, H. (1989) *The Rhodesian Front War: Counter-Insurgency and Guerrilla war in Rhodesia, 1962-80*. Mambo Press, Gweru.

Fauvet, P. (1984) "Roots of Counter-Revolution: The Mozambique National

Resistance", *Review of African Political Economy*, No. 29, July 1984.

Fauvet, P. & Gomez, A. (1982) "The Mozambique National Resistance", Supplement to *AIM* (MOZ) No. 89, March 1982.

Finnegan, W. (1989) "A Reporter At Large. (Mozambique Part 1)" *The New Yorker*, 22 May 1989.

(1989) "A Reporter At Large. (Mozambique Part 2)" *The New Yorker*, 29 May 1989.

Flower, K. (1987) *Serving Secretly: An Intelligence Chief on Record, Rhodesia into Zimbabwe, 1964-1981*. John Murray, London.

FRELIMO (1978) *Historia de FRELIMO*. FRELIMO, Maputo. (1987) *Mozambique Briefing No. 5. The Roots of Armed Banditry*. FRELIMO, Maputo.

Geffray, C. & Pedersen, M. (1986) "Sobre a guerra na provincia de Nampula e conse-quencias socio-economicas locais", *Revista Internacional de Estudos Africanos*, No. 4-5, January-December 1986.

(1988) "Nampula en guerre", *Politique Africaine* No. 29, March 1988, Special edition (Mozambique: guerre et nationalismes).

Geffray, C. (1990) *La Cause des Armes au Mozambique. Antropologie d'une guerre civile*. Editions Karthala, Paris (forthcoming).

Glaser, T. (1989) "Country Reports-Mozambique", *The Courier* (Lomé Convention magazine) No. 114, March-April 1989.

Hall, M. (1990) "The Mozambican National Resistance (Renamo) : A Study in Destabilisation of an African State", *Africa*, Vol. 60, No. 1, 1990.

Hammond, P. (no date) *The Frontline Fellowship Story*. Frontline Fellowship, Newlands (RSA).

Hanlon, J. (1984) *Mozambique: The Revolution Under Fire*. Zed, London.

(1986) *Beggar Your Neighbours: Apartheid Power in Southern Africa*. James Currey, London.

Hastings, A. (1974) *Wiriyamu: My Lai in Mozambique*. Orbis, New York.

Henrikson, T. (1983) *Revolution and Counter-Revolution. Mozambique's War of Independence 1964-1974*. Greenwood Press, Connecticut.

Hodges, T. (1979) "Mozambique: The Politics of Liberation", in Carter, G. & O'Meara, P. (eds) *Southern Africa: The Continuing Crisis*. Indiana University Press, Bloomington.

Hoile, D. (1989) *Mozambique: a Nation in Crisis*. Claridge Press, London.

Howe, H. & Ottoway, M. (1987) "State Power Consolidation in Mozambique", in Keller, E. J. & Rothchild, D. (eds) *Afro-Marxist Regimes: Ideology and Public Policy*. Lynne Rienner, London.

Isaacman, A. (1976) *The Tradition of Resistance in Mozambique*. Heinemann, London.

(1986) "The Malawi Connection", *Africa Report*, November-December 1986.

Isaacman, A. & Isaacman, B. (1982) "South Africa's Hidden War", *Africa Report*, November-December 1982.

(1983) *Mozambique. From Colonialism to Revolution, 1900-1982*. Westview, Boulder, Colorado.

Jardim, J. (1976) *Mocambique-Terra Queimada*. Intervencão, Lisbon.

JODD. (1985) "Interview. Sec. -Gen. Evo Fernandes, Mozambican National

Resistance", *Journal of Defense & Diplomacy*, Vol. 3, No. 9, September 1985.

Johnsson, P. & Martin, D. (1989) *Apartheid Terrorism: the Destabilization Report*. The Commonwealth Secretariat in association with James Currey, London.

Jordan, B. (1988) "Mission Mozambique: SOF Escorts Missionaries out of Combat Zone", *Soldier of Fortune*, January 1988.

Kaplan, I. (1977) *Area Handbook for Mozambique*. US. Government Printer, Washington, D. C.

Knight, D. (1988) *Mozambique Caught in the Trap*. Christian Aid, London.

Legum, C. (1988) *Battlefronts of Southern Africa*. Africana, New York.

Magaia, L. (1988) *Dumba Nengue: Run for Your Life (Peasant Tales of Tragedy in Mozambique)* . Africa World Press, Trenton, New Jersey.

Maier, K. (1989) "The Battle for Zambezia", *Africa Report* March-April 1989.

Martin, D. & Johnson, P. (1986) "Mozambique: To N'komati and Beyond", Johnson, P. & Martin, D. (eds) *Destructive Engagement —South Africa at War*. Zimbabwe Publishing House, Harare.

McKenna, B. (1987) "Renamo: Freedom Fighters' Agenda for Victory", *Soldier of Fortune*, May 1987.

Metz, S. (1986) "The Mozambique National Resistance and South African Foreign Policy", *African Affairs*, October 1986.

Middlemas, K. (1979) "Mozambique: Two Years of Independence", in Centre for African Studies (ed) *Mozambique*, Edinburgh University Press.

Minter, W. (1989) "The Mozambican National Resistance (Renamo) as described by Ex-Participants", *Development Dialogue* 1989, No. 1.

Mondlane, E. (1983) *The Struggle for Mozambique*. Zed, London.

Moorcraft, P. (1987) "Mozambique's Long Civil War: Renamo — Puppets or Patriots?" *International Defense Review*, No. 10, 1987.

Morrison, J. (1987) "The Battle for Mozambique", *Africa Report*, September-October 1987.

Munslow, B. (1977) "Leadership in the Front for the Liberation of Mozambique, Part 1", in Hill, C. & Warwick, P. (eds) *Southern African Research in Progress: Collected papers: 1*. Centre for Southern African Studies, University of York.

(1983) *Mozambique: the Revolution and its Origins*, Longman, London.

Nesbitt, P. (1988) "Terminators, Crusaders and Gladiators: Western (Private & Public) Support for Renamo & Unita", *Review of African Political Economy* No. 43, Spring 1988.

Newitt, M. (1973) *Portuguese on the Zambezi*. Longman, London.

(1981) *Portugal in Africa*. C. Hurst, London.

Nilsson, A. (1990) *Unmasking the Bandits: the True Face of the M. N. R.* European Campaign Against South African Aggression Against Mozambique and Angola (ECASAAMA), London.

Norval, M. (1988) *Red Star Over Southern Africa*. Selous Foundation Press, Washington, D. C.

Opello, W. (1975) "Pluralism and Elite Conflict in an Independence Movement: Frelimo in the 1960's", *Journal of Southern African Studies*, Vol. 2, No. 1.

Paul, J. (1975) *Mozambique: Memoirs of a Revolution*. Penguin, London.

Penvenne, J. (1989) "We Are All Portuguese: Challenging the Political Economy of Assimilation: Lourenço Marques 1870 to 1933", in Vail, L. (ed) *The Creation of Tribalism in Southern Africa*. University of California Press, Berkeley.

Swift, K. (1974) *Mozambique and the Future*. Don Nelson, Cape Town.

Thomashausen, A. (1983) "The National Resistance of Mozambique", *Africa Insight* Vol. 13, No. 2.

(1987) "The Mozambique National Resistance", in Maritz, C. (ed) *Weerstandbewegings in Suider-Afrika*, Departement Sentrale Publikasies, Potchefstroom University.

Torres, E. (1983) "Moçambique entre dois fogos: a URSS e a Africa do Sul", in Bissell, R. et al (eds) A Africa Num Mondo Multipolar: *Estudos Africanos 1*. I. E. E. I. , Lisbon.

Urdang, S. (1988) *And Still They Dance: Women, War and the Struggle for Change in Mozambique*. Earthscan, London.

Vail, L. & White, L. (1980) *Capitalism and Colonialism in Mozambique*. Heinemann, London.

Wheller, J. (1985) "From Rovuma to Maputo: Mozambique's Guerrilla War", *Reason*, December 1985.

(1986) "Renamo. Winning One in Africa", *Soldier of Fortune*, February 1986.

(1986) "Renamo. Winning One in Africa Part 2", *Soldier of Fortune*, March 1986.

Wheller, P. (1969) "A Document for the History of African Nationalism", *African Historical Studies*, Vol. 2, No. 2.

(1970) "A Document for the History of African Nationalism", *African Historical Studies*, Vol. 3, No. 2.

Winter, G. (1981) *Inside BOSS. South Africa's Secret Police*. Penguin, London.

Young, T. (1990) "The MNR/RENAMO: External and Internal Dynamics", *African Affairs*, October 1990.

Reports

Frelimo (1990) "Draft Amended Constitution, January 1990. Prepared by the Frelimo Party for nationwide debate to be ratified by the People's Assembly". Mozambique Information Office, Dossier No. 3, London.

Geffray, C. (1989) "Erati En Guerre: Genese, Developement et Reproduction De La Situation De Guerre Dans Le Nord Du Mozambique: Districts De Namapa Et Erati". CERDU, Paris.

Gersony, R. (1988) "Summary of Mozambican Refugee Accounts of Principally Conflict-Related Experience in Mozambique: Report Submitted to Ambassador Moore and Dr. Chester A. Crocker", Department of State Bureau for Refugee Programs, April 1988.

Hammond, P. (1986) "Mozambique Report — Eyewitness Testimonies of Persecution And Atrocities", Frontline Fellowship, Newlands (RSA).

LAD, WCC, CICARWS (1988) "Mozambique", November 1988.

Minority Rights Group (1985) "Jehovah's Witnesses in Africa", Report No. 29.

Minter, W. (1990) "The National Union for the Total Independence of Angola

(UNITA) as described by Ex-Participants and Foreign Visitors. Research Report submitted to the Swedish International Development Authority (SIDA)". Georgetown University, Washington, D. C, March 1990.

Letters over Clarence-Smith, G. (1989) "The Roots of the Mozambican Counter-Revolution" in the *Southern African Review of Books*.

Cahen, M. August/September 1989: December 1989/ January 1990.

Clarence-Smith, G. June/July 1989: August/September 1989.

Fauvet, P. August/September 1989: June/July 1990.

Minter, W. June/July 1989.

Roesch, O. December 1989/January 1990.

NOTE ON SOURCES

Archive at the Centre for Southern African Studies,
University of York, United Kingdom.

The material cited in this book (field notebooks, Renamo propaganda such as com-
muniqués, statements and political programmes issued by its offices in Heidelberg,
Washington, Lisbon, Nairobi as well as leaflets distributed within Mozambique) has
been deposited at the Centre for Southern African Studies Archive, University of
York. This collection also contains a wide selection of international press cuttings,
pro-Renamo propaganda from the United States, programmes and statements by
Renamo splinter groups, and statements made by Ndabaningi Sithole about
Renamo. There are also examples of pastoral newsletters about Renamo produced
by both the Catholic Church within Mozambique and evangelical groups based in
South Africa and Malawi as well as several unpublished reports about church
involvement with Renamo. The archive also contains copies of articles relating to
Renamo from a wide range of sources.

INDEX